The longing in each of our hearts is to be loved by our father, to intimately know our father and be fully known by him, and receive our father's love. The essence of brokenness is found in the break of relationship which began with Adam and Eve and has passed on to each generation of their sons and daughters ever since. Jesus came to show us how to restore intimate relationship with our heavenly Father. This model necessarily shows us how to restore our relationships with our own earthly father, and our own sons and daughters, who need our love now as much as we ourselves need our own father's love and acceptance.

It is our prayer that this book blesses you mightily. We ask for your continued prayers, manpower and support

Arthur George, Chaplain, Good New Jail & Prison Ministry
Fairfax Adult Detention Center - www.goodnewsjpm-ffx-va.com
McLean Bible Church, December 1998

FIGHT LIKE A MAN

GORDON **DALBEY**

fight like a man

Redeeming Manhood for Kingdom Warfare

Tyndale House Publishers, Inc.
Wheaton, Illinois

This book is dedicated to men of the armed forces, who fought their appointed battle for peace in the past so we might have the security to face our battle today.

Unless otherwise indicated, Scripture quotations are taken from *Today's English Version,* © 1966, 1971, 1976 by American Bible Society. Used by permission.

Scripture quotations marked NIV are taken from the *Holy Bible,* New International Version®. Copyright © 1973, 1978, 1984 by International Bible Society. Used by permission of Zondervan Publishing House. All rights reserved. The "NIV" and "New International Version" trademarks are registered in the United States Patent and Trademark Office by International Bible Society. Use of either trademark requires permission of International Bible Society.

Scripture quotations marked RSV are taken from the *Holy Bible,* Revised Standard Version, copyright © 1946, 1952, 1971 by the Division of Christian Education of the National Council of the Churches of Christ in the United States of America, and are used by permission. All rights reserved.

Scripture verses marked TLB are taken from *The Living Bible,* copyright © 1971 owned by assignment by KNT Charitable Trust. All rights reserved.

Scripture verses marked NEB are taken from *The New English Bible,* copyright © 1970, Oxford University Press, Cambridge University Press.

Scripture verses marked *The Message* are taken from *The Message,* copyright © 1993, Eugene H. Peterson.

Library of Congress Cataloging-in-Publication Data

Dalbey, Gordon, date
  Fight like a man / Gordon Dalbey.
    p. cm.
  Includes bibliographical references.
  ISBN 0-8423-1866-6 (alk. paper)
    1. Men—Religious life. 2. Spiritual warfare. 3. Fatherhood (Christian theology)
4. God—Fatherhood. I. Title.
BV4440.D33 1995
248.8′42—dc20   95-33104

Printed in the United States of America

01 00 99 98 97 96 95
7   6   5   4   3   2   1

CONTENTS

INTRODUCTION
Enlisting in Victory

*May your Kingdom come; may your will be done on earth
as it is in heaven.* Matthew 6:10

Early in 1990 in a groundbreaking PBS special, "A Gathering of Men," poet Robert Bly blasted through the gender-muddling of previous decades with a jarring truth. The average man today, he declared, has learned well from his mother to embrace his "soft feminine side" and become tender and receptive. But he hasn't learned to embrace his more deliberate "masculine side," because his father has been emotionally and often physically absent.

Without a father to secure him in his masculine identity, Bly noted, the man abdicates his own agenda and looks to the woman, as mom, to define his nature and destiny. Ultimately, therefore, he embraces a false feminity and becomes passive.

The secular men's movement set the stage for God's work in men today by redeeming masculinity from the world's polarized view. Authentic manhood, its leaders proclaimed, is neither selfishly aggressive nor irresponsibly passive. Furthermore, it can be embraced only by men willing to face the pain of a broken father relationship.

This crippling "father-wound," which men have suffered for generations, is a wound of absence. It's harder to recognize than other wounds and, ultimately, more destructive.

"I'm still waiting for my father to talk to me about sex and success, money and marriage, religion and raising kids," confessed a *Men's Health* magazine writer, whose father died two years before. "The shame of it is, I don't know a man my age who doesn't feel like he's navigating his life without a map."[1]

You can kill a living organism, such as a plant, in two ways. You can actively destroy it. Cut it down, smash it, beat it up.

But there's another way. You can simply leave it alone. Just don't water it.

Either way, it dies.

Abandonment kills.

The secular leaders have awakened us to the deadly effects of the father-wound in men today. Their drumming in the woods has announced the first-stage agenda for healing: The man must mourn his father, differentiate from his mother, and bond to the company of men.

Indeed, Bly and his counterparts are intelligent enough to know that the awful vacuum in men's unfathered souls must be filled with something authentic, lest we destroy ourselves and women. Since none of us has that "something" to give, it must come from someplace besides men.

"What good does it do to get together with other men?" one man asked who had been talked into attending one of my conferences by his friends. "I mean, if we're all so broken and needy, how can we get something together that none of us has to give?"

This man is close to the Kingdom. He's asking the right questions.

Yet in order to bear authentic masculinity, that "something" we need can't come from women. We've tried that, and it doesn't work.

We men can't heal ourselves (Rom. 7:18). In fact, we need supernatural input. The next move of healing in and among men therefore requires spiritual power. That's what the drums and the chanting of the secular movement promise—but they can deliver only the counterfeit.

Meanwhile, the father-wound remains the major chink in our armor as men, and thereby, the primary entry point for destruction in, among, and through us (Mal. 4:5-6). The wound of father-absence can be acknowledged by simple honesty and stayed by grieving, but it can be healed only by father-presence—which no secular power can provide.

It's one thing to grieve the loss of Dad's presence; it's quite another to replace it with true father-love. Only Jesus, therefore, can heal the father-wound, because only he can overcome our sin-nature and restore relationship with the true and present Father of all men (John 14:6-14).

Only the dignity of sonship can overcome the shame of abandonment (Rom. 8:14-16, Ps. 27:10).

Indeed, in 1994—just four years after Robert Bly's breakthrough pronouncement—a feature article in *Esquire* magazine declared that the men's movement is dead.[2] In "retrospect," it asserted, the movement simply did not "stick" because the self-disclosure and "nakedness of it all" caused "embarrassment" in men.[3]

Just as the American Psychiatric Association in 1973 declared that homosexuality is no longer a disorder—"If we can't heal it, it's not an illness"—so the secular men's movement quickly became overwhelmed by the father-wound.

The men of the world have dropped the sword of truth. It's time for Christian men to pick it up and fight for all God's worth.

Our task is finally at hand: not to curse or worship manhood, but to redeem it—that is, to restore manhood to its true and original definition, as only those who know the Creator can.

Many churches, however, have squandered their witness to the God of reconciliation. They've yielded to the world's polarization of what it means to be male and female, listing to the side of the liberal/feminized god of tolerance or the opposite side, the conservative/masculinized god of judgment.

The church and the world seem able to do only one of two things with the inherent fighting nature of a man—muzzle it by creating a feminized "soft male" model or unleash it through a violent superhero model.

I don't believe that God intended men to be like women. I also don't believe that God intended men to be judging, avenging, and violent—something Jesus never modeled.

I do believe God has called men to be fighters—but fighters of a very different kind from what the world—and many churches—might envision.

God has called men to be Kingdom warriors.

Kingdom warfare, which began when Adam fell, is the battle to reestablish God's authority on earth against our rebellious human nature and our spiritual Enemy, who exploits that to destroy us.

This battle is settled by one question: Do you know God as your father and yourself as his son?

That's the question Jesus answers.

Men who let him, become Kingdom warriors.

Men who do not, become warriors of the flesh, battling for their pride to overcome the shame of our sinful human condition.

Some years ago, I saw a T-shirt from the Christian band Petra that declared, "Get on your knees, and fight like a man!" To my surprise, tears came to my eyes. As I prayed and asked God why, I sensed that this, at last, was the authentic restoration and redemption of manhood that I was called to both become and write about in my books.

My first book, *Healing the Masculine Soul,* aimed to restore the measure of truth in the secular men's movement to its biblical Christian roots. My next book, *Father & Son: The Wound, the Healing, the Call to Manhood,* showed how a man's relationship with his father shapes his relationship with God and his sense of himself as a man.

I purposely avoided the warfare theme in these earlier books. God has been calling out each man to battle—but not while the man's in the hospital, and certainly not before he even realizes he's sick enough to need help (Matt. 9:12-13). Today, however, we must face the battle at hand in order to cooperate fully with

God's healing in and through us. Indeed, the conflict has intensified, both within and about us, to where we can no longer defer God's call to arms.

Escalating sexual sin, from homosexuality and fornication to prime-time pornography; child abuse, from abortion to TV violence; family destruction, from divorce to the loss of extended families; resurgent racism in all colors; addictions, from drugs and alcohol to their religious counterpart in cults and "Christian" legalism—all indicate clearly that powers beyond our human abilities to discern and overcome are destroying us.

This increasing destruction reveals the world as not only unable to heal our brokenness but unable even to affirm any standard by which the need for healing can be recognized. In a startling example, the American Psychiatric Association in 1994 took the next logical step after removing homosexuality from its list of disorders, and declared that pedophilia is no longer a disorder—unless what the individual is doing sexually to the child causes the individual "distress."[4]

With the Enemy so graphically in our faces, it's easy for Christian men to abandon the fight entirely. The good news, however, is this: God is still in charge. The intensity of the battle today reflects not the Enemy's initiative, but rather, his counteroffensive, a reaction to an even more powerful—though often unnoticed—movement of God among men.

The flak is thickest when you're over the target.

Father God is still the Initiator, and he's been building his army, searching the countryside, and gathering his battalion for a major offensive.

He came in the person of Jesus to begin recruiting.

And he's alongside us today in the Holy Spirit, calling and equipping us for his victory (John 14:16-17, 26).

Unlike the armies of the world, however, Jesus has been enlisting not just "a few good men," but the many of us sinners who have been wounded unto death by the powers of the world.

We have experience in enemy territory. We know Satan's stratagems best, since we've wrestled most deliberately with his temptations and attacks. Most important, however, we've been forced to discover we can't save ourselves and therefore have begun to know and trust Father God's saving power.

Without that trust, we're easily defeated in Kingdom warfare because we won't train for victory (1 Tim. 4:7-8). We'll seek pumped-up battle cries but shun the deep inner work of healing that would seal our armor and thereby allow Jesus to prompt his authentic victory cry within us.

It's like refilling a leaky tire on your army jeep; it rides great out into battle, but when you meet the Enemy, it's flat again.

You're not just stuck; you're dead.

Men who haven't let the Father take them to the Cross won't dare recognize the battle at hand, because they haven't received the Father's resurrection power to win it. Rather, they will hide their wounds, often behind a religious facade.

Indeed, a men's movement that does not begin surrendered at the Cross can only become ingrown and capitulate to false spirituality—thus beckoning the old spirits of male idolatry, from misogyny to militarism.

This book is not for the man who wants to charge out into battle as a way of compensating for or avoiding his inner brokenness, but rather it is for the man who has dared face himself honestly enough to realize his own strength can't save him from its effects.

In fact, the true Kingdom warrior has begun to discover that surrendering his inner brokenness to Jesus is the authentic induction into the Father's army and the gateway to his destiny. He can face his father-wound, but it no longer defines him, because he's begun to allow the Father God to define him as a true son (Rom. 8:14-16).

He wants to prepare for his part in the Father's victory.

For you who have persevered through God's boot camp of truth and allowed him to redeem your brokenness for his purposes—such as through divorce, serious illness, fathering failures, or addiction recovery—this book will confirm and hone your readiness to move ahead into the battle God has set before us. For others, it will stir you to recognize the battle at last, confess your unpreparedness, and join the many other men who have begun to seek healing.

In order to accomplish Jesus' mission *through* us, however, we must first begin to let him accomplish his mission *in* us. The Father who loves his sons doesn't send a man into battle with huge chinks in his armor.

Indeed, men often come to me complaining that their spiritual life has become boring and unproductive; "I don't feel like God's calling me to any task at all," someone once said to me.

"You may well be right," I replied. "If he loves you, he won't send you out to battle so wounded you'll get wasted. He may be waiting for you to get up on the table and let him operate. Are you willing to set aside your agenda? Are you willing to ask the Father not, 'When will I see your destiny and victory?' but instead, 'What do you want to heal in me to prepare for my part in it?'"

The army requires basic training before ordering a recruit into battle. You enlist in the Lord's army when you become a Christian and give your life to Jesus—not just so he can bless you immediately with material goodies, but eternally, with the privilege of being reshaped in his image.

That process of reshaping is the making of a Kingdom warrior. In it, the Enemy's strikes at a man of God become like a sculptor's chisel, which at last bring forth the true and godly man from within the stone.

To be a man is to be a son, even of Father God. To fight like a man is to engage life's struggles with all the resources of your inheritance (Gal. 4:6-7). The conflict that we see in the world around us today therefore reflects the timeless battle in every man's heart to be restored to relationship with the Father—which releases those resources unto victory.

The apostle Paul described this battle graphically to the ancient church at Rome:

> I know that good does not live in me—that is, in my human nature. For even though the desire to do good is in me, I am not able to do it. . . . So I find that this law is at work: when

I want to do what is good, what is evil is the only choice I have. My inner being delights in the law of God. But I see a different law at work in my body—a law that fights against the law that my mind approves of. It makes me a prisoner to the law of sin which is at work in my body. What an unhappy man I am! (Romans 7:18, 21-24)

This despair at being wholly unable to do what you know is best for you plagues men even today. We "want to do what is good" as husbands, fathers, brothers, and citizens, but we can't.

The average man today longs to feel secure in his manhood. But he's afraid to face his sin-nature, which sabotages that security, because he's already overwhelmed by shame from having been abandoned by Dad.

But Dad, meanwhile, had been abandoned himself by his own father and was therefore unable to confirm manhood in his son. The man today is thereby hamstrung by a deep, generational shame that whispers relentlessly, "You're not a real man like the others."

Betrayed by relationship, a man often takes refuge in technique and grasps after control. Desperate for manhood, angry for not getting from Dad what he needed to secure it, he becomes vulnerable to a host of worldly—and even religious—counterfeits, which promise to silence the voice of shame, restore his control, and render him a "real man" at last.

When the True abdicates, the False plunders.

And so men today extol the sanitized, civilian question of manhood, "How do I do it?" It's too fearful to let the abandoned boy ask the authentic, warrior question—like the apostle after his above confession—"Who will rescue me from this body that is taking me to death?" (Rom. 7:24).

We're not ignorant. We're dying.

Meanwhile, however, most Christian teaching for men today simply tells us what we should do and why, the terrible consequences for not doing it, and perhaps even the wonderful benefits of doing it.

It's basic, Old Testament teaching—an appropriate and essential reminder of God's standard to an unprincipled, pagan society. As such, it's altogether right and necessary—but, like Moses without Jesus, not wholly sufficient (John 1:17).

It won't, therefore, win the battle at hand.

The Kingdom warrior proclaims not only the life of Jesus, but also his death (1 Cor. 11:26). He heralds not only what God has told us to do but also the deadly human condition from which Jesus came to save us—namely, that we can't do it. That confession alone frees a man at last to know the One who does it, and thereby, to walk in victory.

As he lets the Father crucify his pride, the Kingdom warrior exchanges his broken human spirit for the Father's Holy Spirit. He thereby becomes an agent for resurrection life and destiny as he battles to restore the Kingdom of God within and among us.

But what, in fact, is your destined role in that battle? Who, indeed, enlists men as Kingdom warriors? Does the Father really have orders for us all? Will he train and supply us to carry them out?

To ask the question is to risk hearing the answer—even from the apostle: "Thanks be to God, who does this through our Lord Jesus Christ!" (Rom. 7:25).

This book, therefore, is not about how to be a man, but rather, knowing the one who rescues and restores men.

It's not even about how to be a warrior, but rather, surrendering to the Commander of the Lord's army.

You won't learn a technique here; you'll remember your longing for a relationship.

You won't be exhorted to obey; you'll be invited to trust. You won't be commanded to do right; you'll be freed to be real. You won't be warned to be strong; you'll be promised your Father's strength.

And if you're honest, you'll be battling for your life.

ONE

First, We Surrender

*Yet the Lord still waits for you to come to him so he can
show you his love; he will conquer you to bless you,
just as he said.* Isaiah 30:18, TLB

*While Joshua was near Jericho, he suddenly saw a man standing in
front of him, holding a sword. Joshua went up to him and asked,
"Are you one of our soldiers, or an enemy?"
"Neither," the man answered. "I am here as the
commander of the Lord's army."
Joshua threw himself on the ground in worship and said,
"I am your servant, sir. What do you want me to do?"
And the commander of the Lord's army told him,
"Take your sandals off; you are standing on holy ground."
And Joshua did as he was told.* Joshua 5:13-15

THIS is a story for men of our time.

To stand with Joshua on the threshold of Jericho is to know at
once the terror and the grace of a Kingdom warrior.

Here we see the newly appointed commander of the Israeli
armies poised on the brink of his first and most important battle

in the Promised Land. The very future of God's people hangs in the balance.

Joshua and his people have just crossed the Jordan River and celebrated the Passover meal. But while the memory of God's saving hand in Egypt is fresh from the feast, Joshua is very likely terrified. On his shoulders alone rest the decisions of the momentous battle ahead.

If only Moses were here! Joshua must have thought. *He'd just talk face-to-face with God, get the winning battle plan, give it to the army, and we'd go out and win.*

But his mentor Moses is gone, and Joshua hasn't yet developed his own intimate relationship with God.

The Father, however, has not abandoned his servant. As Joshua paces nervously outside the Israeli encampment, suddenly an imposing figure with a sword appears. Joshua demands he identify himself as friend or foe, and the figure replies, "I am the commander of the Lord's army." In other words, "Whether I'm for you or against you depends on whether or not you're surrendered to the Lord."

And so Joshua, the commander of the army-in-the-flesh, at last meets his spiritual counterpart and authentic Mentor: Jesus, the Commander of the Lord's army.

We can scarcely imagine Joshua's relief as he "threw himself on the ground in worship": "Oh, praise God! Thank you, Lord, for showing up at the eleventh hour! I was afraid you'd left me alone! Oh, please—now give me the battle plan!"

The Commander of the Lord's army, however, does not give his earthly counterpart the battle plan, but rather, something more important, more primary. Before directing how to engage the Enemy, he says, "Take your sandals off; you are standing on holy ground."

The text is simple and direct. Without hesitation—convicted of his own inadequacy, overwhelmed by the grace of his Commander's presence, and anxious to do whatever necessary to overcome his fears and win the battle—Joshua "did as he was told."

Listen to the story: *In order to engage the Enemy boldly, you must first engage your Father God humbly.*

Surrender to Jesus defines God's victory.

Boot camps in the armies of the world teach the recruit submission and obedience. Both allow for conditional or temporary agreement, even distrust; neither implies transformation of the inner man (Rom. 12:1-2). "When the war's over, I'm out," the recruit can rationalize as he salutes his sergeant.

Jesus, however, allows nothing to be held back. He takes away everything you have, and he'll restore to you only those things that fit his purposes in your life—and even then, only when you're ready to regard them as such.

The war to which Jesus calls men is the Father's battle to restore his Kingdom authority on earth as it is in heaven—that is, to restore relationship with himself, against our rebellious human nature and the Enemy who would use that to seduce us from him. This conflict is part of life in this fallen world. It doesn't end until Jesus returns.

Christians are "baptized into union with [Jesus'] death" (Rom. 6:3). In the Father's army, you can't store your sports car and civilian clothes and hope to pick them up after boot camp. You're in for life.

The Enemy Within

The soldier of the world fights only to defeat the enemy; when the enemy surrenders, his job is done. He fights for "peace" as the cessation of hostilities—and leaves the rest up to the politicians.

But as armed conflict in this world reflects an internal political conflict, so the battle in men's souls reflects a larger and deeper spiritual battle. The Kingdom warrior fights not only against the Enemy of God, but against sinful human nature in himself and others.

The Enemy's strategy has been simple since the Snake seduced man: "Cut the man off from the Father, and he'll eventually strut right into my hands." Indeed, when left to our own devices, we're easily seduced because our sin-nature—inherited from Adam's fall—leads us to do just that.

In Jesus, however, God "changed us from enemies into his friends and gave us the task of making others his friends also," the apostle Paul declared (2 Cor. 5:18).

The Father has staked his very Kingdom on earth upon us; he wants the whole man as his own in order to cover and preserve the man in battle. Indeed, whatever part of the man is not surrendered to the Father God becomes a chink in his armor, giving the Enemy access to destroy him.

To become God's warrior, you must therefore want restored relationship with the Father. To spark that desire, God commonly uses the pain of broken relationship with your earthly father.

That's why healing the father-wound is the key to godly manhood.

Disobedience and Distrust

Even as Adam fell when the Snake challenged God's credibility, so disobedience and rebellion are rooted in distrust.

Men who have learned by painful experience not to trust their fathers won't readily trust God. Because they haven't learned trust, they can't surrender. They may know submission to Dad, even obedience because of his power to punish resistance and coerce—but they haven't dared surrender to him.

Kingdom warriors today can learn to trust God by facing him and surrendering to him their pain from Dad's abandonment.

False warriors have learned to mask their fear of that pain and distrust of the Father God with a facade of righteousness, often by exhorting other men to "obedience." Such dishonesty among Christian leaders undermines our "task of making others his friends also." Our sin-nature seeks an excuse to reject Jesus, and too often the church itself provides it.

It's easier to command men to obey than to earn their trust. To obey, you have to know the system; to trust, you have to know the man. Commanders who know religion order men to obey; those who know the Father invite men to trust. In their own character growth, Kingdom warriors seek first to be trustworthy, not dominant. Indeed, God called Abraham "righteous" not when he obeyed God, but rather when he "put his trust in the Lord" (Gen. 15:6). Only then could God count on Abraham's obedience in the long run—not as a one-shot, bite-the-bullet effort, but as a natural outcome of his surrendering.

And so the old hymn exhorts not "Obey and Trust," but rather, "Trust and Obey." Similarly, God prefaces the Ten Commandments with a statement of what he has done in our history to earn our trust: "I am the Lord your God who brought you out of Egypt, where you were slaves. Worship no god but me" (Exod. 20:2-3).

Submitting to and obeying God, then, are secondary effects of surrendering—through which a man's heart is transformed to *want* God's authority in his life.

A man respects integrity. He's drawn to other men who live the life they promote—who "walk the talk." Trustworthy leaders, therefore—from fathers to generals—don't have to command men to obey them. Their authority is rooted in their character, not in their threat to punish. That's why knowing the Father God's true character sets us free from the law (Gal. 5:1-6).

The more risky the venture, the greater a man's fear, and so the more trustworthy the leader must be. Mere appeals to law and duty can only overcome so much fear in a man; when the risk escalates to his very life, he must follow a man and not merely a doctrine. Even as a private wants to know the sergeant who orders him into battle, Jesus secures the personal relationship with the Father that prompts us to obey him.

As God's Commander-in-Chief, Jesus spoke "with authority" (Mark 1:22) when he taught men to trust and give up their lives to the Father, because he was ready to do that himself on the cross.

Men who are distrusted, on the other hand, are not obeyed—often with tragic consequences.

During the Vietnam war, for example, President Johnson fabricated reports of an enemy attack upon U.S. ships in the Gulf of Tonkin. Similarly, his successor, President Nixon, lied about his role in the Watergate break-in. Both chief executives demanded military obedience of young men—who refused when they could not trust their president.

Thus, the Vietnam era defense secretary, Robert S. McNamara, who pushed to escalate the war, confessed in his 1995 book, *In Retrospect: The Tragedy and Lessons of Vietnam*, "We could have and should have withdrawn in late 1963"—when only seventy-eight Americans had died. Blaming himself and his government associates, including President Johnson, for "a series of blunders that led to tragedy," he declared that the war, which eventually claimed fifty-eight thousand lives, made Americans cynical about their government. He then lamented that such "cynicism makes Americans reluctant to support their leaders in the actions necessary to confront and solve our problems at home and abroad."[1]

Without trustworthy old warriors to lead young men, righteous resistance degenerated into adolescent rebellion. Today, we reap the terrible harvest of that deception in a generation of aimless, angry young men. Witness the youth-market ads: true masculinity, engaged and bright, is wimpy; false masculinity, disaffected and sneering, sells.

Exhorting men first to "submit to God" and "obey God's Word" ignores the wound that makes them reject God in the first place. In fact, it only fuels rebellion in those who recognize their wound and creates a "yes-man" legion of false warriors among those who do not.

The man who wants to pursue his destiny against the popular tide of rebellion must surrender to Jesus his painful longing for a perfectly trustworthy father. This usually happens as a man sees more clearly the Enemy's destructive intent and his own inability to save himself from it. Indeed, the Enemy is defeated most convincingly when a man turns him, in effect, into a servant of God who drives men desperately into the Father's arms.

Victory in Surrender

I once took my son, a squiggly, "do-it-myself" toddler, to the zoo and worried that he would get lost and harmed among the crowds and animals. To my horror, as we approached the lion's cage, he suddenly bolted and ran ahead excitedly. I was about to yell, "Stop! Come back to Daddy!" but to my surprise the lion did the job for me. One timely yawn from that awesome beast, and the little boy stopped dead, spun on his heels, and came tearing back to me, arms uplifted and crying, "Daa-dee!" He insisted on holding my hand the rest of the day.

No amount of my exhorting, threatening, or punishing John-Miguel could have prompted him to surrender to me so completely. As a father, I say, "Thank you, lion!"

When the Enemy attacks at our weak spots, we can panic, much as zebras scatter when the lion attacks, leaving each one an easy target. Or we can run to Jesus—together, in his Body—arms lifted and crying out for the Father. Indeed, we can say, "Thank you, Satan, for pointing out that chink in my armor. I'm a lot more effective as a warrior now that I've taken it to Jesus!"

As another has said, "If you haven't met the Enemy, it's because you're going in his direction."

When you decide to stop cooperating with the Enemy and following him into destruction, you turn around—the root meaning of *repent*—and face him at last. At that point, you surrender either to the Enemy's jaws or the Father's arms.

It's your choice. At that point, no one need command you to "obey God's word"; you know you either do it or die.

Men who never get sick enough, however, never go to the doctor—and never get healed. If you never face your lethal self-centeredness from which Jesus died to save you, you never meet him. Therefore, you never know the Father or the calling he created you to fulfill. The prostitutes and tax collectors, on the other hand, were more manifestly sick unto death—and thereby became Jesus' most faithful recruits (Luke 19:1-10).

To the warrior of the world, therefore, "surrender" signals the end of the battle, after the outcome has been determined and the loser yields. For the warrior of God, surrender precedes the battle and determines its outcome. For insofar as a man is surrendered to Jesus, he will walk in God's victory. In the world, losers surrender to the enemy's greater power; in the Kingdom of God, winners surrender to the Father, whose power is greater even than the Enemy's (Luke 12:4-5).

Some of us—usually the stronger, more accomplished—take longer than others to realize the irony of this truth: Victory begins with surrender. In fact, we are more susceptible than women to scorn that truth, simply because our larger physical and economic muscles allow us to feel more powerful than women.

The flesh deceives us: Our own human strength is no match against our spiritual Enemy.

Pride and Hidden Wounds

While a Peace Corps volunteer among the Igbo people of Nigeria in the mid 1960s, I once heard a friend say, "There is no such thing as a small snake."

A single bite from the smallest, newly hatched West African snake will kill the biggest man. Similarly, even the "smallest," most unheralded evil spirit can overwhelm the most healthy and esteemed man.

The man who would engage spiritual reality must begin with humility—even as Joshua took his shoes off when he heard God say, "You're in territory ruled by powers far beyond that which your pride has allowed, and only I can save you from them."

Tragically, most of us men cling to our own strength and scoff at snakes until we are bitten—perhaps by divorce, addiction, or serious illness—and must at last confess the truth: We are creatures of surrender. The question for our lives is not whether we will surrender, but rather, to what or whom?

The apostle Paul therefore declared,

> Sin must no longer rule in your mortal bodies, so that you obey the desires of your natural self. Nor must you surrender any part of yourselves to sin to be used for wicked purposes. Instead, give yourselves to God, as those who have been brought from death to life, and surrender your whole being to him to be used for righteous purposes. (Rom. 6:12-13)

A soldier surrenders only when he has nothing left to hold on to but his life. Thus God promised Jeremiah, who had surrendered wholly to him, "I am bringing evil upon all flesh, says the Lord; but I will give you your life as a prize of war" (Jer. 45:5, RSV).

Surrendering to Jesus is just the beginning. It's joining the army, not retiring from service. If I break my leg one day and give my life to Jesus the next, I can't expect that my leg will instantly heal. I pray for healing, but still go to the doctor.

Indeed, even publicly confessing your faith does not ensure that you'll remain wholly surrendered to Jesus afterwards. If that were true, all born-again Christians, their families, and churches would be pure reflections of virtue!

I once pastored near a community hospital that invited neighbors to become a "community hospital supporter" by donating money and attending occasional public relations meetings with the head surgeon and administrators. Many Christians join the church, similarly, as a "Kingdom supporter." They donate money, attend meetings, endorse the pastoral administrator, praise the Head Surgeon, and enthusiastically recommend their hospital to others.

But they've never gone in for an operation themselves. They've never let Jesus do, in fact, what he came to do, namely, draw them back into relationship with the Father by exposing and forgiving their sin and healing them from the effects of others' sins against them.

To bar Jesus from your deepest wounds is to expose them to the Enemy; to hide them is to hand them over to the Prince of Darkness, who will use the opening to sabotage God's purposes in you.

But, you may protest, "I've never taken any hurts to Jesus, and I'm doing just great!"

The Enemy bides his time—and fattens men for the kill.

Fight or Flight

Steve, in his mid-forties with two grown children, had worked his way up to an influential position in his business and was being considered for the senior elder position in his church of several thousand members. He and his wife had each become a Christian while in college and met before graduating on a church-sponsored retreat.

Steve told me that, during their premarital counseling with the college pastor, his wife mentioned she had been sexually molested as a girl.

"Don't worry," the pastor declared. "That's all been taken care of on the cross. Now that you're Christians, things of the past can't harm you anymore."

Indeed, on the cross Jesus flung wide the doors of heaven's hospital. But you still have to walk in and get up on the operating table.

Twenty-five years later, when Steve had finally reached the threshold of community esteem and significant ministry, the Enemy struck. After the children left home, he said, his wife announced that she hated all men, refused any counsel, and filed for divorce. Church members were shocked and disheartened, and officials barred Steve from all leadership; his Christian witness at work was destroyed.

For Kingdom warriors, surrender to Jesus does not mean putting on rose-colored religious glasses, but rather, daring to face head-on the world's brokenness—even in yourself and your wife—because you trust your Commander is with you.

The world—as embodied in our sinful human nature—can offer only two responses to pain, namely, "fight or flight." These might more aptly be called our animal nature. When a dog is threatened, it either lashes back or runs away. The powers of the world can't conceive of any other option, and these two responses remain preeminent within us—revenge or retreat.

Our God-created human spirits, however, harken unto a deeper call than the world's fight-or-flight (Rom. 12:17-21). When our revenge has upped the ante and prompted a vicious cycle of more destructive response, when our retreat has cost us loss of self-respect and relationship with others, we cry out, "There must be another way!"

And indeed there is.

We can surrender to Jesus.

The Father has sent Jesus as the Way—the only safeguard against running away from life or charging into it angrily.

He's not a formula for changing others, but the Way to stay open, even in your pain, and let God change you.

He's not a scheme for getting what you want, but the Way to let God have what he wants in your life.

He's not even a way to restore your relationship with the other person—who is free to reject your efforts—but the Way to deepen your relationship with the Father God, who alone can reconcile our human brokenness.

For Jesus chose neither flight nor fight when attacked. He could have fled the religious authorities and enjoyed a long and happy life teaching and healing in the remote countryside of Galilee (flight). Instead, he "made up his mind and set out on his way to Jerusalem" to face his attackers head-on, even knowing they would crucify him (Luke 9:51).

At the same time, he could've destroyed his enemies with a word (fight). His focus in the battle ahead, however, was forecast by an immediate confrontation in the very next verse. That night, Samaritan villagers refused to let Jesus and his disciples stay among them. Like a Clint Eastwood movie in religious garb, the disciples asked angrily, "Lord, do you want us to call fire down from heaven to destroy them?"

But Jesus did not face off against the Samaritans and challenge them, "Make my day!" Fortunately for those of us who are sinners, Jesus can't be pushed off-center by rejection and goaded into revenge. Instead, "He turned and rebuked [his disciples] and said, 'You don't know what kind of a Spirit you belong to, for the Son of Man did not come to destroy men's lives, but to save them'" (Luke 9:55).[2]

Dare we let him?

In surrendering to the Father and going to the Cross, even for those who reject and deny him, Jesus became God's Way of resolving conflict. He demonstrated that a son of the Father does not seek pain—Jesus begged God to take the cup of suffering from him—but neither does he flee when it beckons his destiny.

Jesus stayed open, remained vulnerable, refused to hide from the pain in his calling. He was willing to face the pain because he trusted that his Father would stand with him in it. Even as it hurt him unto death, he kept the door open for God to stay in control and fulfill his destiny (Phil. 2:6-11).

This is a word for all men struggling against the flesh.

Dan, a thirty-five-year-old schoolteacher, came to me after his wife left him for another man. "Sometimes, I just want to shut down to women forever," he told me. "But I have to trust the Father's got something better for me if I can only let him use this awful pain to bring up whatever needs healing in me. I know I can't just shut down to women and still stay open to him like I need to be.

"I know I'm not ready yet for another woman. So I just ask the Lord to keep me open, and I wrestle it out with him day by day. I get counseling, talk with other guys, and have them pray for me; I get my physical exercise and do the best I can at work.

"I tell the Lord how much it hurts. But whatever it takes, I don't want to go through this again—so I'm going to stay on the operating table for the whole operation."

Surrender to Jesus is neither masochistic running after pain, nor cowardly running from it, but running into the Father's arms in the midst of pain. That allows him to bear your wound and you to receive his life rather than the world's destruction.

Unlike Dan, most men wounded by women consider only the animal response—and either lash back with verbal or physical abuse, or withdraw by shutting down emotionally. All too often, Christian men put a spiritual spin on the animal way, wielding Scriptures to detail the woman's sins or justify their own shutting down.

We try everything but the truth—which only emerges through surrendering to Jesus.

God's Option: Surrender

I used to keep a file folder on news articles about men in responsible positions—policemen, clergy, politicians, sports heroes, media personalities and the like—who either committed violent antisocial acts (fight) or suicide (flight) after being rejected by a woman. I stopped, simply because I ran out of file space for so many articles. If any disease claimed as many men's lives, it would be declared an epidemic.

I wrote this chapter before the O. J. Simpson trial began. While writing it, however, I read a front-page *Los Angeles Times* headline and subhead: "Broken Romance Writes Tragic End to Bright Future: Friends and family of officer are shocked by murders and his suicide."[3]

In this case, twenty-four-year-old navy ensign George Smith had been voted "best all around" by his high school class six years earlier. When his sweetheart and fellow officer Kerry O'Neill broke off their engagement, he shot both O'Neill and her companion, former navy star quarterback Alton Grizzard, and then killed himself as well.

Again, the apparent extremes of fight or flight both avoid surrender to Jesus—and therefore are flip sides of the same coin. They're equally ineffective. The man who vows, "I'll never date, marry, or get close to a woman again," (flight) generally harbors intense anger (fight). He shuts down and withdraws from confrontation because he feels inadequate, then ends up going for the fists, gun, tongue-lashing, or "Bible bullets" to compensate.

"Because she hurt me so badly," he rationalizes, "I'm justified in my response"—no matter how animalistic.

In fact, however, he's made the woman into an idol. Instead of a "suitable companion to help him" fulfill God's calling (Gen. 2:18), the woman has become the caller. He lives life—or destroys it—in response to her, often because he has not had a father to draw him into life beyond Mom.

Historically, therefore, when we had so turned away from God to our animal nature that we could imagine no scenario of conflict resolution other than "fight or flight," the Father sent Jesus to save us from its certain destruction. Until a greater power born of a deeper truth entered the world, alienation and violence remained business as usual among us men—even as for the young military man George Smith.

Surrender to Jesus allows the authentic saving Power to enter;

pride keeps you closed and creates a false sense of security in your own power. "I live in a high and holy place," God declares, "but I also live with people who are humble and repentant, so that I can restore their confidence and hope. . . . There is no safety for sinners" (Isa. 57:15, 21).

One evening years ago, these truths became a life-or-death lesson for me. Just two nights before, I'd taught a church group these insights on dealing with resentment and that morning had put my teaching into practice.[4]

For some time, I'd been hurt badly by someone I trusted, and all my attempts to speak directly with the person only deteriorated into further hurting. I had prayed with other men for accountability and begged Jesus to stay me from my natural impulse to run from the pain. Still, my fight-or-flight nature was consuming my best energies as I either shut down emotionally or entertained fantasies of revenge.

On my knees, I asked Jesus to clarify for me which hurts from that person needed his healing. I offered up each painful incident to him and asked, "Give me your heart, Lord. Show me any wound that prompted this person to hurt me like that." With that, I saw in my mind's eye that person—often as a little child—hurting and crying out for comfort and healing.

I found myself weeping for the person and then praying fiercely on this person's behalf to be set free from the bondage of those hurts.

I hasten to add: This process is no license to reestablish relationship with the other person, but indeed, a faithful letting go. It cleansed me and prevented my resentment from hindering the Father's work in that person's life, and it allowed the Father to get on with his work in my life.

In fact, my sense of release that morning was so exciting that I asked the Lord to dig into my memory for other resentments I might be carrying toward any other persons—and we dealt with those similarly. Afterward, I put in an exhilarating afternoon of writing.

That evening, I laced up my running shoes energetically and set out on the neighborhood route I'd jogged for years without incident. Breathing deeply, I found a comfortable stride under the streetlights and reflected on the day's events. After some time, I came to a broad but darker street that sloped gently downward, and I enjoyed the "coasting" feeling as I simply savored the sense of "rightness" in what I'd taught and experienced.

Moments later, my house appeared ahead under the clear sky and bright stars. The air beckoned crisply. *Why not go another circuit?* I thought—and, buoyed by the day's success, ran on by.

What a breakthrough day! I thought, shaking my fists triumphantly as I turned a corner. *Praise God!*

No cars passed as I loped along, enjoying the vitality of the moment. A while later, the street headed upward, leveled, and then the broad, downward-sloping street stretched before me. A streetlight far ahead reflected dimly in the dewy asphalt, and a picture of my driveway finish-line came to mind. I headed for the middle of the broad, empty street, enjoying the sense of freedom.

Behind me, a dog's bark shot out in my direction. Accustomed to barking from behind backyard fences as I jogged past, I disregarded it and thought to go a little easy on my right knee, which had been hurting a bit over recent weeks.

To my surprise, however, the bark became louder and suddenly was joined by a quick clicking sound on the pavement behind me.

Before I could turn to see, a leaping shove of weight slammed against my side. I stumbled as a blur of tan fur and white teeth flashed before me. At once I drew up as the dog—which I recognized immediately as a pit bull—fell snarling viciously at my feet.

Startled, I stood panting in the vast and empty middle of the dimly lit street and watched, horrified, as the dog quickly gathered itself and crouched low. In a flash, it leapt at me again with a loud yelp, teeth bared.

Instinctively, I threw up my arm for protection, and the dog clamped its jaw just above my wrist. As its teeth bore down, I shouted at the top of my voice, and it let go, dropping about a yard in front of me and scrambling for balance to leap again.

Terrified, I realized instantly that no one from the nearby houses would likely hear my shouts or come to my aid. Out in the middle of the street, no stick or stone lay at hand for a weapon. My soft-soled running shoes would be no defense; to run from the swift dog, even if I had not been exhausted after doubling my regular distance, was out of the question.

Pain shot through my arm. Trembling, I glanced down and saw my running jersey shredded and spotted with blood.

My eyes darted hopelessly from one side of the street to the other and came back to the dog's face—eyes narrowed, ears back, teeth bared—and saw evil as naked as ever I have seen it, like a huge snake's head, tensed and ready to strike.

All thoughts fled from my grasp as the dog quivered and crouched lower for its spring.

"Stop!" I heard myself pleading desperately—and then, with determination, "In the name of Jesus, stop!"

The instant the word *Jesus* sprang from my lips, a veil seemed to part, and by a new and holy instinct I knew at once what to do.

Utterly terrified, absolutely powerless, I surrendered.

"Jesus," I whispered, looking away. As the dog let out a sharp yowl and lifted its forelegs to leap, I dropped my arms helplessly to my side.

In that unforgettable split second, more intense in both horror and peace than I have ever before known, all fear and tension swept out of me. Quietly, I stood there—whether seconds or minutes I can't say.

I only know that when I looked down again, the dog had not leapt after all, but was still coiled and growling in front of me.

"Jesus," I said again, this time calmly, and looked directly into the dog's burning eyes: "Jesus, Jesus, Jesus."

Hesitating yet, it growled once more, looked around, and then stood there just looking at me. Clearly, it was over. With a snort, the dog turned awkwardly and trotted off into the night.

Dark and empty, the vast asphalt pavement surrounded me, glimmering faintly from the distant streetlight. I sighed, strangely nonplussed. Looking again at my arm, I lifted it and made a fist, then stretched out my fingers. Dark streaks of blood spotted my shredded sleeve, but the wound was not bleeding badly. *Painful,* I remember thinking, *but not long from being healed.*

I was still about a half mile from home, and the night air on my sweat-soaked jersey suddenly seemed cool. Holding my hand up to reduce circulation through it, I began running again, slowly at first, and then up to my usual pace.

In my spirit, meanwhile, a strange battle was taking place. One part of me seemed waiting, still poised either to run or fight. I thought of suing the dog's owner. In my imagination, I saw an instant replay in which the dog leapt at me and I smashed his head to a pulp with a vicious karate kick.

Wincing, I consciously rejected all these impulses and images; indeed, they seemed only to hover like the dross in an annealing furnace, surfacing only to drain away before a pure and underlying peace unlike any I had ever known.

Reigning over every stride was the Moment.

Terrifying, glorious, it came back to me. The dog had been ready to jump, that was clear. What, indeed, if he had? In my imagination I saw it leap again—and bleeped the thought away. Completely helpless . . . not one bit of protection . . . and yet . . . and yet . . .

As my driveway came into view at last, it struck me: What a graphic example of precisely the lesson I had taught at church! Clearly, any attempt on my part before the vicious dog either to defend myself or run away—the sum total of my animal/natural responses—would only have given the dog more power over me and caused me greater harm. The newspaper had reported several killings nationwide by pit bulls in recent months, and in each case, the victim had tried to get away.

I had no natural human strength of my own to save me, and only when I had accepted that fully and turned instead to Jesus, was I saved.

I drew up to the driveway and stopped, panting lightly. In fact, I realized, I had been forced to reject the fight-or-flight response, neither seeking revenge nor running away, and so become other-than-animal myself. In reaching instead for Jesus, I had experienced graphically the fact that Jesus gives us power over animal nature—not only its fearful, self-centered component within us, but its vicious and destructive component without.

Awestruck, I sat down on the front porch step and savored the openness and strength I felt growing within me. In that moment, I realized that my prayers of compassion that morning for ones who had hurt me were also an integral part of the day's amazing lesson.

In praying for the other's brokenness instead of lashing back, I had essentially risked the other's continued aggresson. Isn't that why we hesitate to forgive? Having given myself to Jesus, however, I was willing to risk his bringing about some other result than an escalating Ping-Pong volley of revenge.

Just as with the dog.

As I sat there on my front stoop, I realized that my self-centered human nature was trying through fantasies of retaliation to regain the control I had yielded to Jesus. Indeed, my natural self told me that I surrendered to the dog and was, therefore, a coward.

To remedy such shameful behavior, I should strike back with "my power"—a stiff lawsuit against the owner or carrying a club while jogging next time in hopes of bashing in the dog's head.

As a chill from the night air struck me, I sighed, rose, and went inside for the most cleansing shower I have ever experienced.

Certainly, in order to protect myself and others in the future, I knew I would need to report the incident to the authorities. When I later did, I met others who had complained likewise, and the city enforced our request for proper restraints on the dog.

But city hall could not save me from the murderous dog that night when I stood alone before it. I could easily have been killed. I was determined, therefore, to learn everything the Lord could teach me from it.

Shortly after, I told a friend about the incident, and he immediately demanded, "Are you telling me that when evil attacks, you should just give up?"

Puzzled at first, I hesitated and prayed quickly for understanding. "Yes, I am," I said at last. "In fact, when the Enemy attacks, you must give up—not to the Enemy, but to Jesus.

Clearly, I didn't surrender to the dog, but to Jesus. If I'd surrendered to the dog, I wouldn't be here to tell you about it."

The dog had indicated its intention to destroy me. In surrendering to Jesus, I had allowed him to indicate clearly his intention to save me. He is Jesus—Y'Shua in Hebrew, literally, "God saves."

The difference between surrender and passivity is Jesus.

Certainly, God doesn't deliver you from all pain and suffering if you just call out to him. After all, Jesus called out to God from the cross, but he was still crucified.

What, then, does calling out to Jesus accomplish? It takes your pain out of the Enemy's reach and places it in God's hands, to use for his purposes.

Indeed, in the days that followed, I began to see that the death of self, which I tasted in the presence of the vicious dog, is kin to the cross, on which Jesus renounced both cowardice and revenge and gave up his natural human self to the Father. On Good Friday Jesus did not surrender to Death, but rather, to Father God. Nor did he surrender to the flesh. Indeed, yielding neither to cowardice nor revenge, he fulfilled his destiny:

> He was humble and walked the path of obedience to death— his death on the cross. For this reason God raised him to the highest place above and gave him the name that is greater than any other name. (Phil. 2:8-9)

Modern secular therapies that urge the dying person to "make peace with" or "give in to" death, are therefore an evil deception that draws souls into eternal darkness. For a child of God to surrender to death is truly the end of life, for death is "the last enemy" (1 Cor. 15:26).

But for those who have already surrendered to the Father by giving themselves to Jesus, even as he gave himself to the Father, death is the final surrender of the natural flesh to God—as terrifying, perhaps, as a killer dog—but as promising, certainly, as the resurrection of Jesus, "the pioneer of [our] salvation" (Heb. 2:10, RSV).

19

Judith MacNutt, psychologist and wife of author Francis MacNutt, recounts the advice of a friend: "If a child loses a loved one, don't ever tell him or her, for example, 'God took your daddy.' Instead, tell the truth. Say, 'Death took your daddy—and Jesus took your daddy from death'."

That is, when I surrendered to Jesus, the dog surrendered. So does the Enemy of God surrender when he knows that we have placed ourselves fully in the hands of his Conqueror.

It's time to renounce our own fight-or-flight power and surrender instead to the Father God, so he can fill us with his power.

Since Adam broke relationship with the Father, we've fought like animals—and it's destroying us.

It's time to fight like a man.

TWO

Knowing the Commander

*The time is coming when I will make a new covenant with the people
of Israel and the people of Judah. . . . None of them will have to
teach his fellow countryman to know the Lord, because all
will know me, from the least to the greatest.* Jeremiah 31:31, 34

*"Now that you have known me," [Jesus] said to them,
"you will know my Father also, and from now on you do know him
and you have seen him."* John 14:7

*And eternal life means to know you, the only true God,
and to know Jesus Christ, whom you sent.* John 17:3

AFTER a year, the late-night nursings were beginning to exhaust
Mary, and I knew it was time for Dad to take over.

I didn't look forward to being awakened randomly at night. I
admired Mary's perseverance, but I'm a heavy sleeper. "I don't
know how you do it," I often said.

Now it was time to find out.

I confess I balked at nighttime feedings partly because John-

Miguel always awoke crying, "Mommy!" I felt like a second-fiddle mom—and not a very good one at that.

In fact, I started out more hindrance than help. John-Miguel's cries were not loud enough to wake me, but they did wake Mary, who soon learned that only a well-placed elbow in my side would bring me to consciousness.

The elbow and relentless cries for "Mommy!" were not pleasant motivators, and at the first nighttime whimper I began bargaining with the Lord. I prayed. I rebuked spirits. I begged. I was ready to deal. *Please, Lord, make him sleep! It's better for the baby, after all. I'll write an extra hour a day. I'll increase my tithe!*

But still the cry for "Mommy!" wailed on.

Yawning, I rolled out of the sack and stumbled into John-Miguel's bedroom. *Maybe it won't be all that bad after all,* I told myself, and took a deep breath. "Daddy's here!" I announced hopefully. "It's OK!"

To my pleasant surprise, the room fell silent. *Well, that wasn't so hard!* I thought, and confidently stepped toward the crib.

"MOMMMMMYYYYY!" Shattering my eardrums along with my ego, the cry blasted forth with renewed vigor.

Startled, I stopped—then sighed. Gingerly, I picked the boy up and put him on my shoulder.

Week after week, bottle after bottle, I pushed on through the cries for Mommy—dutifully, if not lovingly. Soon, however, I began to enjoy just holding my little son. Before long, I was praying for him, even singing my prayers softly at times. On a few especially tough nights, we walked out on the patio under the stars and talked about moons and dogs and raisin bread.

And then late one night, it happened.

Lost in heavy sleep, I stirred as a strange sound tapped lightly on my ear.

"Daa-dee . . ."

My eyes flickered open, closed again. Shifting, I reached to pull the covers higher.

"DAA-DEE! DAA-DEEEEE!"

Bold and full-throated, the small voice pierced the dark morning stillness like a bugle.

My eyes exploded open. Lurching from the bed, I raced into John-Miguel's room and scooped him up in my arms. "That's my man!" I cried out, laughing and lifting him high above my head. "Hallelujah! That's my man!"

"What's going on in there?" Mary called out sleepily from back in our bedroom. "I didn't even wake you up, and you're in there making all that noise?"

Sheepishly, I lowered a confused and bleary-eyed John-Miguel to my chest. "I'm not sure exactly what's going on," I called back. "But . . . it's OK. I mean, it's good."

I held my son against me at last and smiled. "Real good," I whispered, shaking my head. "Real good."

The Cry of the Masculine Soul

What, indeed, stirred—even leapt—within me that night when I first heard my son cry out, "Daa-dee!"?

Partly it was my joy, certainly, after waiting so long for him to acknowledge the bond between us. And yet, when I had rejoiced fully and both he and Mary were asleep again, I lay in bed staring at the ceiling in awe, gripped by something deeper. I was identifying with the cry of my son. In his baby's voice I heard something I recognized in myself.

I believe every man harbors that cry deep within his masculine soul, awaiting the night. It's the primal, human cry for centeredness and security in a dark and broken world. "Save me!" we cry.

We cry not for a technique, principles of faith, or moral standards, but for a person—indeed, for our Father.

Even as Jesus cried, "Abba!" a man's cry for "Daa-dee!" stirs the heart of the Father God like no other. *That's my man!* I imagine God's proclaiming, as the angelic chorus sings, "Hallelujah!":

23

For all who are moved by the Spirit of God are sons of God. The Spirit you have received is not a spirit of slavery leading you back into a life of fear, but a Spirit that makes us sons, enabling us to cry "Abba! Father!" In that cry, the Spirit of

God joins with our spirit in testifying that we are God's children (Rom. 8:14-16, NEB).

The most gaping hole in men's armor today is our not truly knowing God as our Father. Therefore, we don't know we're sons. The Enemy tells us we're slaves, and instead of silencing him with God's truth—"I'm my Father's son!"—we hush the cry for "Daa-dee!" and trudge through life in shame (Gal. 4:1-7).

I never commanded my son to call out for me. I never threatened to punish him if he didn't. In fact, he didn't cry out for me until I'd demonstrated my trustworthiness, by hanging in there with him night after night. When a man dares look at his own brokenness, therefore, he begins to appreciate that Jesus has literally "hung in there" for him. Then he's ready at last to trust God, to cry out, "Abba, Father!"—and become a Kingdom warrior.

The warrior must know the commander in order to trust him and persevere in battle. Victory for a broken human spirit requires more than just following commands, like a slave. Indeed, troops who receive life-or-death orders from generals and admirals they've never met personally often give their commanders nicknames—which, though not necessarily endearing, nevertheless foster relationship.

In World War II, for example, such colorful handles as General "Old Blood-and-Guts" Patton and Admiral "Bull" Halsey allowed servicemen to bond emotionally with their superiors and thereby overcome a fear of being expendable to them.

To the extent that a man knows God and experiences that spiritual bond, he knows to whom he belongs and what he's made of—and so, knows himself. The man who knows God as Father is overwhelmed by his love, wooed into submission, and thereby given the courage and inner resources to become all he was created to be.

To the extent that we don't know God, however, and haven't experienced him in our lives, we have difficulty trusting him, we choose not to surrender ourselves to him, and we lack confidence in his call to battle.

Throughout the Bible—in the Lord's Prayer itself—God is portrayed as our Father who loves us. No more endearing "nickname" draws a warrior into deeper relationship with his commander than "Daddy."

And that's what Jesus called God.

In fact, Jesus' calling God his own Father beckoned such radical intimacy that it frightened and angered the religious folks who had kept God at a safe distance. "My Father is always working, and I too must work," Jesus answered the religious leaders who challenged his healing on the Sabbath. John then notes:

> This saying made the Jewish authorities all the more determined to kill him; not only had he broken the Sabbath law, but he had said that God was his own Father and in this way had made himself equal with God. (John 5:18)

Sadly, the average Christian man today doesn't know the God he worships, largely because he hasn't learned to truly know his earthly father. Many fathers withdraw emotionally and/or physically from their sons. The notion of drawing close to a God called "Father" stirs anxiety and fear in a man without a close earthly father; he either feels left out and inadequate or he feels pain that he would much rather forget.

Often when a man has prayed through fear and anger toward his father for forgiveness, he at last cries out, "Who are you, Dad? I just want to know you!" (John 14:8). For the male child, this cry springs from the fundamental question, Who am I? For indeed, a man knows in his masculine soul that his identity mingles with that of his father, the man whose very name he bears.

Wounded by Dad

Sam, a successful creative writer at forty-three, told me he struggled for years trying to fulfill his engineer father's desire for him to be a scientist. "I guess Dad was just trying to make sure I had a secure job," he said. "But it turned out in college I kept getting better grades in English than in calculus or chemistry."

Sam dutifully majored in math, moved far from home, and taught high school math. "I felt guilty whenever I spent time writing," he said. "So I wrote long letters to friends instead of stories." One day, while visiting his parents, Sam was rummaging through the attic and came upon a thick college literature text filled with underlines and comments in the margins. Leafing to the front cover, he was startled to see his father's name on the book.

"I ran downstairs to see Dad," he said. "I asked him, 'Is this yours?' He looked at it and said matter-of-factly, 'Oh yes, that was my favorite course in college.' I guess times were tough when Dad was in school, and he never could allow himself to pursue what he really liked best. But knowing that literature was his favorite course in college really freed me up. After that, I didn't have to feel disloyal to Dad for doing what I really wanted in life."

A man suppresses most diligently in his son what he has disallowed in himself. Sam's father had enjoyed literature so much that he had to work hard to suppress that joy and instead get a paying job in hard times. The voice that said, "Go ahead and find out if your love for literature reflects your true calling!" could not be tolerated. He had not taken his pain to the Father God and grieved that loss of freedom as a young man. Suppressing that pain in himself kept him from recognizing and affirming it in his son.

Another man may complain, "But my dad hurt me so badly and just destroyed our family; there wasn't anything good in him I'd want to claim."

My wounded brother, listen: No matter how badly your father hurt you, Jesus died for him. No matter how thoroughly sin overcame him, and even overflowed from him into you, something good from Father God's heart will have shone through his life. Granted, that may be hard to see. Indeed, it's not visible to a little boy who lashes back with condemning caricatures, but only to a real man—that is, one surrendered to the Father himself, and therein able to see the truth beyond his own pain.

In fact, recognizing all the good traits in your father is a treasure found only by men willing to work for it. Every boy wants a father he can look up to; certainly this longing stems from the human longing to praise the Father God.

Recent years have seen a flood of articles lamenting the loss of heroes in today's culture, which seems to enjoy debunking more than esteeming. But the lack of heroes among us simply reflects our lack of fathering—and the debunking reflects our grief.

If a boy's first and foremost hero disappoints or betrays him, he'll take his hurt and anger out on other heroic portraits, scorning all pretense of masculine achievement and trashing it with a vengeance. A society of father-wounded boys fosters either the iconoclastic antihero like Bart Simpson, or the unreal superhero, from Rambo to Spiderman—the all-powerful, immortal alter ego of every unfathered boy's dreams.

Missing in such a society is an affirming portrait of a real man—in all his shortcomings and strengths, his joys and pains, fears and accomplishments. The Bill Cosby TV sitcom some years ago was a rare exception and became so popular because it sought to fill that vacuum.

A boy who experiences this at home—who is listened to, respected, protected, and apologized to as well as disciplined with love by his dad, simply has no need for the world's false father images.

Dad, I need you to be good, every boy says in his heart, *because I am an extension of you in my world.*

On the sandlot ballfield as boys, a common challenge among us was, "My dad can whip your dad!" Each of us was seeking honor for his father as a means to self-esteem.

A father can disown his son in an effort to avoid the pain of his mistakes, but no son can emotionally disown his father. He can change his last name, move thousands of miles away, refuse to have anything to do with Dad. But he remains his father's son and longs to affirm—and to be affirmed by—Dad.

This is the truth that sets a man free to affirm and praise his Father God. Worship, in fact, might properly be called "Bragging about your Father"! The absence of men from worship, therefore, may simply reflect their disappointment in Dad. On

27

the other hand, worship comes alive when you know your Father is present and good. Thus Carol Wimber, wife of Vineyard Anaheim founder John Wimber, noted the turning point in their church's growth when they began singing songs *to* Jesus instead of just *about* Jesus.

Jesus waits for a man to fall on his knees before him and cry out, "I want so much to affirm my dad, but he's hurt me so badly—Jesus, come and heal me so I can see my dad as you see him, forgive and let go of my resentment, and get on with the life you've called me to!" But too often, he doesn't trust that Jesus has either the desire or the power to heal his father-wound. And so, instead, he curses God for giving him such a father.

We all make choices at times that hurt our sons, and only the Father God can heal and redeem the effects. Though the entire focus of God's saving action in this world is to "restore the hearts of the fathers to the sons and the hearts of the sons to the fathers" (Mal. 4:6), this can only be done insofar as men get up on the emotional/spiritual operating table and surrender to him.

In his masculine soul, every man knows that his own self-esteem depends upon his esteem for his father. If Dad is looked up to by other men, and my experience as his son confirms that's justified, I feel tremendous pride: *The man who links me to the larger world, with whom I am intrinsically identified, is good. Therefore, I am good.*

On the other hand, an abusive father, or one whose private actions toward his son belie his popular image as hypocrisy, prompts terrible shame in a boy. "Everyone at church thinks my dad is such a loving guy, so 'understanding' and 'affirming,'" one college student told me disgustedly, "but he's never once told me he loves me or is proud of me."

Translation: "What's so bad about me that makes me not as good as all the others Dad cares for?"

I wonder: Could this be the source of rabid fan loyalty for the home ball team? Athletics can be a vehicle for gaining masculine respect in the world. A winning home team therefore promises to overcome the shame of father-loss.

If Dad doesn't usher me into respectability among men, I identify instead with the ball team. They're "my team" among other teams, even as Dad is "my father" among others. If they win, I feel like a winner until the next game; if they lose, I get depressed and feel like a loser, as I felt around Dad.

The Enemy lurks with a real and specific agenda for the man who does not take his father-wound to Jesus.

I once ministered to a man mired in self-doubts. As we talked, he scorned every activity popularly associated with men, from football games to electronics; he was terrifed of any urge to strength in himself, even to improve his skills and advance in his career; he had allowed others to take advantage of him and felt inadequate and fearful in relationships with women.

Not surprisingly, he described his relationship with his father, who had lived at home during his boyhood, as "pretty well nonexistent." Resentfully, he added, "In fact, he was basically a wimp, especially around Mom."

Clearly, this man had conformed his whole life to his father-wound, and I felt confident as we began to pray that the Lord would begin significant healing. Yet I was startled by what happened. When I asked the Holy Spirit to show us any workings of the Enemy from which he was ready to be freed, the word *man-hating* came to mind.

Puzzled, I waited—and it came back a second time.

I'd battled that spirit in women, especially those who had been sexually molested or otherwise abused by their fathers. As a male authority figure—whether teacher, counselor, or minister—I had often seen healing begin as I offered the woman a safe place to vent her anger. Then she could see its ultimately destructive effects on herself and thus seek deliverance.

But what could it mean for a man to be oppressed by a man-hating spirit?

As I prayed for wisdom, I knew. To hate the father is to hate the primary reflection of masculinity to the boy. Because the deeper, natural, authentic impulse is to love the father—to need and long for his affirmation—the boy/man requires supernatural power to shut that impulse down and instead hate him. "At your service," the Enemy offers. "I'll provide the protection you need to make sure you're closed off to your father—and even feel strong doing that!"

Hatred is a cover-up for powerlessness, creating a false sense of strength when the truth is frightening.

In his bargain, however, the Enemy doesn't tell you the hook—the catch-22—that the same man-hating spirit that erects an emotional wall to defend against your father will scorn and undermine any expression of your own masculinity.

As a pastor and counselor, I've discovered that a man-hating spirit is therefore very common among men who act out homosexually. At first, I'd assumed their turning away from women simply reflected a hatred of women.

But nearly all of the men I have ministered to with homosexual compulsions have been abused either physically or emotionally as boys by an older male. They therefore harbor destructive impulses toward that male—and through that experience, toward both men in general and their own masculinity. In his 1995 autobiography, for example, Olympic diving champion Greg Louganis revealed his homosexuality and AIDS diagnosis, then described how he was physically abused by his stepfather, and subsequently abused sexually by an older man.[1]

Those who affirm their homosexual orientation have obviously not taken that wound to Jesus, and it remains an open door to the Enemy. Thus, they are easy targets for a man-hating spirit, which eventually fills them with a self-hatred as men themselves. This self-hatred enlists them to undermine authentic manhood—which would dare face the truth. This explains the angry militancy in the homosexual movement today, and its shift from civil rights to advocacy.

The commandment "honor your father" is therefore designed to ensure that a man honor his own manhood—not that we are to put on rose-colored religious glasses and deny the pain from Dad, but rather, that we deny the Enemy a chance to perpetrate his man-hating spirit among yet another generation.

Acknowledging your father's shortcomings and his wounding you does not dishonor him; indeed, it enables a son at last to see his father realistically, as Jesus sees him, and move through forgiveness into genuine relationship as men.

In order genuinely to know his earthly father, a man must therefore see deeper than his own hurts. He must see his father not as a little boy, but rather, in the fullness of truth—that is, as Jesus sees him. And that requires a level of surrender that allows Jesus to begin transforming the man himself.

The man who asks to see with Jesus' eyes must eventually see his own sin. This is God's boot-camp of mercy, which will lead him to stop judging Dad long enough at last to affirm and appropriate his father's genuine virtues.

Searching for Dad

Because the father-son bond is intrinsic to manhood itself, a man who has never met his father often feels a growing urge to do so as he approaches midlife, when he no longer has the energy to shoulder defenses and run from the truth. His suppressed boyhood longings may surface in dreams, or perhaps while watching a movie or hearing a song, many of which reflect the father-hunger in men today.

In *The Empire Strikes Back*, for example, Luke Skywalker is shocked to meet his father in Darth Vader; in *The Last Crusade*, Indiana Jones discovers new strengths as he adventures with his aging father; in *Field of Dreams*, a man is freed emotionally as in the spirit realm he plays baseball as a boy with his deceased father; in *Backdraft*, a fireman's two sons boldly follow in his footsteps.

Popular songs such as Paul Overstreet's "Seein' My Father in Me," Mike and the Mechanics' "In the Living Years," George Strait's "Love without End, Amen," Chet Atkins's "My Father's Hat," Johnny Cash's "A Boy Named Sue" all portray a man's boyhood and adult longing to be close to Dad.

Usually, a man is at first ashamed of this childlike vulnerability in needing his father. But that openness is precisely the avenue through which he meets Jesus, who has come to bring each man to his true Father.

Indeed, if a man trusts the Father God's love and call, he not only seeks his healing among prayer partner, counselor, and men's fellowship; ultimately, he seeks to learn more about Dad.

Bill, for example, was a forty-two-year-old doctor whose father had left the family when he was a toddler. Married, with three children, he came to one of my conferences and told me he had suffered all his life from deep anxieties and lack of self-confidence, frustrating not only himself, but also his wife and all who knew and respected him. His mother had told him while he was growing up, "Your father didn't care about you and said he never wants you to contact him."

After reading my books, he decided to pray with a group of men at his church, one of whom turned out to be a private detective. Eventually, Bill hired the man to see if his father might still be alive. Searching social security files and other documents, the investigator found his father, living just a few hundred miles away.

"After a lifetime of anxiety over this man who apparently abandoned me, I suddenly had his phone number right there in my hand," he told me. "I was terrified. Now all the fear, the resentments, the anger, the hurt, the longing came back with a vengeance. Of course, I remembered my mother's warnings all my life against contacting Dad. But I knew the ball was in my court now, and I could never look myself in the mirror again if I backed off."

After praying further with the men, he called.

"My heart was pounding like it would crack my ribs," Bill said. "But then, there was this voice on the other end saying, 'Hello?'

"'Hello,' I said, hardly able to get the word out. 'This is Bill Foster. I think I'm your son.'

"There was dead silence, and I almost lost it. As I fumbled for what to say next, before I could begin I heard him crying. 'Oh Bill,' he said. 'I can't believe it. Where are you?'

"I told him where I was and a few things about my job and family. 'Can I come see you?' he asked right away. That kind of caught me off guard, coming so quickly and after all Mom had warned me against. But I didn't skip a beat. 'Well, sure,' I said.

"We talked for a couple of hours, and it turned out my mother hadn't told me the whole truth—he said he'd always loved me and wanted to see me, but every time he'd tried to contact me, Mom had hidden our tracks.

"Can you believe he got in his car that afternoon and drove straight through the night to see me?"

I could, indeed. Most fathers don't leave the home because they hate their sons, but because of marriage problems. The boy, however, can't see that. He thinks, *Dad has left me because he doesn't like me.* The boy often feels guilty: *There must be something wrong with me to make Dad leave. In fact, I must've caused the problem between him and Mom.* Hence, the shame in children of divorce.

Excitedly, I asked Bill if he would tell his story to the other men at the conference.

"Before all this, I'd have been too scared to get up and say anything before a bunch of men," he declared. "But I'm ready now!"

Indeed, being restored to relationship with his father had confirmed Bill as a man among men. Here was a warrior in training.

I'll never forget the reverent hush at the conference later as Bill stood before several hundred men and told how he waited up that night, pacing around the house—until just after dawn he heard the crunch of tires on his gravel driveway and raced to the door.

The little boy in every man's heart choked back a tear as Bill told us of seeing his dad get out of the car that morning. Hesitantly, the two men walked toward each other.

"I just couldn't take my eyes off his face," Bill said. "Sure, there were the wrinkles and gray hair, but his eyes, his chin—I just knew that was my father."

Then suddenly, there in the gravel driveway, the old man opened his arms. And at forty-two years old, Bill rushed at last into his father's embrace.

After several days of stories, tears, laughter, and fishing with his dad, Bill felt a new sense of himself. The two men agreed to call regularly and visit again soon, and his father went back home.

Bill, however, knew the battle was not over. Indeed, to secure his healing, he would need to speak the truth with love to his mother. With covering prayer from other men and much courage of his own, he did so, and was given a heart to forgive her.

Bill's attitude toward his children changed first. "Now I can be a father myself," he said.

Being a father will surface your father-wound, but it can also help to heal it. Knowing the heart of Father God, after all, is a man's healing. An honest man knows he doesn't have within himself the wisdom and strength his children need from him. When he goes to Jesus for it in their behalf, he'll receive the Father God's heart.

"Before, I'd pretty much backed out of my children's lives as if I really didn't matter to them," Bill said. "Seeing how much my own dad matters to me has changed all that. Now, I want to know them and get involved with their lives."

Bill's wife, meanwhile, was overjoyed. "He's just so much stronger, more secure in himself," she told me. "The angry outbursts over little things—the pouting, the moody withdrawing—all have been fading away. He's even been talking about leaving the clinic and starting his own practice. I guess you could say he's growing up."

She sighed and smiled. "And at last, I don't have to be the strong one all the time. I feel a lot more like a woman."

Certainly, not every "contacting-your-father" story works out so well as Bill's. Yet I share it here because I believe it confirms the Father God's intent in our time to "turn the hearts of fathers to their children and the hearts of children to their fathers" (Mal. 4:6, RSV).

In fact, like Bill, most men today have never met their fathers—that is, truly engaged them emotionally. Many men grew up with fathers present physically, but absent emotionally. "Being there" is not enough; fathers must be engaged in their children's lives.

Occasionally, a man will tell me, "But my father's dead, so all this father-wound stuff really doesn't apply to me." But suppose I shoot you in the leg, and then I die right afterwards. Whether I'm alive or dead, you still have a wound in your leg and had better go to a hospital. If you don't, your wound remains an easy target for the Enemy, and you'll be crippled. It doesn't go away with the one who wounded you.

Whether a man's father is alive or dead, he's still his father's son, and he is deeply influenced by his father's life.

How can a man make peace with a father who has passed away? He might contact relatives or others who might have known him.

One man I know flew from California to the East Coast to visit his father's eighty-eight-year-old sister in a nursing home—with a tape recorder and a stack of tapes.

"I decided this was for my son as much as for me," he declared. "I was pretty low-key until she began talking about 'Grandma.' It took me a second before I realized 'Grandma' would've been born sometime before the Civil War! I knew then that I was onto something hot.

"That thin little lady could hardly move, but she gave me a treasure: a look not only at my dad, but generations that shaped him—and me."

If you can't find either your father or others who knew him, you can pray with your Christian brothers for the Father God sovereignly to reveal those aspects of your earthly father's character essential to his purposes in you. Because not knowing the father leaves such a critical chink in a man's armor, the Holy Spirit wants to show this to a man and will do so if he sincerely asks. Pray and ask God, "What do I need to know about my father that would help me become what you've called me to be?"

From Betrayal to Trust
This journey of relationship with the Father is booby-trapped with self-preservation and pride. Any man who has tried it knows it can't be done alone. And indeed, God has provided: For becoming a son allows a man to see himself as a brother among other, fellow sons of the Father.

A man who never received godly fathering, however, can't trust other men because he hasn't learned to; the first man he loved and needed betrayed him. But if he has the integrity and courage to follow his need and fear to the Cross—where all his human powers to save himself fail—he'll meet his Savior there. He'll discover at last his true Father and destiny as a son.

Learning to overcome this fear of other men—to trust the Father and move ahead together in victory—requires a man to commit himself to a small ongoing support group of fellow warriors (see my chapter, "The Wolf Loves the Lone Sheep" in *Father & Son*). Among other men similarly wounded by the world and redeemed by the Father, he can feel safe when he's open and vulnerable—without fear of being judged, criticized, or advised. Such an emotional sanctuary, like an operating room protected from germs, allows the Great Surgeon to heal his son.

The average man today, however, is afraid other men—especially his son—will discover his inadequacy, reject and leave him, even as his father abandoned him as a needy boy.

When the truth hurts, pride lurks.

Longing to be included in the fellowship of men even as a little boy longs for Daddy's embrace, a man naturally grasps after something ostensibly strong to hide his vulnerability.

We're ready now to look at the most powerful temptation to which most of us succumb, the false sword that appears so righteous at first, but which has become the Enemy's chief deception among religious men.

It is, in fact, the Enemy's ultimate weapon, brandished only when men have begun drawing close enough to the Father to become a threat.

And so, of course, it killed Jesus.

And so, of course, it kills his men even today.

THREE

Battling False Religion

The teachers of the Law and the Pharisees are the authorized interpreters of Moses' Law. So you must obey and follow everything they tell you to do; do not, however, imitate their actions, because they don't practice what they preach. They tie onto people's backs loads that are heavy and hard to carry, yet they aren't willing even to lift a finger to help them carry those loads. Matthew 23:2-4

Come to me, all of you who are tired from carrying heavy loads, and I will give you rest. Take my yoke and put it on you, and learn from me, because I am gentle and humble in spirit; and you will find rest. For the yoke I will give you is easy, and the load I will put on you is light. Matthew 11:28-30

CRIPPLED by insecurity at home and at work, Tom had written to a Christian men's ministry for help. In response, the organization sent him a list of "biblical manhood" standards, which he posted enthusiastically in his office.

"For a few days, I was pumped up," he said. "But then one morning, I took a really honest look at those standards and realized I fall far short of them. I was really crushed.

"I used to wonder if I'm a real man; now I read that list and know I'm not. I feel like a wimp wanting to take it down, but I just hang my head in shame every time I look at it."

Religion becomes false when—as Tom discovered—it claims to restore men to right relationship with God, but in fact sabotages it. False religion exhorts men to a standard of behavior without overcoming the brokenness that keeps us from being able to achieve it. Thus Jesus chastised the Pharisees for laying burdens on men without lifting a finger to help them. Indeed, such religion destroys men today—like Tom—even as it crucified Jesus, thus betraying its source in the Destroyer.

The late Walter Trobish—perhaps the first Christian to take men's wounds seriously—divided his seminal 1983 book *All a Man Can Be* into three parts: "The Suffering Man," "The Man Reacts," and "The Free Man." "I intentionally did not entitle the third part of this book 'The Ideal Man' or 'The Man Who Is Human' or even 'The Man As He Should Be'," he declared:

> If I had done that, I might have put on already overburdened men even more demands that would have increased their frustration. By laying before them higher ideals, I might have made men feel more like failures, tempting them to give up completely. The result might be discouragement, even despair.[1]

Emanating from the Father of Lies, false religion is rooted in false father-love, based upon performance instead of identity— that is, upon what you do rather than upon whose you are. It tells men what to do, but can't show us who does it.

Indeed, false religion abandons relationship with the Father for the false security of the Law—thereby making men slaves instead of sons. As Paul proclaimed,

> But when the right time finally came, God sent his own Son. He came as the son of a human mother and lived under the Jewish Law, to redeem those who were under the Law, so that we might become God's sons. To show that you are his

sons, God sent the Spirit of his Son into our hearts, the Spirit who cries out, "Father, my Father." So then, you are no longer a slave but a son. And since you are his son, God will give you all that he has for his sons. (Gal. 4:4-7)

I learned this distinction shortly after my own son was born. Thanking the Father one morning for John-Miguel, I felt an overwhelming surge of love fill my heart. I knelt down, and in that moment, I knew that no matter what the powers of the world might throw at him, I would defend my son with my life. A strange mixture of joy, strength, and fear then swept over me.

As I knelt, a question popped into my mind: *Why do you love him?*

Startled—and frankly unsure—I paused. And then, another question followed: *Is it because he performs so well and does so much for you?*

Sensing the drift, I had to smile. *No,* I thought. *All he "does for me" is fill his diapers and cry all night!*

Then why do you love him?

I hesitated. *I guess . . . because he's my son.*

That's all?

Again I hesitated, and then sighed. *Yes, Father. That's all. I love him so much it scares me. Just . . . because he's my son.*

I waited, but "heard" nothing for a minute, as if the Father were letting that truth sink in.

And then, like a bolt, it struck me: *Why do I love you, Gordon?*

Patently obvious, the answer nevertheless terrified me. As I knelt frozen in fear, I realized how much I had invested my life in trying to please God with my "performance" offerings. As from a spiritual earthquake, I could feel the foundation of my self-image begin to crack. Could I really trust God to love me—indeed, would I remain his son?—if I stopped trying to earn his favor?

As I continued to pray, I realized Jesus was urging me, even as the Pharisees: "Go and learn what this means, 'I desire mercy, and not sacrifice.' For I came not to call the righteous, but sinners" (Matt. 9:13, RSV).

Translation: "My son, I love you just because you're mine,

created in my image. I love you so much it scares me—because I'm committed to you forever, and you might trash my love by setting me up as a tightwad tyrant and trying to earn it—when in fact I've given my life so that you may simply receive it.

"I don't demand you do as I say in order to get my love; I give you my love in order that you might do as I say.

"Receive it, my son."

In that moment, I realized that I want my son to presume upon my love, to take it for granted. I don't want him striving anxiously to please me in hopes of earning my love. Otherwise, sooner or later he'll hate me for withholding the love he needs, and he'll act that out in ways that ultimately sabotage his manhood.

It's harmful not to give a son what he needs to fulfill his calling. But it's demonic to criticize him for not "living up to his potential" while withholding from him the love that would enable him to do so. As Jesus charged the Pharisees, that's laying an unbearable burden on him without lifting a finger to help.

False religion proceeds largely from men who lacked true father-love as boys and who therefore lack as men both the courage to face their brokenness and the trust to take it to Father God. Consequently, they sacrifice time, energy, and money to win the Father's favor, but have no mercy to give—because they're too proud to seek it.

As long as a man believes he can work to achieve the Father's love, he can believe he's in control. If he can't, he has to trust the Father to love him unconditionally.

For a generation abandoned by Dad, that's terrifying.

"Give me the rules, principles, and laws instead," the flesh cries out. "Show me how I can make it happen!"

The story is told of an especially intelligent and accomplished man who died and stood before heaven's gate. "What's the password?" St. Peter asked him.

It must be something religious, likely from the Bible, the man thought. "The Lord is my shepherd!" he declared hopefully.

"Close, but that's not it," St. Peter replied.

"Our Father, who art in heaven?"

Again St. Peter shook his head.

Realizing the password to heaven could be any of a thousand religious phrases, the man shrugged in dismay. "OK," he said, "I give up."

"Welcome," St. Peter said at last and opened the gate.

The Pharisees, as Jesus said in the above text, were right. But they were not real. That is, they were not honest about their needs, weaknesses, and limitations, and therefore could not proclaim God's provision, power, and freedom. They knew the Law, but not the Father; they had mastered religion, but feared relationship.

As a result, they could not mediate the Father's Spirit to others as men. Instead, they burdened men with impossible performance standards, but refused to witness out of their own brokenness to the Father, who alone can enable men to keep them.

Fleeing from the Truth into the Lie

Because they were afraid to know the Father God, the Pharisees did not know mercy. As shepherds, they beat their sheep with the crook—an instrument designed rather to pull the animals back to safety.

It's cruel to beat a man with a lie. But it's demonic to beat him with the truth. Sheep beaten by the wolf flee to the shepherd and are saved; those beaten by the shepherd's rod flee to the wolf and are devoured.

You can take refuge from a lie in the truth. But when someone lashes you with the truth, your only apparent refuge is in a lie.

During the social upheaval of the sixties, for example, national leaders amid the Vietnam debacle whipped young men with the lie: "The Vietcong threaten our way of life; if you are loyal Americans and real men, you must therefore go and kill them." Navy doctor Tom Dooley, sadly lost in homosexuality and longing for esteem in his lonely Southeast Asia post, fabricated stories of Communist savagery in his best-selling books—all conjured to win fame on the anti-Communist bandwagon.

Young men overcame the shame of disobeying their elders and seized the higher moral ground by proclaiming the truth: That in fact, Vietcong leader Ho Chi Minh, though no saint himself, had nevertheless sought a political order based upon our own Constitution, and that the U.S.-supported South Vietnamese leaders were corrupt.

But then the old men played their trump card: "You're not a man unless you're a warrior!" they smirked.

We were stunned—because in our masculine souls, we knew it was true. The old men had taught us no vision of the warrior besides their own guns-and-coercion "macho" image, and they thereby hoarded the masculine currency. We had self-righteously rejected theirs as a false warrior, but had no more authentic vision ourselves with which to replace it. The apparent options were terrifying: We could either embrace a false manhood, or be emasculated.

Desperately, we fabricated our own heroic passivity, retreating from shame behind flowers and a smokescreen of drugs. Diligently aimless and ultimately self-destructive, we thereby fled from the old men into the waiting arms of the true Enemy.

A pervasive contempt for old men short-circuited a profound longing for Dad's affection and approval and beckoned a man-hating spirit.

For example, men who haven't dealt with their own sexual insecurities fear the man lost in homosexuality and beat him with a lie: "You're not a man, you're despicable, and therefore not worthy of living." In desperation, he righteously takes refuge in the "Gay Pride" movement, which declares the truth his broken masculine soul longs to know: that he is a valuable human being.

Or, they beat him with the truth: "You're a sinner! You're going to hell if you don't stop your homosexual behavior and become righteous"—that is, "like us." Fleeing the religion police, the man takes refuge in a lie: "God made me this way, therefore it's good! Acting out homosexually makes me righteous because it sets me apart from those hateful Christian bigots!"

Christian men have abandoned the truth to the "Gay Pride" movement, which speaks a word of dignity to men laboring under a tremendous shame. We can reclaim that standard by saying to its audience, "Yes, you are a valuable person, and I will defend you in that truth, even against other Christians. God loves you—whether you stop or continue your homosexual activity. In fact, he has come in Jesus to offer you ultimate dignity as his son. If you let him, Jesus can free you from homosexuality and restore you to the true manhood we all long for."

You don't have to have homosexual desires yourself to add, "I, too, know what it's like to struggle with sexual insecurities."

You just have to be honest—and willing to surrender your fears to Jesus so he can ground you in true manhood.

I once met with a group of men to plan a men's conference, and a leader noted that our event would very likely be picketed by gay protesters. "So what?" another said. "We know what the Scriptures say about homosexuality, and we'll just tell them the truth!"

Stunned by such nearsightedness, I sat speechless.

"Well, I just thought we ought to know that's likely to happen," the leader added, turning to proceed with other business. As the others sat quietly, I leapt into the vacuum to talk about the wounds that foster homosexuality and suggested we all might benefit from learning more about it.

One other participant rose and spoke in agreement, and then the room fell silent. Awkwardly, the leader thanked the two of us for our input and proceeded with other business.

The silence, however, had spoken loudly: "We're afraid that getting close to those men might surface some brokenness in ourselves, and we don't believe Jesus can heal either them or us. It's easier to hide behind the Bible than engage them as fellow sinners."

Sure enough, the protesters turned out for the event, and in the absence of Kingdom warriors, the powers of the world mocked us. The next day's local paper featured a front-page picture of a conference-attendee holding his Bible under the face of an angry gay demonstrator.

You don't have to beat broken men with the truth or shove it in their noses to make them believe it. You just have to love them enough to demonstrate it.

Like Jesus.

You can't save a man from sin, but you can show him the Savior. To the extent that you're secure in the Father's truth yourself, you can communicate the love that inspires it. You can sit down with a brother lost in homosexuality and listen to his story, even weep with him—so that when his acting out has caused him enough pain to want something better, he'll flee to the Shepherd and not the wolf.

Performance Religion

False religion, like sin, brings life to our proud human nature—but it brings death to men's souls, especially when enough men allow it to become entrenched in the culture.

I grew up, for example, without ever having seen an adult male confess his wrongdoing and ask forgiveness—whether pastor or president, cowboy, movie star, or schoolteacher. Real men, I concluded, don't make mistakes, especially those who would lead or inspire other men.

As a young man in my late teens, I began thinking about becoming a minister. Having attended a variety of churches, I concluded that Jesus is the Model Human Being whom any man can emulate if he only tries hard enough. The problem is, most people are just lazy.

The minister's job, as I saw it, is to model goodness like Jesus—that is, to lead others by example to be as good as you. Of course, all Christians are supposed to model goodness, but ministers get paid for it. Clearly, you have to be better than the rest in order to be a professional good guy.

Last but not least, in order to get people to do as you, you have to get them to like you.

After a decade of refinement—if not denial—I pronounced myself prepared for the ministry: educated, morally upright, friendly, hardworking, knowledgeable, entertaining, and anxious to please.

At age thirty, I went to Harvard Divinity School and confirmed my ministerial self-esteem by winning the preaching prize two out of three years.

At age thirty-three, I graduated from seminary and began pastoring, with great plans to uplift my first congregation.

At age thirty-five, I met Jesus and began preaching about his power to heal and transform lives—at times without respecting the congregation's theological boundaries. I panicked as people began not to like me anymore. "You're not the pastor we hired," a deacon warned. In time, a vigilante committee was formed to oust me.

At age forty, I made amends to those I had offended. I'll never forget walking up those driveways at night, knocking on parishioners' doors with clammy hands, and going in to ask forgiveness for judging them.

Soon thereafter, I realized at last that the deacon was right. With respect for my congregation and my own calling, I resigned. Within weeks, what remained of my model self-image crumbled in divorce, and I was out on the street looking for a room and a job.

Professionally, financially, and emotionally, I was dead.

Spiritually, however, I was at last coming alive. You have to die, after all, before you can be "born again" (John 3:1-13).

I had no cards left to play the religion game. It was time to face the truth I'd avoided my whole life: I can't do it right.

The powers of death were chafing to finish the job—even as the pit bull months later—and I had no power to resist. The only choice in my life was which way I would choose to die. I could either die alone and ashamed or take a chance on Jesus' resurrection power and die with him (Eph. 1:18-20).

The Enemy had done his job; I no longer had any resources to hide from Jesus.

It was time to know the Father.

You get paid to play religion; but you pay everything you've got to know the Father.

I was already a Christian. Years earlier, during the charismatic renewal, I had given my life to Jesus and preached "spiritual gifts" to the church. But now it was time to preach the Good News: "The Great Physician has come at last—and we get to be operated on first!"

I surrendered to the Father my ministry, marriage, and public esteem, begging him to use my brokenness as an opening to enter my heart and clean it out.

King David's warrior prayer became a habit: "Search me, O God, and know my heart; test my thoughts. Point out anything you find in me that makes you sad, and lead me along the path of everlasting life" (Ps. 139:23-24, TLB). I read and memorized Scriptures, fasted, went to a counselor, got a prayer partner, kept a journal, read books, committed to an accountability group, prayed, prayed, and prayed.

A pastor friend with a large parsonage took me in, and I performed weddings and funerals to pay my bills. After three years, I had written two book manuscripts but couldn't sell either.

My desert season turned out to be longer than I'd planned—but long enough for me to trust Jesus and to realize that the Father was making me his warrior precisely in that crucible of my pain. Indeed, when at last I had nothing left to offer him but my brokenness—when I was fresh out of resources with which to earn his love, when there was nothing left of myself to trust—I began to trust my Father's love.

Before, I'd kept myself at a distance from the church, judging it for drawing so many broken men. In reality, everyone else's brokenness threatened me because I hadn't taken my own to Jesus. Today, I have no problem committing to an organization filled with broken men—as long as they're coming to get healed and not to hide from their brokenness.

Hard trials cure an honest man of performance-oriented religion, as they convince him he can't perform—and thereby force him to rely on God's strength. As another has said, "You don't find out that Jesus is all you need until Jesus is all you have."

During that season of refining, I began to understand Paul's confession:

> So far as keeping the Jewish Law is concerned, I was a Pharisee. . . . But all those things that I might count as profit I now reckon as loss for Christ's sake. Not only those things; I reckon everything as complete loss for the sake of what is so much more valuable, the knowledge of Christ Jesus my Lord. For his sake I have thrown everything away; I consider it all as mere garbarge, so that I may gain Christ and be

completely united with him. I no longer have a righteousness of my own, the kind that is gained by obeying the Law. I now have the righteousness that is given through faith in Christ, the righteousness that comes from God and is based on faith. All I want is to know Christ and to experience the power of his resurrection, to share in his sufferings and become like him in his death, in the hope that I myself will be raised from death to life. (Phil. 3:5, 7-11)

The Kingdom warrior has learned—often from painful experience—that he can't do what God commands. Righteousness, as Jesus said, is a burden too hard to carry by yourself.

Such self-honesty allows the Kingdom warrior to know that neither can he put others right with God—not even by exhorting, shaming, or otherwise coercing them. Rather, the finest he can do to help them carry the burden of righteousness is to humbly point them to the Carrier. And so, like Jesus on the cross, he dares humbly to offer others his own brokenness and vulnerability as an invitation to the Father's heart.

Thus Paul proclaimed,

Freedom is what we have—Christ has set us free! Stand, then, as free people, and do not allow yourselves to become slaves again. . . . Those of you who try to be put right with God by obeying the Law have cut yourselves off from Christ. You are outside God's grace. As for us, our hope is that God will put us right with him; and this is what we wait for by the power of God's Spirit working through our faith. For when we are in union with Christ Jesus, neither circumcision nor the lack of it makes any difference at all; what matters is faith that works through love. (Gal. 5:1, 4-6)

That is, when we men are in union with Christ Jesus, we're free from the shame of not being able to do what God says. Neither "biblical principles of manhood" nor the lack of them makes any difference at all; what matters is having faith that the Father's love works in and through us.

Tragically, most Christian men today don't know this freedom Jesus died to give us. We therefore have cut ourselves and others off from God's grace.

Hiding behind the Law

Mark, an architect in his late forties who chauffeured me from the conference site to my hotel one night, was a graphic example. We had chatted awhile about fathers and children when suddenly he clenched a fist on the steering wheel. "I just don't understand why, after all these years in a Christian family, my daughter wouldn't have more virtue!" he exploded.

His twenty-year-old daughter, he said, lived at home while attending college locally and was "just getting more and more rebellious." One evening the week before, she told him about a man she'd met who worked a late shift, and declared that she was going to meet this man for a date when he got off work at 3 A.M.

Determined to teach his daughter "biblical values," Mark had previously taken a course on Christian parenting from a nationally known ministry and thought he was prepared. "I did just what the course said," Mark declared. "I read her the Scriptures about purity and told her how she was demonstrating unbiblical values, questionable morals, and a total lack of integrity. Then I asked her, 'What kind of Christian witness do you think that kind of behavior makes?'"

Mark shook his head in disgust as he pulled up to the hotel curb. "She just stomped out to her car and took off!"

As Mark simmered in the seat beside me, I hesitated. *Lord*, I prayed, *do you want me to speak honestly?* Sensing no check, I took a deep breath.

"I can hear your frustration, brother," I offered, "and how badly you want things to get better between you and your daughter. I think the Lord really wants to honor that desire in you—in fact, I think it's his Spirit speaking in you.

"But I need to tell you: I've heard the Scriptures, I've heard the Law, and I've heard the judgment. But I haven't heard the father."

Mark looked up, puzzled. "What do you mean?"

"Do you love your daughter?" I asked.

"Of course I do!" Mark declared, an angry furrow creeping into his brow. "That's why I took that course and wanted to ask you for help!"

I sighed. "Then why didn't you tell her?"

"I don't get it!" Mark shot back. "Here's this attractive twenty-year-old girl going out in the middle of the night with some guy she just met. She needed to know that goes against all Christian values!"

"Frankly," I said, "she already knew that if she was raised in a Christian family. What she needed to know was that her father loves her. If that were my daughter, I'd be afraid for her safety. I'd tell her, 'Honey, I'm your father and I love you. I've always loved you, since I first held you in my arms when you cried as a baby! I love you so much I don't want to see you get hurt.'"

I paused as Mark sat quietly, weighing my words. I took another deep breath and continued: "I'd say, 'You're a woman now and old enough to choose what's best for yourself. I can't stop you from doing what you want, but I have to say I'm scared for you. I know you want to date and find the right man. I want that for you, too, and have prayed for a man who can appreciate how beautiful you are inside and out.

"'But what you're talking about here makes me afraid you'll miss out on that. Maybe you're afraid of that yourself, and that's why you're taking such risks. Whatever, I was a young man once, and I can tell you that most guys would assume a woman is looking for sex if she agrees to a first date at 3 A.M. I don't want to judge this particular guy, but as your father, I ask you to give him a chance to demonstrate his intentions.

"'Please, ask him to meet you at another, early evening time. If he really cares about you, he'll honor you and be glad to do that; if he doesn't, he'll take off, and you'll have saved yourself a lot of grief.'"

"I think I see what you're getting at," Mark admitted. "But what about that course I took? I mean, those were Christians teaching it."

"It's sad," I said, "but people who teach like that don't know the Father—they just know law and religion. You can't afford to hide behind law and religion if your daughter's endangering her life. Jesus showed us the Father behind the Word; come on out and show her the love behind the law. She's beyond the age when you can control her behavior—but no woman's ever too old to be moved by her Daddy's love."

Mark hesitated, then sighed. "I don't think I've ever really just told her how much I love her like that."

"My brother," I said, "that could be why she's rebelling."

We sat quietly for a minute, and I decided to push ahead. "Why do you think you haven't told your daughter how much you love her?"

Mark dropped his eyes, turned, and looked out the side window. "I guess," he said finally, "somewhere along the line I got the idea my love didn't count for much with her."

"That must really hurt," I offered. "But my educated guess is that she dropped back to test you and see if your love depends on her doing things just right or is really unconditional and from your heart. If she did that—and most women tell me they do—she's got a healthier sense of self-protection than you realize!

"Frankly, if she knows she's safe and secure with your love, she's a lot less likely to take foolish risks with other men."

Nodding, Mark turned back and looked at me. "Do you think it's too late for me to tell her?"

"I think you're scared she'll reject you—and no man would blame you. She might. But just suppose your dad were alive and called you tonight and said, 'Mark, I want to tell you how much I love you.' Regardless of what you'd do about it, how would you feel?"

Nodding, Mark smiled thinly. "I'll do it."

"You're on the front line, brother," I said, putting a hand on his shoulder. "But you're a real warrior—and you're ready."

I then prayed and asked the Father to honor Mark's courage, to give him his heart for himself and his daughter, and to prepare both of them for the time when Mark would reach out to confess his love as a father.

"You know," I added as I got out of the car, "you underestimate the impact of a father's love. My guess is that's because you haven't dared face how important your own dad's love was to you, and therefore, how badly it hurt you not to have it. If that's true, I really hope you'll let the Lord lead you through that grief so you can know the real power in loving your own children."

Mark had been a Christian for twenty years. But that night he began to know his Father. As a result, he could give his daughter a chance to know her Father, too—whether or not she could say yes to him in that moment—because her Dad had demonstrated his love.

Did it work? Did father and daughter live happily ever after?

I don't know—I never saw Mark again. I only know that hiding behind the Law doesn't work, that loving openly and dangerously is how Jesus works.

False warriors read the Bible anxiously for passages to hide their brokenness—because they don't trust the Father to be either merciful enough to forgive or powerful enough to heal. In fact, such distrust often leads men into New Age spirituality: "Give me an answer that will make me feel better!" The fortune-teller gives knowledge but not trusting relationship with the Father.

Kingdom warriors, on the other hand, read the Bible hopefully, to surface their sin so they can take it to Jesus and get healed for the battle.

Like the Pharisees, Mark at first placed the burden of righteousness on his daughter without lifting a finger to help her. He was safe hiding behind the Law.

But when he surrendered his scriptural arsenal designed to bomb her into submission, he left himself wide open to be rejected, just like Jesus on the cross. Mark loved his daughter as Jesus loves her, thereby becoming a living word of God himself: "Love one another, just as I love you" (John 15:12).

From a biblical view, in fact, your relationship with God can't be separated from your relationship with other persons. As John declared,

> We love because God first loved us. If someone says he loves God, but hates his brother, he is a liar. For he can't love God,

whom he has not seen, if he does not love his brother, whom he has seen. The command that Christ has given us is this: whoever loves God must love his brother also. (1 John 4:19-21)

To hide from each other, as Mark hid at first from his daughter, is to hide from God. The most graphic sign that a man does not know God is that he does not truly know another person. For example, often he may lust after a woman's body to avoid the more fearful emotional intimacy with her, or miss the full experience of Christian brotherhood by limiting his relationships with other men to business or sports encounters.

When God confronted Adam after he ate the forbidden fruit, he clearly could have said, "You're right, Father. I did it. The Snake just sounded so good. I thought I knew what's best for me, but I know now that only you do. I thank you for setting that boundary to protect me, and ask you to forgive me for distrusting you and breaking it."

But shame and fear of punishment intervened. And so instead, he passed the buck to Eve—demonstrating thereby that he did not know God as his merciful Father.

Consequently, his relationship with Eve was truncated. No longer could he be naked and not ashamed (Gen. 2:25) with her as before the Fall; instead of openly disclosing themselves to each other for better or worse, suddenly they "realized they were naked, so they sewed fig leaves together and covered themselves" (Gen. 3:7).

Thus hidden from each other, they hid from God (Gen. 3:8).

Not knowing God caused Adam not to know the woman and prompted the punishment upon men thereafter that destroys intimacy. That is, the man was condemned to rule over her (Gen. 3:16) and thereby forfeit the original joy of her intimacy as a "suitable companion" in a common destiny (Gen. 2:18).

American revolutionary Thomas Paine wrote, "Government, like sin, is a badge of lost innocence." Similarly, the Law is a stopgap substitute for the Spirit, who flourishes amid a trusting and innocent relationship with the Father.

As boys, we men have learned that to be vulnerable is to get hurt, and afterward no advocate will present your case convincingly to your adult antagonist. We grow up anxious for protection from others; hence, the legal system. Indeed, the vast proliferation of lawyers and overflowing court dockets today simply reflects our inability to function in relationship—that is, to trust each other and settle differences by ourselves face-to-face.

Adam and Eve never needed the Law in their Garden Paradise. Even as civil law is necessitated by and accommodates our lack of relationship as citizens, God's Law is necessitated by and accommodates our lack of relationship with him. The need for the Law embarrasses him—and directs the Enemy to a gaping chink in our armor.

Hence, the Pharisees and false religion.

So far as it's designed to save us from our sinful nature, the Law is only as good as we are bad. The worse our behavior, the more valuable the law becomes as a counterpoint.

The apostle Paul therefore scolded the early Christians for going to pagan courts. Because we who have surrendered to Jesus and received his Spirit have been set free from the fleshly maneuverings of our sin-nature, we can "submit [ourselves] to one another because of [our] reverence for Christ," (Eph. 5:21) and abide his judgment. "The very fact that you have legal disputes among yourselves shows that you have failed completely," Paul chided. "You have been purified from sin; you have been dedicated to God; you have been put right with God by the Lord Jesus Christ and by the Spirit of our God" (1 Cor. 6:7, 11).

In other words, in the Fall we sacrificed intimacy for control—like Mark with his daughter. We distrusted God and listened instead to the Snake, who promised us godlike power.

The "knowledge of what is good and what is bad" (Gen. 2:9), which we gained through disobedience, however, led us to distrust each other. Having rejected God as Author and Mediator of our relationships, we needed to protect ourselves from each other.

Thus we seized upon his Law not as a loving revelation of how we function best, but rather, a handy way to protect ourselves from being shamed, to cover up our sin and appear righteous.

The Law became a big fig leaf behind which to hide our true selves from God and one another.

Through the Cross, therefore, the Father has offered to exchange the reality of his power for the illusion of our control.

Our flesh prefers the Law—even today alienation has become a major Enemy stronghold over men. Its inroad is an epidemic alienation from Dad, and its most common vehicle in churches is performance-oriented religion, which alienates us from each other.

Having clung to the Law to distance ourselves safely from each other, we haven't dared let go long enough to let the Spirit draw us into trusting relationship—even as we hunger for it. And so we allow the Law to define our relationships, as in roles and hierarchy. But law, meanwhile, has no power to restore authentic relationship; a plaintiff and defendant rarely become loving friends through their lawsuit, even if they agree the settlement is just.

In fact, the Law can't really protect you from getting hurt. It may make a mugger think twice before acting, and perhaps ensure that he's punished if he's caught. But he can still mug you, no matter how severe the law is against it.

Law, therefore, offers a false security. It may put a criminal in jail, but it can't keep him from wanting to commit crimes. Hence, over three-fourths of prisoners leave jail only to commit further crimes and return.

Through the Cross, God said clearly that it costs more to build loving relationships than to proclaim and enforce the Law. But while churches are busy teaching courses on "Christian values," any honest person knows, as another has put it, that values are caught, not taught. Even as your tennis game improves by simply watching a pro play, you largely internalize Christian values by drawing close to someone who lives those values.

So, even as God became flesh in Jesus and dwelt among us, his Law is internalized through relationship, not edict or exhortation.

That's why Jesus excoriated the Pharisees for not doing what they taught.

Indeed, that's why Mark's daughter walked out on his sermon. It's the difference between verbally spanking your daughter with "Christian values" and giving her the love that would allow her to demonstrate them. A woman who loves herself, after all, does not go out on a first date at 3 A.M.

A father teaches his children to love themselves by loving them himself.

Similarly, God's Law can convict, but it can't transform. It can tell you what's a sin and what happens if you sin, but it can't stop you from sinning. As the apostle Paul noted, "No one is put right in God's sight by doing what the Law requires; what the Law does is to make a man know that he has sinned" (Rom. 3:20).

Jesus did not offer his life as a Band-Aid. He did not come simply to shore up the Law's flimsy security, but rather to reveal the authentic and lasting security to which the Law witnesses—namely, being a beloved son of the Father.

Thus Paul continued, "But now God's way of putting people right with himself has been revealed. It has nothing to do with law, even though the Law of Moses and the prophets gave their witness to it. God puts people right through their faith in Jesus Christ" (Rom. 3:21-22).

The Law therefore exposed our sin, but could not overcome its effects. That is, it can convince men that we are sinners, but not that we are sons. That's the Spirit's job.

With nothing else to mediate our relationships, we could fear one another and, at best, curb our anger for fear of punishment. But we couldn't trust each other—and when we tried and got wounded, we had nowhere to go for power to reconcile.

Therefore, we could not stay in relationship.

We could not love.

Until Jesus came to save us.

Beyond Religion: From Judging to Loving

We human beings are a dangerously unpredictable lot. I couldn't guarantee Mark, for example, that his daughter would welcome his expression of love, any more than the Father could guarantee Jesus we'd welcome his.

It's risky to drop your guard and love; you might get crucified.

That's why true love requires not fantasy and hormones, but faith and courage.

It's why true love is for warriors, not romantics.

The Kingdom warrior therefore loves fiercely and boldly. Through surrender, he learns to have faith not in his daughter or any other human being—or even in himself—but in his Father. His love isn't shaken, therefore, by what another person does or doesn't do.

It always appears safer to judge than to love. Certainly, it's easier. The story of Mark and his daughter, however, reflects the larger truth for us all: Your life is in danger as your sinful human nature constantly entertains a date with the darkness, and you can't afford to hide from the Father and each other behind law and religion.

It's just too late; the darkness is upon us—even within us.

The Kingdom warrior knows that judging in an effort to control others is a cheap, and therefore, false security. Like Jesus, he invests himself instead in the more promising—albeit more costly—battle to love.

Someday I'm going to go to a televised ballgame and unfurl a banner in the grandstand that says, "John 3:17: For God did not send his Son into the world to be its Judge, but to be its Savior."

After surrendering his control at the Cross, like Jesus, Mark chose instead to risk being wounded more deeply in order to provide his daughter with the security to choose her own safety.

That's Father-love.

The Kingdom warrior gives up his right to judge for the privilege of loving, fighting for the other's salvation by opening a way for the Savior.

In surrendering your own spirit to Jesus, you give the Father God a chance to work through his Spirit. That's the very best a man can do on behalf of another.

You don't have to clobber them over the head with the "Word

of God." Rather, you have to become a living word of God yourself.

That is, you have to surrender to let his Spirit work through you. Then, you can demonstrate love for others and invite them to its Source. They're free to say no; but if they do, you don't grieve alone. Jesus weeps with you.

The Kingdom warrior does not hide behind the Bible from his fear of the truth or of otherwise getting hurt. Rather, he allows the Word of the living God to call him out into a world crying for love even as it crucifies the Lover—and indeed, to encourage him by reminding that even when saying, "Yes, Lord" hurts him unto death, his Father stands with him.

Like Mark with his daughter, he has learned to trust—as the apostle Paul urged the Galatians—not in his human power to coerce through shame, but rather, in "God's Spirit working through our faith." What matters to the Kingdom warrior insofar as he is "in union with Christ Jesus" is not law that works through condemnation, but rather, "faith that works through love."

That's how you learn the difference between judging and loving.

Judging the Sin, Loving the Sinner

In order to learn the difference between judging and loving, you must surrender to Jesus and let him love you to death. Until you know that's all you can do, nothing you do will help (Rom. 7:24).

The man who refuses to face his own captivity to sin not only refuses to let Father God heal his father-wound; indeed, he projects his "dad insecurity" onto the Father God.

When he enters a church and hears people worshiping "the Father," he reverts to a familiar mind-set. It's simple: The Bible tells you what you have to do to please this Father, so you just do what the "Word of God" says, and exhort others to do it, too.

The deception in such a "faith" becomes readily apparent to any honest man when he faces the truth of Romans 7:14-25, that is, when he discovers he's incapable of doing what God says—and therefore, needs a Savior.

Without such self-honesty, a man clings to a performance-oriented faith fabricated by "those who try to be put right with God by obeying the Law" that thereby short-circuits grace and leaves him "cut off from Christ." Such false religion preys upon our epidemic longing for Daddy's love coupled with an unwillingness to trust the Father God to provide it.

Kingdom warriors, however, have a different hope: not, as the apostle Paul warned, that we will put ourselves right with God, and this is what we work for by the power of our determination working through our efforts. Rather, "our hope is that God will put us right with him; and this is what we wait for by the power of God's Spirit working through our faith."

Our sin breaks relationship with the Father, as Adam discovered, and opens the door to the Enemy:

> Don't think that the Lord is too weak to save you or too deaf to hear your call for help! It is because of your sins that he doesn't hear you. It is your sins that separate you from God." (Isa. 59:1)

So the father-wound did not begin—as the secularists speculate—at the Industrial Revolution, when dads began working away from the home, but at the Fall, when the man turned away from God, his true Home.

Indeed, the wounding between fathers and sons today is a reflection of that Original Wound; we haven't known how to father our children since Adam because we have cut ourselves off from the "Father, from whom every family in heaven and on earth receives its true name" (Eph. 3:14-15).

Because our father-wound reveals the very fall of humankind itself, it can't be healed by mere exhortation. We men are sick unto death. We need healing to the core and can't do it ourselves.

Jesus did not come to exhort us to perform better, but to give us himself, that he might perform through us. In suffering and dying for us, he paved the way for his Spirit to help us act differently. He did everything he could do to show he's with us, ready and able to draw us back to the Father to fill our self-centered human nature with his Holy Spirit.

Even today, he's waiting for us to do the only thing we can do—namely, surrender to him.

In effect, the Manufacturer has sent out a product recall notice: "There's a flaw in your vehicle that will kill you. Bring it back and get it fixed." Even as the manufacturer doesn't expect us to fix the car ourselves, we're not held accountable for being unable to do what God tells us. If we could, we wouldn't need a Savior.

The Father who created (manufactured) us can handle our sin. Indeed, he's already done that on the cross. What he can't handle is our unwillingness to bring it to him. And so he declares,

> I was ready to answer my people's prayers, but they did not pray. I was ready for them to find me, but they did not even try. The nation did not pray to me, even though I was always ready to answer, "Here I am; I will help you." I have always been ready to welcome my people, who stubbornly do what is wrong and go their own way. (Isa. 65:1-2)

A Society Given to Law

Men who haven't faced their father-wound see God as an arbitrary and unapproachable Tyrant and therefore seek to exhort, coerce, or threaten others to keep his Law. Men who have taken their father-wound to the Cross have seen God as Father and therefore seek to help men know his love so they will want to keep his Law.

Fearful of losing control, we have been unwilling to know God truly, and have given ourselves over instead to the law to mediate our relationships and coerce "moral values." Ironically, the cost for thus avoiding relationship is increased lawlessness—that is, a generation of men who have precious few internalized values and little sense of what is truly best for themselves, much less for others.

Until relatively recently in our society, we have enjoyed a consensus of moral values, often enforced by shame. As a boy in the 1950s, for example, I recall people whispering when a classmate's parents were divorced. But the superstructure upon which this moral consensus rested was a hybrid false religion, that is, a host of secular organizations and institutions that promulgated a moral code but lacked any power to help people keep it beyond punishment for failing.

Thus the Boy Scouts, for example, could exclude boys with homosexual tendencies, but had no idea either what causes homosexuality or how to overcome it. Amid such a broad consensus, dads who lacked relationship with their own fathers and, consequently, with their sons, could rest assured that social institutions would hide their inadequacy and pick up the slack for them.

No more.

The limitation of the law to alter men's behavior is becoming clear to any objective observer of our society—bursting with prisons and lawsuits. And although Jesus two thousand years ago knew and provided for this ultimate flaw in legal systems, men who purport to follow him today cling to them as if Law, and not he, were life.

When Christian men become as fierce in pursuing healing as in defending the Law, real men will begin coming to church. When we become more determined to proclaim the Father's love than to pronounce his judgment, they'll line up to get in.

We're now ready to see the simple but powerful truth about God's authority that our rebellious human nature refuses to grasp—and that the Enemy is hell-bent to hide.

FOUR

From Law to Love

*The law always ended up being used as a band-aid on
sin instead of a deep healing of it.* Romans 8:3, *The Message*

*For God is at work within you, helping you want to obey
him, and then helping you do what he wants.* Philippians 2:13, TLB

. . . not because you must, but because you are willing.
1 Peter 5:2, NIV

WHEN you know your Father loves you, you want to do what he
says because you know it's best for you.

End of rebellion.

Enter the Kingdom warrior.

It's that simple.

It's not easy, however, for a generation of men abandoned by
their fathers.

Indeed, why wouldn't a man want the very best for himself?
Because he doesn't know his father loves him. A boy, after all,
derives his sense of self-worth from Dad. If he doesn't think Dad

loves him, he concludes, "I'm not worthy of love"—and he will choose his lifestyle accordingly.

Biblical morality is not a tool for controlling others, but a reflection of the Father's heartfelt longing for his children's safety and fulfillment.

Your Father God loves you. He wants you to know where he designed you to go, and how to get there. Therefore, he's given his Law—not as a tyrant, for his good alone, but as a Father, for your own good. "Don't worship other gods," he says in commandment number one (Exod. 20:3)—not to indulge his ego, but rather, because only he knows you inside and out. Other spiritual powers or gods will mislead and manipulate you, but only he loves you and can fulfill the purpose for which you were created.

The Father's love, that is, dissolves the stone-wrought Law so it can be absorbed into your bloodstream, be assimilated into your being, and minister life (2 Cor. 3:6). Thus, he wants you to have his love; indeed, he'll do anything for you to have it, even sacrifice his Son—because without it, you can't do what his Law says is best for you.

Then you can't be his warrior—and his Kingdom suffers that loss.

The average man today, however, doesn't associate law with love—likely because he didn't feel loved by dad-the-lawmaker as a boy. Even when he agrees the law is necessary, or even good, he most often believes that only punishment can uphold it—because that's what he experienced with Dad.

But what if both you and your dad have a heavenly Father whose "love endures forever" (Ps. 118) and, indeed, who has sent his Son to take upon on himself the punishment of the Law? In that case, we uphold the Law not as slaves, for fear of being punished, but as sons, who enjoy access to the Lawmaker-Father's very heart:

> We have, then, my brothers, complete freedom to go into the Most Holy Place by means of the death of Jesus. He opened for us a new way, a living way, through the curtain—that is, through his own body. (Heb. 10:19-20)

At times I become impatient with my son's "interruptions." And then I recall a touching photo from the early sixties: President Kennedy has turned away from the country's most powerful men in the background and is bending down to reach out as his toddler son "John-John" bursts into the hallowed Oval Room.

No matter how compelling our sin-nature, no matter how shameful the sins we have committed, no matter how busy God may be with apparently larger concerns, we can burst right into the throne room like "John-John" and hop onto the Father's lap, confident of his undivided attention and heartfelt love.

That's good news—but only for those who have faced their sin honestly enough to want it.

Jesus did not come to abolish the Law, but to fulfill it (Matt. 5:17). That is, he accomplished what the Law sought to but couldn't—namely, restored relationship with the Father. The Father God's goal through the cross wasn't simply to change your behavior. He'd already sent Moses to do that with the Law, and it didn't work. What did Jesus accomplish that Moses didn't?

"God gave the Law through Moses, but grace and truth came through Jesus Christ," John declared (John 1:17).

The Law illuminates our brokenness. It shows a man where he's missed the path. Yet, it was not designed to make us try harder, but rather, to die faster. The more seriously you take the Law, the sooner you surrender to Jesus—because the sooner you realize you can't keep it, the sooner you realize that you need your Father's mercy and grace.

But there's something even better than the Law. The Father sent Jesus after Moses in order to draw you into relationship with himself—as if to say, "If you surrender to my Son, you'll experience how much I love you, and therefore, love yourself enough to want the best I have to give you."

That is, you won't short-circuit your destiny by settling for the world's false security and fleeting pleasure. You'll do what the Father says because you want to become all he created you to be.

The Kingdom warrior is consequently a pioneer, even an adventurer. He asks not, "How can we men sustain the old and deadly way of punishment?" but rather, "How can we move out in the 'new and living way' that Jesus has blazed for us on the cross?" (Heb. 10:20, RSV).

These questions became graphically real to me just before John-Miguel's first birthday, when we began taking walks together around the block.

Months earlier—with absolutely no coaching from me—one of his first words had been "truck."

"Is it in the testosterone?" Mary asked, amused and amazed.

I don't know. I only know that, as a normal, tactile, concrete-thinking toddler, he wanted to go out in the street and touch every truck that passed. As I held one hand, he would lean and reach out his other hand to the street, crying, "Truck! Truck!"

Eventually, the tugging increased until I had to kneel beside him on the sidewalk and put my arms around him. Immediately, an urge arose within me—was it testosterone?—to spank him and shout, "No!"

And yet, as the truck whooshed by us, my fear was overwhelmed by a deep sense of love. I found myself not only holding my son protectively from the street, but drawing him affectionately to myself.

Restraint merged with love—and I balked.

Arrows of shame struck me at once from within: *Don't wimp out! Take control and show your strength! You're the father. If you love him, hit him and say no! Be a man and do your job! You're supposed to force him to obey—it's clearly for his own good! Do you want him to get killed by a car?*

Still, I hesitated. His impulses were not malicious or even mischievous. Indeed, how could I punish my son for wanting to touch a truck? As Mary suggested, it's in his makeup as a boy. The issue, rather, was somehow to separate the good desire to touch a truck from the false satisfaction of running out into the street.

64

His tender one-year-old sensibility was incapable not only of seeing the larger danger in the street, but also of appreciating any larger agenda behind Daddy's hitting him. His little mind could only reason, "Daddy and I are enjoying walking together. Why is he hitting me for wanting to do something fun?" Such a boy won't enjoy life later as a man.

More important, he'll entertain crippling self-doubts. "If I'm not doing anything wrong," he reasons, "it must be that Daddy just doesn't like me." That is, "Why doesn't Daddy love me anymore?"

Thus, shame overshadows relationship with the father.

Certainly, I don't want my son to get hit by a truck. But the bargain was absurd: Should a boy have to give up Daddy's love in order to be safe? Indeed, for a child, safety *is* Daddy's love.

The man who hasn't looked honestly at his own boyhood longing for Daddy's love can't recognize himself in such thoughts and will discount them as fanciful, even extravagant. In shutting down his father-longing, he trades Father God's love for the more apparent security of the Law. He abdicates the call to Kingdom warfare, the call to venture beyond the fears of losing Dad's love and come into his destiny as the Father's son.

On the sidewalk, meanwhile, I could only pray, *Father God, help! You know I want to be a good father. I want to make John-Miguel feel safe* and *loved. I want him to fear the moving truck, not me. Show me how to do it!*

As John-Miguel protested, wriggling in my arms, I "heard" no answer but an aching love in my heart.

Uncertain but deliberate, I hugged him firmly and looked him in the eye. "Daddy loves his boy," I said. "Truck big! BOOM in street! Hurt boy! Big owwy! John-Miguel stay on sidewalk with Daddy. Daddy loves his boy. Carry boy on street. No owwy. Boy happy. Daddy happy." The wiggling stopped—was it just because there were no trucks at that moment?—and we walked on. Soon I spotted a parked truck and pointed to it.

"Truck! Truck!" he shouted excitedly, stretching for it as I picked him up and carried him over.

"Daddy loves boy," I said, squeezing him gently. "Daddy carry boy. Truck stopped. Truck OK. Boy touch truck."

Hesitantly, reverently, John-Miguel reached out and caressed the truck's red tail-light as I held him in my arms.

Thereafter on our walks, whenever I picked him up and stepped out into the crosswalk, I held him especially close to me to communicate both love and protection. "Daddy loves his boy," I would say. "Daddy carry boy on street. No owwy. Daddy happy. John-Miguel happy."

After a few times, he got the idea. When a truck or car approached, without my saying a word he stopped walking ahead and drew close to me. As he held onto my leg, I knelt down and hugged him, and together we enjoyed watching the car whoosh by, and even made our own engine noises.

I continued to lift him up at corners and tell him, "Daddy loves his boy," as I carried him across the street. Eventually, we came to one corner, and to my pleasant surprise—without my saying a word and before I could bend over—he turned to me and lifted his hands: "Daddy carry boy!"

Hallelujah!

Yet the true test was yet to come.

Several days later, we were playing with his tricycle in the front yard, and the phone rang. Intending to jump inside and take the call only for a second, I said, "Daddy go phone. Boy stay on grass." The call turned out to be engaging, and after a minute I caught myself in fear and raced back out front.

Sure enough, John-Miguel was standing on the sidewalk looking out at the street. A few cars were passing by and I was about to shout at him—but a compelling sense of restraint came over me. Instead, I ran out on tiptoes close enough to where I could grab him if necessary, prayed, and waited to see what he would do.

He hesitated—I could almost see his mind turning over the options—and then finally turned back toward the house. As he climbed onto his tricycle, he saw me. Straining to seem casual, I walked over, knelt down, and hugged him. "Daddy loves his boy," I said, sighing deeply. "John-Miguel stay grass and sidewalk."

Matter-of-factly, he nodded. "Daddy carry boy street."

"Yes," I said, smiling and holding him closely. "Daddy carry boy street."

Knowing the Law by Knowing the Lawgiver

Today, a year and a half later, John-Miguel still stops at street corners for me to pick him up. In fact, far from running amok for lack of "godly discipline," he's become a watchman for other children.

Recently, my wife Mary came home with him from play group and said that when the program had finished, John-Miguel and many of the other children ran out of the classroom. The mothers raced out after them, but Mary did not. One mother passing by said to her, "Aren't you scared your boy will run out in the street?"

Mary was not. Still, when she got outside, she was surprised to hear John-Miguel's shouting anxiously at several children who were already at the edge of the sidewalk: "NO! Stay on the sidewalk! Come back! Don't do it! Don't go in the street!"

This is how through the Cross the Father God deals with our behavior. When I surrendered to Jesus my goal to change my son's behavior, and invested instead in our relationship, he changed his behavior—seeking the best for himself, and even for others.

John-Miguel has convinced me that true father-love frees you from a fear of punishment and allows you to internalize the Law for your own well-being—and consequently, for the well-being of others.

Indeed, that's what the Father accomplished in Jesus, after promising centuries earlier,

> The time is coming when I will make a new covenant with the people of Israel and the people of Judah. It will not be like the old covenant that I made with their ancestors when I took them by the hand and led them out of Egypt. Although I was like a husband to them, they did not keep that covenant. The new covenant that I will make with the people of Israel will be this: I will put my law within them and write it on their hearts. I will be their God, and they will be my people. None of them will have to teach his fellow countryman to know the Lord, because all will know me, from the least to the greatest. I will forgive their sins and I will no longer remember their wrongs. I, the Lord, have spoken. (Jer. 31:31-34)

As the apostle Paul comments,

> We have confidence in God through Christ. . . . It is [God] who made us capable of serving the new covenant, which consists not of a written law but of the Spirit. The written law brings death, but the Spirit gives life. (2 Cor. 3:4, 6)

Suppose, on the other hand, that I had simply spanked my son and yelled "No!" when he first wanted to run out into the street. "The law," he would conclude, "exists to placate Dad. I can't trust him to give me the best, namely, the fun of running out to the trucks and cars." He therefore would decide, "It hurts to get spanked, and I feel alone and afraid when he yells at me and pulls away. *As long as Dad's around*, I'll do what he says."

Like ancient Israel, the Law is in the Book, but not in his heart.

The boy learns obedience, but not trust; law, but not relationship.

If you keep the law, not for your own good, but just for your father's approval, you can discount the law if you can discredit your father. Since every dad is a sinner, that won't be hard to do. In order to disobey Father God, even Adam needed only the Snake's rationalization that God is a jealous egomaniac. Similarly, in the sixties, a generation of men who convicted their fathers of racism, militarism, and sexism leapt into self-destructive rebellion and immorality.

The law, therefore, prompts rebellion precisely as far as it short-circuits relationship. The law can confer rank, but only the Spirit can confer sonship (Rom. 8:14-16).

Lacking heartfelt relationship with the Father, the Israelites couldn't discern his loving intent. Therefore, they readily believed the Snake's lie that the Father was withholding the best from them. "How come the pagans get to have all the fun?" they essentially complained. Thus groaning under the Law, they "did not keep that covenant," succumbing to the seductive pleasures of their pagan neighbors (Jer. 2:23-25).

Without relationship with the father, exhortations to "moral behavior" only foster shame, which beckons rebellion.

What happens when Dad has laid down the law but is not present to enforce it—for example, when the boy is running out with all the others after play group? Clearly, he's free at last to do what he thinks is best for him—and heads right for the street.

Two weeks ago, John-Miguel and I were driving home from a city playground along a busy, four-lane thoroughfare. As we passed through a particularly run-down section of town, I was shocked suddenly to see a little boy, perhaps two, teetering on the curbtop not two feet from cars speeding by. "Oh, no!" I exclaimed. "Look at that little boy!" Heart pounding, I asked Jesus to protect the boy as I signaled quickly and lurched into a gas station at the next corner.

"Where is the little boy, Daddy?" John-Miguel asked. "Where are we going?"

"The little boy is playing back there near the street," I said, leaping out of the car and locking the doors. "It's dangerous, and Daddy needs to go help him. You will stay here by yourself for just a little bit. Pray to Jesus. I'll be right back."

Strapped in his carseat, he nodded matter-of-factly, and I dashed off around the corner.

To my relief, the boy had stepped back from the curb but was still walking aimlessly in the grass between the curb and sidewalk. He didn't respond to my questions in toddler-ese, but I managed to get him to go across the sidewalk and sit beside the run-down apartment building where he likely lived. Spotting a pay phone across the street, I ran to call the police.

When an officer had been dispatched, I raced back to John-Miguel and drove back to the apartment building driveway to watch the boy and wait.

"Is the little boy OK?" John-Miguel asked immediately as I jumped in the car.

"Yes," I said, pulling quickly out into traffic. "The boy is OK. I called the police to come and help him." Seconds later, as I pulled into the apartment driveway and turned to see that the boy was still sitting safely, I noticed that John-Miguel was sitting with his brow knit.

And then, with a simple question, he cut through my emergency agenda to the heart of the issue.

"Where's his daddy?" he asked, puzzled.

Where, indeed?

A flush of emotion swept over me as I realized how casually my son assumed every little boy is protected by his father, how deeply he had internalized the notion that relationship with Daddy is the primary issue when danger threatens.

"I . . . I don't know . . . where his daddy is," I said, swallowing deeply as some primal longing, even profound joy for my son and our relationship together, broke forth. "But the policeman is coming, and he will be OK."

When moments later the police officer had taken over the situation and I hit the freeway on-ramp, I let my tears come. For several minutes, I thanked the Father for knitting me and my son so closely.

And then I sensed God's deep grieving for so many, many of his sons for whom the simple question "Where's his daddy?" goes unanswered. I wept for men teetering on the boulevard curb before the driving powers of death—in sexual promiscuity, drug addiction, abusive religion, unethical business deals.

Men who have never known a father's love don't know what's best for them, because dad's love is what's best for every boy. Thus, they don't know where their eternal Daddy is: right beside them, with a mighty hand and an outstretched arm (Deut. 6:20-21).

Consider the Christian teenager whose father has never talked openly and honestly with him about sexual desire and godly love for a woman. He's heard sermons on "biblical truth" and "sexual purity." But without father-love, his hormones proclaim, if only in his dreams, a far more compelling vision of what's best for him. As long as he goes to church and lives in a home where it's shameful to mock God, he bites the bullet and puts up with "Christian" restraint.

But what happens a few years later, when he's a bachelor out of the house and old enough to do what he wants for himself on Sunday? The Snake speaks, and he readily agrees that it's better to leave the church, get out from under its shame, and attend faithfully to his "sexual needs."

Fast-forward to when he's on a business trip away from his family, and some attractive woman comes on to him. For good measure, throw in a fight with his wife earlier, before he got on the plane.

All external restraints are gone; in fact, the external impetus is to forget his quarrelsome wife. No one would ever know but himself; a colorful truck is hurtling by, and Daddy's not there to shout "No!" and spank him. Indeed, here's his chance to show that spanking, shaming dad once and for all who's boss of his own life.

The long-run outcome of a man's inner battle with God's will reveals whether the Law has moved from the Book into his heart—that is, whether he knows his Father loves him.

Will he say, "Father, this looks good, but I've experienced your love enough to trust you when you say it's destructive. I want your best for me, Father, so I give up to you. Take over and help me put all my energies toward straightening things out with my wife"?

Or will he say, "Forget you, Father, and all your guilt trips— I'm gonna run out and touch that truck!"

As author Larry Crabb has noted, in effect the Snake seduced Adam by arguing, "The Father's holding out on you. He told you not to eat from that tree just because he doesn't want to cut you in on the best of life." In fact, however, the Father just wants to protect his son from opening up to the Enemy.

But the proud urge to deny our limitations and be as gods ourselves plays into the Destroyer's hands, and we exit Paradise to the Snake's laughter.

In other words, a man who hasn't drawn close enough to Jesus to know the Father can't bank on the Father's love. Like a son cowering before an arbitrary, angry, and distant dad, he dares not trust the Father and doubts that God's Law is for his own good.

And yet, even worldly men commonly accept that law is for your own good.

When we lived in Los Angeles, for example, nearby Olympic Boulevard was repaved, and for several days only a center yellow line divided the two-way, six-lane width of black asphalt. Driving in L.A. is life threatening under the best of circumstances, but negotiating unmarked, three-car-width blacktop with hundreds of other cars was suicidal. After narrowly avoiding several accidents in just a few blocks, I stayed off Olympic until all lane marks were restored.[1]

No man would say, "Some tight-sphinctered guy up in the highway department put in those lane marks to take away our freedom because he just doesn't want people to have any fun driving!" Rather, we assume the lane marks are put there by someone who wants the best for us, namely, a safe trip.

God's Law is the lane marks on the highway of life, which enable us safely to get where we're designed to go.

Know your Commander: He's not a cosmic killjoy who burdens us with laws and restrictions simply to deprive us of any pleasure. He's a loving Father who shows us the boundaries within which we function best, so that we might enjoy the true and ultimate joy of becoming the men he created us to be.

The flesh is right: If you follow Jesus, you won't have the good life.

You'll have the best life.

Discovering the Love behind the Law

Jews celebrate God's commandments at the festival of Simchas Torah—literally in Hebrew, "Rejoicing in the Law." Visit your local synagogue and watch—join in if you dare!—as people dance and sing over God's Law, carrying the scroll around, embracing and kissing it as a dance partner.

"Happy are those who . . . find joy in obeying the Law of the Lord," begins the very first hymn in Jesus' hymnal (Ps. 1:1-3). "They are like trees that grow beside a stream, that bear fruit at the right time, and whose leaves do not dry up."

Yet the flesh balks. How many men find joy in keeping the commandments—in not stealing, in turning their eyes from a woman's legs, in honoring a hurtful parent? In fact, if these were naturally such fun, God wouldn't have needed to command us to do them. And so the world's blessing of pleasure—proffered by

virtually every movie, TV commercial, and popular magazine—
is promised to the self-indulgent man who breaks God's Law.

The world does not know the Father's love (John 1:10).

The early church proclaimed Good News to a world blinded
by sin and trapped in self-destructive rebellion: not more laws,
but rather, freedom from the burden of laws that mere human
strength can't keep. What we must do in order to live, we can't;
but God has come in Jesus to do it through us.

Thus, the apostle Paul chastises those who preach striving
after the Law, calling them "false brethren . . . who slipped in to
spy out our freedom which we have in Christ Jesus, that they
might bring us into bondage" (Gal. 2:4, RSV). Indeed, he proclaims, "Freedom is what we have—Christ has set us free! Stand,
then, as free people, and do not allow yourselves to become slaves
again. Listen! I, Paul, tell you that if you allow yourselves to
become circumcised, it means that Christ is of no use to you at
all" (Gal. 5:1-2).

At the same time, Paul wisely exhorts us not to "let this
freedom become an excuse for letting your physical desires rule
you" (Gal. 5:13). The Father's freedom from the Law is freedom
to surrender to his Spirit and no longer to the compelling,
destructive desires of the flesh.

My Volkswagen Golf came with a manufacturer's manual that
tells me to put in 4.4 quarts of oil when I change it. I am "free,"
however, to put as much oil as I like in my car. No one from
Volkswagen International will come to punish me if I don't put
in 4.4 quarts.

I could say, "Nobody's going to tell me how much oil to put in
my own car! I paid for it with money I earned. It's mine. I mean,
you just have to interpret the manual right. It's too soft, not
conservative enough, because the guy's aiming to please custom-
ers. I'm going to put in two quarts of oil and no more."

I'm free to do it my way.

But the engine soon overheats and dies.

On the other hand, I could say, "The manufacturer's manual is
too restrictive, not liberal enough. The writer meant well, of
course, but we educated men understand that the manual was

written in Germany a few years ago, and therefore, just isn't really appropriate for me as an American in the 1990s. I want to be nicer to my car, and put in eight quarts."

I'm free to do it my way. But the seal blows, and again, the engine overheats and dies.

The Bible is the Manufacturer's manual.

In it, my Creator blesses me by telling me how he created me to function best. Today, at age fifty, I want to know that. He's given me free will to choose otherwise, but I don't have time or energy to waste playing adolescent games.

I want to get on with my destiny.

Therefore, I want to know my Father, who designed it.

I want what the apostle Paul prayed for the early believers:

[I] ask the God of our Lord Jesus Christ, the glorious Father, to give you the Spirit, who will make you wise and reveal God to you, so that you will know him. I ask that your minds may be opened to see his light, so that you will know what is the hope to which he has called you, how rich are the wonderful blessings he promises his people, and how very great is his power at work in us who believe. (Eph. 1:17-19)

Conservative or liberal, the man who does not trust relationship with the living God will ultimately accommodate the Bible to his own brokenness and miss the apostle Paul's blessing. He'll either put in too much oil and dilute the Bible to suit his own desires, or too little oil and quench the Spirit from it. Either way, he sabotages God's purposes in and through him.

So I trust the manufacturer has told me how the car runs best, and I put 4.4 quarts of oil in my car. I comply—not because I'm a wimp who can't think for myself, but precisely because I have a strong sense of my own best interest. I don't want to burn out my engine; I want to get where I'm going.

It's simple.

But not easy for men who don't trust Dad.

Be warned, therefore: Men who fear being known, and who

therefore don't want to know the Father, won't appreciate your tugging at their mask.

"You will be expelled from the synagogues," Jesus warned his followers, "and the time will come when anyone who kills you will think that by doing this he is serving God. People will do these things to you because *they have not known either the Father or me*" (John 16:2-3, italics mine).

In the spring of 1993, I was blindsided by a review of my book *Father & Son* in the evangelical journal *Christianity Today*. In it, the reviewer condemned me for saying that real men want relationship with the Father and therefore won't abide religious programs that focus on Law and principles as a substitute. "According to Dalbey," he declared, "real men need not keep the ten commandments."[2]

On the contrary, real men don't settle for knowing the commands over knowing the Commander. Again, we are not slaves, but sons (Rom. 8:14-16).

Significantly, in his further sweeping objections to the men's movement, the reviewer shared no hint of any struggle in his own life as a man—thus hiding from his readers and reflecting the very fear of relationship that fuels such misperceptions.

To those laboring under the Law, any witness to the Father's love will always appear extravagant, permissive, licentious—because it reminds their shame-laden spirits what they long for but have convinced themselves they can never have. Indeed, when they've punished themselves long enough for wanting it, they'll crucify the One who bears it.

Biblical commandments, in fact, are demonstrable truth given by a loving Father to his children after establishing his enduring, saving relationship with them. Scriptures that exhort obedience follow upon reminders of God's trustworthiness; it is the God who "brought you out of Egypt, where you were slaves" (Exod. 20:2) who commands you to "worship no god but me" (Exod. 20:3).

To the Christian reviewer of my book and to all my believing brothers, I simply say: Trust your Father God. You are his son. He loves you. His commandments are for your own good. When you doubt that—as the flesh often does—ask him, complain to him, engage him.

Jesus did. The night before he was crucified, he sweat blood, asking the Father to pass the cup of crucifixion to someone else, and making "his prayers and requests with loud cries and tears to God" (Heb. 5:7).

Engaging the Father in such vulnerable, honest relationship allows you to hear the Father's loving intention clearly in his time and way. Then you won't want to sin and settle for less than he's created you to be. You'll love yourself as much as your Father does.

That's the Law fulfilled.

It's what today's unfathered men are longing for.

Relationship with the living Father God can't be synthesized. A man whose father has abandoned him to laws, rules, and religious principles can only become angry in time. The masculine soul in every boy cries out the truth: "Even the best laws can't substitute for a dad who embraces me, listens to me, plays with me, who loves me enough to make me want the best for myself."

Much law-breaking among men can be traced to this rebellious anger at the father for "not being there for me" as a genuine person. If dad is not emotionally or physically present, a man lashes out at what has become the most tangible "father presence" to him—namely, the law. Prisons, therefore, are filled with unfathered men (see my chapter "Seeking the Brown Ooze" in *Father & Son*).

Certainly, a primary way of knowing God is by reading his Word, the Bible—an absolute necessity if a man is to be centered, apart from his own rebellious human nature. God's written Word is the ultimate standard by which all human behavior is properly judged. It saves a man from sabotaging his destiny.

Someone has said that the difference between reading the Bible and engaging the God who wrote it is the difference between reading a sex manual and making love.

When Religion Replaces Relationship

When I was a boy at my first Vacation Bible School, I learned a joyous song that I've hummed through tough times even as an adult: "The B-I-B-L-E / Yes, that's the book for me! / It tells me of / his wondrous love, / The B-I-B-L-E!" Some forty years later, I was shocked and dismayed, while visiting a believing church, to hear precious Sunday School children singing instead the middle lines, "I stand alone / On the Word of God."

How graphic, and how destructive: Religion has replaced relationship; self-righteous alienation has eclipsed the Father's heart. May almighty God forgive us for dumping our distrust of God onto our children instead of daring to trust his love.

The living God has recorded his historical words and actions in the Bible as an invitation to relationship with him now. The sin-nature in every man, endorsed by Dad's abandonment, balks at the Father's invitation. We either rebel outright and reject the Bible's authority, or we set the stage for future rebellion by reducing it to an impassive list of do's and don'ts.

Hence, the fraudulent "liberal-conservative" church split. On the left, God becomes the politically correct Eternal Creator, Nurturer, and Sustainer. On the right, he is the religiously correct Lawgiver and Enforcer. In the hearts of men, however, God remains, now and forever, Father.

In the Father's eyes, we're all just sinful, wounded sons, too proud to face the truth about ourselves, hiding our shame behind exhortations to "do it right!" Striving to be religiously correct is the same as striving to be politically correct. Both are rooted in the shame of not being able to make ourselves correct/right before God (Rom. 3:21-24).

Everyone tells us to be right. But nobody invites us to be real because nobody knows what real is anymore.

Because we don't know the Father.

Indeed, other books besides the Bible can stimulate you intellectually, and other religions promote similar standards of ethical and moral behavior.

Sadly, however, many Christians seem to think the uniqueness of Christianity lies in its moral values—as if all the other world religions actually advocated stealing, adultery, lying, and the other "thou-shalt-nots" of biblical Law. Christianity, however, is distinguished not by its moral standards, but rather, by how they are achieved—not by what Christians do, but by Who does it.

In fact, Christianity is distinguished from all other religions not by a principle, but a Person.

His name is Jesus—in Hebrew, "God Saves."

Without his life, death, and resurrection, we don't know God as the one who saves us, and there is no Christianity.

He makes us righteous by canceling out our sin and drawing us back to the Father. As we surrender to him, we are freed from the shame of being unable to do what we're designed to do.

Christianity bears good news and bad news. The bad news is, you can't do it. The good news is, Jesus has done it.

The fearful human effort to appear righteous and hide our sin, therefore, denies the work of Jesus and comprises false religion—which eclipses the Father God's love with the dark shadow of law and punishment. Indeed, it slanders the Father God's character as One who seeks primarily revenge instead of righteousness.

Yet the Lord proclaimed,

> Turn away from all the evil you are doing, and don't let your sin destroy you. . . . Get yourselves new minds and hearts. Why do you Israelites want to die? I do not want anyone to die. . . . Turn away from your sins and live. (Ezek. 18:30-32)

In misrepresenting Father God, false religion beckons the Father of Lies, the Enemy who requires continual human sacrifice.

On the cross, Jesus made the one and only human sacrifice required. We don't have to do anything else ourselves to gain the Father's love. In fact, we can't; he has sacrificed all that's necessary to cover our sin. Nothing you or I do, no matter how religious, righteous, or moral, can add to or improve upon Jesus' sacrifice.

We can only fall humbly at his feet and receive it.

That's how relationship with the Father begins, even as Kingdom warriors are inducted.

That's how a man learns his Father God loves him. John declared: "This is what love is: it is not that we have loved God, but that he loved us and sent his Son to be the means by which our sins are forgiven" (1 John 4:10).

Even as reading this book might help you know Gordon Dalbey, meeting me personally would open a whole new dimension to our relationship. Early in my teaching ministry, after my first book came out, men would often comment after a retreat, "Now that I've heard and talked with you, your message comes across a lot more powerfully than when I just read your book."

And so it is with our Father God.

I treasure the times men have shaken my hand and said, "Though I appreciate the content of your teaching, it's who you are that ministered to me most powerfully—your honesty and vulnerability."

And so it is with our Father God.

Obviously, what a man says can't be divorced from who he is; his words reflect the spirit within him.

And so it is with our Father God.

Indeed, the glory of living in this present age is that the Father's very Spirit has been poured out upon humankind—the same Spirit who enables us to know Jesus, and thereby, the Father himself (John 14:6-10; 15:26).

But will we let the Spirit do his work?

The Spirit Gives Life

I had almost finished this chapter when by holy coincidence I dusted off a book from my shelf written in the late 1960s by the pioneering Kingdom warrior Robert Girard. Stifled by his performance-oriented church upbringing and dismayed as a pastor at how readily he nevertheless fostered that in his own congregation, Girard determined to seek a renewal of his faith. Described in his book, *Brethren, Hang Loose*, his journey offers a remarkably up-to-date blueprint for the battle at hand today.

In a chapter titled, "The Letter Killeth, but the Spirit Giveth Life," he declares,

> In Christ, at the cross, the old system was annulled. Laws and rules (even God's) aren't the issue any more under the new

covenant (Rom. 7:6). The new system under grace produces "newness of life" because it isn't based on a confrontation with cold commandments I can't obey—it's based, instead, on a living, personal relationship with the Holy Spirit.

Under the New Covenant, Girard says, "it's all different":

> It's not conformity, it's relationship with a Person. It's not my failure, it's his success. It's not me working for God, it's God working through me. It's not . . . the letter, but the Spirit. Not death but life. Not I but Christ. Not trying but trusting.

This life in the Spirit, which fulfills God's goals for us, is released in us totally on the basis of faith. Trust. Dependence.

It's a whole new ball game. And it can't be played by the old rules.

From this perspective, Girard portrays the Father God's life-changing prescription for the church:

> As long as we operate the church or any of its agencies as institutions set up to teach the learners how to act like Christians, how to conform to the "acceptable evangelical norm," how to perform in the Christian manner, we shall not experience the fresh life we are seeking. Because we will still be "living under the law," intent on teaching the flesh how to look and act like it is living in the Spirit—even when that is not true.

The church must teach people "how to go on with Christ" once they have surrendered to him:

> True, most are told to get baptized, to get busy, to begin witnessing, to pray, to read their Bibles and to join the church. But that's still elementary. Most will begin to do these things because they see them as good things to do. But these "good things" become an experience of death instead of life for multitudes of Christians, because they spring not from the life of the Spirit within, but from the same old

human nature trying in the same old way to be good and to produce good works and to conform to an outside standard. It gets old and stale and dissatisfying and frustrating after a while—and unproductive. Because it's not from the Spirit at all. It's from the flesh.

Telling people over and over that they are born again doesn't bring renewal. Preaching the super-performance standard of Jesus and the apostles doesn't do it.

The preaching of law (even "New Testament law"), getting people to ask, "What would Jesus do?," carefully setting up the church organization and meeting structure and outreach pattern to conform to that of the New Testament Church—none of these things will assure renewal.

Only when Christians and their churches learn (are taught) how to walk, in personal life and together in the Body of Christ, in utter dependence on the Holy Spirit, controlled by the Spirit, led by the Spirit, and in the energy of the Spirit, will we begin to touch the fringes of genuine life and renewal.

We think we have the Scriptures down pat. We know the law of God and the written do's and don'ts. . . . From the Bible we can prove what is right and what is wrong. We can explain the doctrines that accompany our theological position. We know how to be orthodox. But Life (with a capital "L") eludes us. Because we haven't caught the sweeping New Testament truth that all of Christianity and all in the church and all in the Christian life functions rightly only in the context of personal relationship to, and control and empowerment by, the Living Holy Spirit.[3]

I read these words today, almost twenty-five years after they were written, and am undone. I know so many men who surrendered to Jesus during that amazing season of harvest in the seventies. What, in God's name, has happened to us that we've lost sight of Jesus and become so mesmerized instead by principles of manhood and striving after standards of "godly" behavior? Like the apostle Paul writing to the Galatians, my heart cries out,

> What magician has hypnotized you and cast an evil spell upon you? For you used to see the meaning of Jesus Christ's death as clearly as though I had waved a placard before you with a picture on it of Christ dying on the cross. Let me ask you this one question: Did you receive the Holy Spirit by trying to keep the Jewish laws? Of course not, for the Holy Spirit came upon you only after you heard about Christ and trusted him to save you. (Gal. 3:1-2, TLB)

The trail has been blazed.

But we must start at the beginning.

How, then, do we move into this vital, upending, renewing relationship with the Father God, which the living Holy Spirit beckons?

Why, indeed, do we fear it so much?

FIVE

Loved without Strings: When Pinocchio Becomes Real

I RECENTLY read my son the old classic *Pinocchio,* and was startled to see how aptly it portrays the relationship between manhood, law, and the father's love.

In the story, the carpenter Geppetto longs for a son in his old age—that engaged me right away!—and makes a puppet he calls Pinocchio. A "fairy godmother" grants the wooden figure life, but not flesh and bones. To become a real boy, she says, he must "prove himself brave, truthful, and unselfish," and she leaves Jiminy Cricket with him as her on-the-spot spokesman.

Pinocchio wants to become real, but worldly pride traps him in falsehood—luring him into a circus as a "stringless marionette" feature act, where he scorns Jiminy Cricket's warnings and gets thrown in a cage (Rom. 7:24). When the fairy comes to rescue him, he lies to her, and his nose grows. Unwilling to face his wrongdoing, Pinocchio is unreal. Thus, he is unable to discern truth. He gets lured from there to "Pleasure Island," where "naughty boys get turned into donkeys" and face at last very real consequences for their rebellious self-centeredness.

This time, his spiritually appointed "conscience" Jiminy Cricket saves him before he becomes fully transformed into the stubborn, self-centered animal. Humbled and repentant at last, he returns home with donkey ears and tail as a bodily warning— only to find Geppetto has left to find him and been swallowed by a whale.

Determined to atone for his rebellion, Pinocchio goes to the ocean and—reminiscent of Jonah—swims into the whale's belly. There, in the monstrous depths, he meets his father at last. To escape, he builds a fire, and the monster sneezes them both out; as the boy bears the old man to shore with the monster in hot pursuit, he fulfills the fairy's requirements and becomes real.

Certainly, Pinocchio begs comparison to the biblical story of the Father God and ourselves as his sons. The boy was created to be a source of joy to his father, but he allows the powers of the world, both within and without, to sabotage his destiny. Yet the power who gives him not only vitality but real life in serving others seeks after him and intervenes to offer him restored relationship with his father.

To become real, the story says, you must know love without strings attached—that is, not wooden as a puppet, stiff and manipulated by external principles, but flesh and blood as a son, responsive to internal needs and longing. Like Adam, Pinocchio enjoyed that in the beginning with his creator/father. But he had to face the deadly power of the world and succumb to its temptations in order to become real enough to value his father's love.

Like Pinocchio, we're easily lured by the pleasures of the flesh to become trapped as animals instead of free as beloved sons. Ashamed of how we've rejected the Father's love, we lie to ourselves and others. But when at last we see the awful power of the Enemy to deceive and destroy us, we long for the Father and cry out to him to save us.

It is then that we give up on our own righteousness, confess the truth about ourselves, and seek his mercy. At last, in the belly of the monster, we meet him as we are, and by grace, he transforms us (Jon. 2:1ff.).

We become no longer resistant puppets, but pliable sons. Not awkward mechanisms, but grace-full human beings. The Father's heart is within, motivating us; we no longer need strings of law to pull us.

We become real men at last—seeds filled not only with the genetic code of our destiny, but the internal bran to germinate it. Indeed, when planted in the body of Christ, we find the soil to embrace, nurture, and bring it into fruitfulness.

The Law is like the tugs of puppet strings—external jerks that control a man to give him apparent, but not authentic, life. God, even as Geppetto released Pinocchio to stumble in the world, loves his sons; he could pull the law strings and make us do his will, but he wants us instead to be real, so he can have relationship with us.

In sending Jesus, the Father God gives up on the "Old Covenant" of the Law as a way of drawing us to himself (Jer. 31:31-34). He cuts the law strings and sets us free to surrender and enjoy his love—or rebel, and kill him.

Our proud human hearts, however, can't believe in a God greater than ourselves and know we'll kill any who presume to be. "If I can't forgive myself," we reason, "surely God can't either; if I'd destroy anyone who betrayed me like that, surely God will destroy me for doing it to him."

And so religiously, fearfully, shamefully, we keep tying the strings back on, preaching Law, principles, and obedience. The flesh rests its case: It's easier to be wooden than real; safer to be puppets than sons.

True Morality

A generation ago, Christian men were seduced into thinking it's easier just to "lay down the law" and tell young men, for example,

"Don't fornicate because it's wrong. God's Word says so!" But our exhortations only masked our own lack of relationship with God and thereby squandered his credibility among an entire generation today.

Men who don't dare to know Father God, who made that Law, can't lead their sons into the relationship with him that would allow them to keep it. And so the average young man today scoffs at such lazy theology, which disregards his own will and experience.

"Why does God say not to fornicate?" he demands. "My body tells me it's great! I mean, what's the big deal?"

What, indeed?

Join me, if you will, on my frontier fantasy (the frontier of parenthood!):

I imagine my son when he's about twelve. I'm driving the car and he's in the seat beside me. I pull up to a stop sign, and on the sidewalk, a woman in a short skirt walks by.

His head turns.

It's time.

That night I take him out for a walk. "I notice you've been checking out the girls, and that's fine," I say. "But as you do that, I want to talk to you about what's going on in your body and spirit. I know that girl in the short skirt today looked good, but I love you, Son, and I want you to have something even better—the best, in fact, that life can offer you."

First, I remind him about the fireplace: how it warms the house on a cold night and is so much fun for roasting marshmallows and making popcorn. "Why do we build the fire only in the fireplace, and not on the living room rug, in the bathroom or garage?" I ask.

"It'd burn the house down!" he scoffs.

"Absolutely." I nod. "What's happening inside you feels like a fire sometimes, doesn't it? If you don't put it where it belongs, it'll burn your house down. But if you do, it'll make your home safe and fun, even a warm refuge from the cold world."

Later, when my son's older and beginning to date, I plan to tell him more of the truth: the way we relate physically to each other affects our emotional and spiritual bonding. If you hit someone, for example, that makes them afraid of you, so you pull away. A hug, on the other hand, makes you want to be close.

The more sexually physical you get with the girl, therefore, the more bonded you become emotionally and spiritually, and the harder it will be to break the relationship. As the most intimate physical act which beckons the power of creation itself, sexual intercourse is therefore reserved for lifelong commitment only, under the authority of the Creator God (1 Cor. 6:15-17).

I'll reassure him that God will bring him a "suitable companion" to help him fulfill his destiny—even as he brought me his mother. I'll urge him, therefore, to commit his bachelor season of celibacy to discerning his gifts and calling, so he can recognize a suitable woman by her own, matching destiny.

"A lot of women will turn you on sexually," I want to say, "and so will the one God brings you. But the more you know what God created you to do, the more the field of women narrows. In fact, the more you want to get on with your destiny, the more picky you'll become about women. That's OK. Decide what you need in a woman, be willing to be that kind of person yourself, and don't settle for less."

We'll talk about how scary it can be getting emotionally close to a woman, dropping your guard and letting her see your faults as well as your strengths. Getting physical, therefore, can be a coward's cop-out that short-circuits real intimacy—which can only come by facing and working through problems and differences.

I'll say, "Perhaps someday you'll be a father, and by grace, you'll have a daughter of your own. You'll love her and want to protect her with all your heart and strength. Treat your date as you'd want a young man to treat your daughter.

"When you respect a woman physically and emotionally, you demonstrate how valuable she is, and she feels very feminine. You've given her something only a man can—and that makes you feel very masculine."

Where appropriate, I'll tell him about my own mistakes and miscues and reassure him that no man gets it perfectly.

I hope we'll talk a lot about sexuality. But while he needs to know the warning of worldly sexuality, I pray I can keep focused on the promise of godly sexuality and not hide my own weaknesses and uncertainties behind the Law and punishment.

Otherwise, he just won't talk with me.

That's my frontier fantasy.

Still, much as I believe my love allows him to listen, and even make him want the best for himself, I know it can't make him do what's best. As long as he has a belly button, he'll still be a sinful human being who needs a Savior.

In fact, even as I rejoiced and wrote our "sidewalk safety" story for the previous chapter, I was struck by a deep pain while praying about it later.

At first, I basked in the glow of seeing how my love had allowed him to exercise positive inner restraint. "That's great, Father!" I prayed excitedly. "Now all I have to do is demonstrate my love, and that will protect him from the temptations to come!"

Long silence on the other end of the line.

I waited, puzzled—and increasingly worried. And then, I sensed the Father's response: *For many years, your love will be enough, even a necessary foundation, and I'm pleased that you are so willing to give it to him. But the time will come when your love will not be enough to deter him from the temptations of the flesh.*

"Wha . . . what do you mean?" I asked, reeling as my bubble burst. In a flash of fear, it struck me how many years I'd wasted as a young man, running from my calling after things of the flesh, hurting others and myself.

I fell on my knees. "But Father," I cried, "if my love isn't enough for when he gets older, there must be something I can do then to keep him on track?"

Almost immediately, I sensed the response:

It is then you shall tell him at last who he is.

Tell him the story of my history in him—through you, your father, and your grandfather unto his spiritual ancestors in ancient Israel— that a love greater than yours might enter the contest in his heart.

Tell him who made him, and the kind of men I used, even the history and sin I overcame in them, that he might be prepared for his own calling.

Tell him he's a man of destiny, that my hand is upon him even as his forefathers. Tell him he can deny it, he can hate it, he can run from it, he can pretend he's someone else. But I, his Father, will have my way with him, even as with you, his father. And as I do, he will rejoice and take his destined place at last as my son, even a brother among brothers, a man among men.

Humbled, awestruck, I wept. "OK, Father," I managed. "I'll tell him."

A man with no past is consumed by the desires of the present. The powers of the world tell him, "Escape the problems of the present by immersing yourself in the future. Make resolutions. Promise improvements. Design plans. Image your success. Create yourself."

The biblical faith tells him, "You are lost in the present because you have lost your past. You do not know where you are because you do not know where your Father has been. Your future is shaky because your past is uncertain. Your branches are stunted because your roots are shallow."

A tree without roots is a tree without fruits.

Only the God of history can be the God of true morality (Heb. 12:1).

Obedience follows upon relationship.

The Fear of Not Measuring Up

Jesus was not sent to reveal morality or restore religion. Moses had already done that. Rather, Jesus came to reveal the heart of the Father and restore relationship with him (John 14:6-11)—which had been broken in the Fall, thereby rendering us utterly incapable of keeping his Law (Rom. 7:14-25) and knowing our true identity as his sons and daughters.

A slave frets over his master's command so as not to make a mistake and be punished. A son, on the other hand, is privy to his father's heart. He's free to ask the Father, "Why is this so important for me to do?" This truth, this question, frames the very heart of the gospel, yet is tragically inacessible to most men today.

As the psalmist cried out, "Deal with your servant according to your love and teach me your decrees. I am your servant; give me discernment that I may understand your statutes" (Ps. 119:124-125, NIV).

Indeed, only the son who trusts his father dares ask Dad to explain. Those who fear questioning God often simply are projecting onto Father God their boyhood experience before a fearfully distant, authoritarian father—that is, they fear he either does not exist, or perhaps worse, has no explanation beyond "Do it or else!"

Even as an adult, the issue remains: "Am I a good boy? Am I doing it right? Do I have a proper, acceptable faith? Do I measure up?"—that is, "Does my father love me?"

This man doesn't know his true Father, who has settled these questions on the cross. Like the Pharisees, he can recite the Word of God, even wield it religiously against others—but he can't truly believe it because he doesn't know the Father who spoke it.

For the truth is this: No, I can't be a good boy. No, I can't do it right. No, I can't have a pure faith. No, I can't do anything to measure up.

But yes, my Father loves me.

What's more, he—who by means of his power working in us is able to do so much more than we could ever ask for, or even think of (Eph. 3:20)—has come in Jesus to meet me in my inadequacy and draw me to himself.

Most men today, even as Christians, don't know this basic truth. And so we labor under the shame of not being able to do what we know we must do in order to win our Father's approval, acceptance, and love. Deep in our masculine souls we cry, like the the apostle Paul in Romans 7:18-19, "Daddy, I'd do what you demand if I could, but I just can't!"

Life in this world knows no deeper despair than this.

I urge you: Dare to remember it. Jesus is God's response to this very cry. To whatever extent you forget its agony and terror, you can't know Jesus, and you will not know the Father God.

Men forget this to the extent that Dad turned away. The

abandonment was just too painful. But the Father God has provided; as the psalmist declared, "My father and mother may abandon me, but the Lord will take care of me" (Ps. 27:10).

Instead of trusting the Father's mercy and openly confessing our shortcomings, too often we remain in the grip of shame and either rebel or redouble our efforts to please.

Because he has denied his deep inner pain just as his father did, however, the rebel eventually embraces a self-righteous politic or program just as shame-based as Dad's. "I'm better than Dad now because, unlike him, I do the right things: I have more truly intimate friends, have a more informed perspective on world events, go to a Bible-based church. . . ."

On the other hand, a man may burn himself out striving to be good. "I can please Dad if I just try harder," he has said as a boy. In its Christian form, such a man eventually must lie to himself and believe that in fact he's keeping the Law 100 percent. Since that's in fact impossible, it can only appear true insofar as he looks better than others. And so, his being good requires that another be not-as-good—even as the Pharisee presumed to thank God that he wasn't "like that [sinner] over there" (Luke 18:11).

Similarly, the "codependent" partner of an addict needs others to sin in order to feel good about himself. He plays the savior, hiding from his own sin behind the more obvious addictive behavior of another.

Such a man's pride and compulsive control blinds him to the Enemy. Indeed, the price of believing you're in charge is believing it's always your own fault when trouble strikes. "This wouldn't have happened," he fancies, "if only I'd had more faith" or "if only I'd been nicer."

Such a man can't face the reality of other people's sinful nature because he hasn't faced Jesus with his own. His vision is truncated and ingrown by fear of rejection. He grasps after his own goodness to save himself rather than trust the Father's goodness.

Isolated and alone, he wonders why nobody else is quite as good as he is. In fact, he sees his loneliness as a confirmation of righteousness, rather than an occasion to seek help.

I want to teach my son by example to trust his father's mercy.

Risking Intimacy with God

Once, after he'd been walking a few months, John-Miguel ran barefoot toward the bathroom where I'd just spilled water on the floor. "Stop!" I shouted to him. A slight turn of his head showed he heard me, but he chose instead to run into the bathroom.

I leapt up and raced toward him. Sure enough, his little foot hit the wet-slick tile and went up in the air. Lunging, I caught his head just as he fell backward onto the floor. Shaken but unhurt, he burst into tears.

As I picked him up and drew him to me in relief, he paused a second and looked at me through his tears with puzzled astonishment, as if to say, "Unbelievable! Dad, you weren't just yelling at me to promote your own authority—you really wanted to save me from getting hurt!"

Clearly, I could have punished him for disobeying my command. But I want him to remember not the shame of his mistake, but the benefit of its instruction. It's harder for me now, but it's an investment in his destiny—and in my own future peace of mind. I'm getting too old to catch desperation forward passes like that!

I would rather he learn that he's loved than that he's disobedient. If the touchstone of his identity from me is "I'm disobedient," I suspect he'll act that out or withdraw in shame. I'm banking, rather, that the more he knows he's loved, the more he'll obey, to preserve his own welfare and not just my self-image.

At the same time, I'll keep on making my mistakes as a dad. If I could be the perfect father, my son would never feel he needed Jesus.

Clearly, a loving father-son relationship like that is risky. The boy could think you're a wimp and reject your authority altogether. He might hate you for your mistakes and never turn to the Father God to learn forgiveness and true manhood.

But when you're out in the middle of the desert, it's just as far back to slavery in Egypt as ahead to the Promised Land.

You might as well push on.

Grasping this simple but often elusive truth frees a man from childish fear of punishment to walk in mature relationship with his Father God. His life energies can shift from seeking to be blameless and avoiding sin, to pursuing his destiny. He no longer cowers from the Father's call in fear of making a mistake. Rather—quite sure he will make his share of human mistakes— he presses on toward his higher calling, open to learn and confident of his Father's mercy (Phil. 3:12-15).

Sin as Self-Destruction

As the scales of rebellion thus drop from a man's eyes, he can see how the powers of the world have seduced him toward destruction and away from authentic manhood. Indeed, he can see how the efforts of the world to change things focus on the one sinned against, because the flesh's main concern is one's own welfare.

To the flesh, justice, for example, means "punishing those who hurt me." And certainly, the one hurt has a right to be compensated by the "hurter."

But on the cross, Jesus demonstrated a new justice, a new hope for transforming this world, by giving up his right to revenge. Jesus wants not only to heal the one sinned against but also to heal the sinner.

This view requires the sinner to realize that *to sin is to harm yourself*, that sin is first and foremost self-destructive, cutting a man off from his destiny and higher calling in the Father.

The Father's goal, therefore, is to convince the thief that stealing denies his own gifting; the adulterer, that lusting after another man's wife short-circuits the greater joy in his own marriage; the murderer, that killing diminishes the value of even his own life.

Moviegoers were appropriately startled in 1993 when Clint Eastwood was awarded an Oscar for *The Unforgiven*. Wondering what made this film so different from Eastwood's blood-spattered others, I went—and was disppointed to see yet another predictably violent western.

And yet this time, the killer feels guilty. Hounded by a sense of unforgiveness unto nightmares and drinking, he counsels a young hotshot gunslinger to turn from violence.

Significantly, Eastwood's character has acted wholly within

man's law, killing on contract to avenge violence against a defenseless woman. The powers of the world promise him no consequences for his killing, and in fact, a cash reward. Yet we see the wrenching internal struggle from his violating a commandment more profound, more authentic than the world's freedom.

Sadly, *The Unforgiven* packages this truth in so much gratuitous violence itself that it's likely lost on the average bloodthirsty Eastwood fan. Dostoyevsky's *Crime and Punishment* is in no danger of being supplanted by Eastwood's film. Yet, in the Hollywood milieu otherwise hell-bent to distort reality, I'll take it as a helpful signpost on the way to knowing the Father.

Recognizing that the killer hurts the killed, the robber hurts the robbed, and the adulterer hurts his spouse—requires no special sensitivity beyond animal self-preservation. But understanding how killing harms the killer, stealing harms the thief, and adultery harms the adulterer, requires a deeper perspective.

You have to see a man with Father God's eyes.

Indeed, to know this truth about sin a man must realize that he's not wired up to do such things, that when he does, he surrenders to the Destroyer and cuts himself off from God and his true self as the Father's son. He refuses the Father's embrace that Jesus died to bring him—and thereby short-circuits the Creator's design, truncates his life, and withdraws from his destiny.

Acts that God calls "sin" bear their own harmful consequences to you the sinner—the most dire of which is cutting you off from God, who alone can save you from their eternal consequences. As Isaiah proclaimed,

> Don't think that the Lord is too weak to save you or too deaf to hear your call for help! It is because of your sins that he doesn't hear you. It is your sins that separate you from God. (Isa. 59:1)

At its best, the law protects citizens. California law, for example, requires that motorists use seat belts. Why? Because it saves lives.

On the cross, however, God has demonstrated a better way to

save human life than law and punishment: Demonstrate that men and women are loved as sons and daughters. Then, they will want to preserve and fulfill themselves. And when they discover they can't do that by themselves, they will call for the Lover.

They will wear seat belts, for example, not because the law punishes them if they don't, but because they don't want to die—and allow the powers of the world to cut short their destiny.

The Kingdom warrior therefore fights not to preserve the Law, but to protect the children of God from harm. That fulfills the purpose of the Law, namely, to keep us from drifting off into the Enemy's hand (Rom. 3:19-22).

Humanly imposed punishment, therefore, from schoolyard detention to prison, is redemptive only insofar as it models the deeper harm sin causes in the sinner's soul—and thereby prompts the offender to repent in order to be healed. When divorced from that truth, prisons become schools for crime, recidivism soars, and a society that doesn't know the Father God trembles behind locked doors.

"Vengeance is mine," God declares. Any punishment of sin designed by men must reflect the deeper reality of the harm sin causes the sinner. Sin, that is, bears more profound consequences than men can devise out of their vengeance (Luke 12:4-5).

If the total effect of sin is God's punishment, if what God outlaws bears no intrinsic harm to the sinner, then Christians can only tell the world, "Shame on you for not doing what God says!" Whereupon, the world understandably responds, "How can we get this egomaniac Father God to stop spanking us for doing things that otherwise make us feel so good?"

That's why telling a man how badly his sin hurts others rarely changes him. Sin is rooted in our incurable self-centeredness; banking on a sinner's altruism is foolish.

A different approach is that used by the twelve-step program of Alcoholics Anonymous, which succeeds in changing addictive behaviors largely by focusing instead on bringing a man to see how his addiction hurts himself. Like the law, loved ones may enforce penalties for the addict's acting out, and may even leave. But the underlying goal is not to avenge their own pain, but to properly disengage from the addict so he can make his own responsible choices.

The addict is notoriously self-centered—that is, self-consumed rather than self-loving—and others are forever reminding him, to no avail, of his misbehaviors.

Finger-shaking at the addict, in fact, only adds to the underlying shame that fuels his addiction. Only when enough people leave the addict to make his own choices and suffer the consequences does he begin to realize how his addiction harms himself. Then, it's his choice to seek help or die of pride.

Some Christians may be offended by this argument, as if it promotes selfishness instead of the self-denial Jesus requires. But self-denial means nothing if you have no self to deny, even as "giving of yourself" means nothing if you have no self to give. When Jesus says, "Love your neighbor as yourself," he presumes that you do love yourself; if you don't, how can you understand what "Love your neighbor" means?

And if a man truly loves himself, is he not regarding himself as Father God does? Therefore, love yourself as much as God does—and you will keep his commands because, like him, you want the best for yourself.

I'm not saying, "Do not obey God," but rather, like the apostle Paul in Romans 7, that you cannot obey God. Face it. Dare first to trust him. Go to Jesus, fall on your face before him at the cross, surrender your pride. Stop running from the truth for fear your sinful nature will be exposed. Quit hiding your brokenness behind religion, exhortation, and standards of performance.

Your Father loves you. He has come in Jesus not to shame you; you can do that quite well by yourself. He's come to save you because you can't do that yourself.

Let him.

The Right and the Real

We don't have to earn the Father God's love; we just have to receive it. Indeed, we *must* in order to become the men he created us to be.

When Peter would not let Jesus wash his feet, Jesus declared,

"If I do not wash you, ... you are not in fellowship with me" (John 13:8, NEB). Peter's "doing for Jesus" looked good, but Jesus recognized in it the self-striving of false religion.

Receiving God's love is unbelievably simple—but not easy. Indeed, our human nature can't believe it because it's so threatening to our pride.

The price for pride, therefore, is an abiding fear that the foundation of your life is a sham and will crumble before the truth. And so you hide from the truth, often behind "religious achievements." You never mature in your relationship with God from slave to son—that is, you burn out striving to do what God says for fear he'll punish you if you don't. The average man knows he can find a TV ball game any Sunday that's healthier for him than that.

Tragically, if a man has exhausted his own resources seeking healing and can find no other men to demonstrate true religion, often he'll take false religion. At least it makes you look good while you die.

He joins a church and dutifully affirms the principles and behavior standards the other men proclaim—but when he begins trying to keep them, he discovers he can't. Because those other men appear so righteously polished and able to do it themselves, he's ashamed to tell them about his inadequacy.

To earn their approval and enjoy their righteous reputation, he becomes enmeshed in their religious charade, himself exhorting newcomers to righteousness even as he's dying inside. The older men thereby help him to hide his brokenness instead of face and overcome it—and thereby keep him from experiencing the grace of Jesus' victory.

As the apostle Paul declared, the man who sacrifices love for law and honesty for performance cuts himself off from Christ (Gal. 5:4). He therefore can't see with Jesus' eyes and forfeits his discernment. He thinks love is a reward for performing well and honesty means "keeping the law."

Today, even as when Jesus came, we men have lived so long with the counterfeit that we can't recognize the Real. Indeed, the Real threatens our illusion of control, and we crucify him.

Law and religion can teach a boy right from wrong, but only a father can teach him real from right.

It's right to obey God's Law.

But it's real to confess you can't.

Only a real father who trusts the Father God enough to face his sin openly—and share that struggle appropriately with his son—can lead his son beyond worshiping him to worshiping the Father God.

I once asked two hundred men, "For how many of you did your father ever ask your forgiveness after he hurt you in any way?"

Six hands went up.

A son learns manliness from his father. This means 97 percent of these men had never been taught that a true man acknowledges his shortcomings and seeks to make amends. Is it any wonder the average man today wants more to save face than to save his soul?

Dad, you'd better be the first to tell your son about your faults. He'll find you out sooner or later, and if you haven't told him with humility, the Enemy will tell him with a vengeance. His consequent distrust and disrespect for you will lead him to distrust and disrespect his own manhood—and later, his son's.

Being real and facing your inadequacies undercuts shame. It forces a man to cry out for a Savior and thereby frames the gateway to relationship with the Father God.

I'd rather be real than right. If I'm real, Jesus can make me right. But if I fancy I'm right, I give the Father little choice but to allow the Enemy his way with me, which will eventually force me to be real. Often, only the Enemy's fierce work of loss and brokenness can crack a man's wall of denial—as through divorce or serious illness. Only then can the Father's loving work of truth and grace enter and restore him.

Loving the Man God Sees in You

When I was writing this chapter, a humbling and powerful insight came to me as I was getting my son ready for his bath one night. (I suspect the Father gives me his best thoughts at such "random" times because if it happened while I was pondering at my desk, I'd be tempted to think it came from me!) In any case, while running the hot water I recalled a recent occasion, similar to several others before, when a professional counselor came to me after a conference and said, "I've appreciated just being around you because you're such a complete man."

I was gracious enough to say, "Thank you," and accept the compliment. But as he left, I turned away from it in my mind. *What a joke!* I scoffed. *Have I really been misleading people so badly? I thought I was more transparent than that! If only he knew how weak and unmanly I feel at times, how often my thought life gets out of control, how immature and lazy I can be. . . .*

The list of my sins scrolled on as I poured the bubble bath into the water.

And then it struck me: That guy was no starry-eyed groupie. He was a certified therapist—a reasonably credible judge of human beings. What if he was telling the truth?

I realized, in fact, that he and the others present that night *did* know of my own brokenness and stumblings because I had shared many examples from the lectern.

How, then, could he possibly say with integrity that I was any sort of "complete man," knowing as he did my shortcomings?

Unless . . . I hesitated, and then, like a cleansing waterfall, the thought cascaded over me: *Unless, indeed, being a man is not a matter of what you do, but rather, of whose you are—not of performance, but of relationship!*

I remembered he also said something like, "You said many things of substance, but what encouraged me most, and what I'll remember most, is just your relationship with the Father—your openness and vulnerability to him, and out of that, with us."

Always doing it right may make a complete god—but not a complete man.

Amazing!

What if I've been teaching the truth?

Flashbulbs popped in my mind.

What if being open and honest with the Father is not a way to achieve the standard of performance that qualifies you as a man;

indeed, what if that kind of authentic relationship with the Father *is* the standard?

I'd been thinking, *These men who think I'm such a complete man just don't know me the way I do.* But suddenly I knew the truth: I don't know myself the way God does. That man was seeing something in me that I could not—something, in fact, that's invisible to a man blinded by the Law.

He was saying, essentially, that authentic manhood is not doing the right thing, but knowing the real Father.

And he was seeing that, even in me!

Hallelujah!

And amen!

SIX

Lest We Fall: From Shame to Sonship

My brothers, if someone is caught in any kind of wrongdoing, those of you who are spiritual should set him right; but you must do it in a gentle way. And keep an eye on yourselves, so that you will not be tempted, too. Help carry one another's burdens, and in this way you will obey the law of Christ. If someone thinks he is something, when he really is nothing, he is only deceiving himself. Galatians 6:1-3

"SUPPOSE a guy in your men's group picks you up in his car, and as you get in, you notice several sex magazines on the back seat. What would you do?"

I had just taught on the warrior's need for small-group covering—prayer protection—and my question opened the topic of holding each other accountable. The immediate responses demonstrated how difficult it is for us men to stand with one another in our brokenness—and how easy, instead, for us to hide behind an onslaught of advice and shame:

"I'd show him the Scriptures about sexual purity."

"I'd tell him real men don't need that kind of thing, and if he'd just get rid of those magazines, he'd realize that."

"I'd ask him how he'd feel if his wife found out."

"I'd say, 'Would you bring those magazines to a men's prayer group'?"

Everyone was righteously angry, but no one dared consider any deeper wound that might be prompting the sin. Significantly, not one man referred to the group itself as a positive resource in responding to a brother's sin. My asking, "Suppose he doesn't listen to you?" only prompted more punitive one-on-one solutions.

The one man who did refer to the group used it as a threat: "I'd tell him if he wanted to stay in the group with us, that porno stuff would have to go."

No one had enough positive experience bonding with other men to say, "We're all in this together, so I'd want to involve the others in the group to find out what's going on and see if we could help the guy."

Shame breeds isolation—even abandonment.

As the apostle Paul suggested to the Galatians, seeing a brother's sin reminds us of our own weakness, and we're tempted to hide that behind judgment and exhortation. That's why it's so hard for us to toss a lifeline instead—in fact, to be a lifeline, with one hand securely in Jesus' and the other reaching out to embrace a brother in his brokenness.

Thus another brother's sin becomes a threat, rather than an invitation, as the apostle Paul put it, to "help carry one another's burdens . . . [and] set him right . . . in a gentle way." We either kick out our brother who sins or shut him down with exhortations to change because his falling reminds us of our own weak sinful nature—which we're ashamed to face because it reveals our inability to save ourselves.

Whatever shame a man does not dump on Jesus, he dumps on others.

Distrusting the Father's mercy and saving power, we open the door wide to the Enemy. Sometimes we drive a brother right into the Enemy's arms.

All because we're crippled by shame.

On the cross, however, Jesus stepped into the shame-filled gap between the fullness of what God wants us to be and the confines of our rebellious human nature. If he didn't, every one of his warriors would be lost to the consequences of their sin, and he wouldn't have an army. He bore the consequences of our falling short, so instead of retreating under its shame, we can advance and conquer in his name.

When I throw myself at Jesus' feet, confessing my sin and crying out for him to save me from it, he takes me to Father God to hold me. We can talk things over together. I can pour out my heart, knowing I'm safe and won't be condemned.

Sure, I need to make amends for things I've done—but he'll even show me how.

And I can look my brother in the eye as a man as I do it.

Accountability without Shame

We must hold accountable a brother in sin. But we must do it "gently"—not because the Father wants us to be wimps, but because we're all tempted equally and could fall just as easily as the next guy. We're judged as we judge others, so we'd better be merciful. "Forgive us our sins, just as we have forgiven those who have sinned against us," Jesus urges us to pray (Matt. 6:12, TLB).

The Kingdom warrior knows we're all in this together, bearing "one another's burdens" as necessary to uphold our platoon. Indeed, if any man thinks he's "something"—that is, so important that he doesn't need other men to bear his burden and call him to account—he'll soon be "nothing." The Enemy will pick him off for breakfast and he'll be a zero on the Lord's scorecard.

A man retreats into the fantasy of being such a pumped-up "something" when he feels the shame of his sin-bred "nothingness," and doesn't allow the Father to restore his true identity as a beloved son. Afraid of his own needs because he doesn't believe his Father will meet them, he dares not draw close to another needy man.

He's like a poor swimmer, afraid to come alongside a drowning man lest he get dragged down himself. He doesn't know Jesus is swimming alongside him, that he can reach one hand to a brother as long as he's first reached his other hand to Jesus, the true Lifesaver. Not having confessed his inadequacy to Jesus, however, he's ashamed to admit it to other men. So he keeps a safe distance and righteously shouts instructions to the drowning brother.

The Law mediates no saving power. Wielding it on a drowning brother only tosses him bricks—and does the Enemy's work for him.

Grace, however, saves unfathered men by restoring us to right relationship with Father God. The dignity of sonship overcomes the shame of abandonment. It thereby frees a man no longer to abandon other men in need.

"If you will let me make the difference in you," God says, "you will make the difference for me in this world."

Treating the Wound That Beckons the Sin

After that group of men had evaluated their first responses from this perspective, one man raised his hand slowly. "I think now I'd say to the guy, 'I know how bad that porno stuff can be for you. I was once hooked on it myself, and it really messed me up. The Lord really had a job on his hands getting me free. I don't want that to happen to you, Brother. I can't stop you, I know—but I'd sure like to talk some about it together.'"

Hallelujah! That's a Kingdom warrior: sacrificing himself— his pride—in another's behalf, surrendering his brokenness to Jesus, and moving boldly into fearful territory.

Again, you don't have to be a biblical scholar to tell a brother, "Sexual temptation, from sex magazines to bikinis on the beach, is a struggle for me, too. We need to fight together."

You just have to be real.

Being real overcomes the shame of not being right. When we're afraid of being judged and rejected, being open with the Father and each other gives the Holy Spirit access to heal and redeem us.

If the Father God loves us and condemns pornography, for example, then pornography is not good for us. When we entertain it, we don't love ourselves as much as he does. The man who indulges in it, that is, doesn't value himself enough to want the most fulfilling expression of his sexuality.

So, to withdraw from and abandon a brother for having sex magazines, or to judge and shame him, is lazy. If you love him, you'll take the time to figure out why pornography is bad for him—and lay down your pride to talk about how you, too, have missed the mark of godly sexuality.

Lazy warriors get killed quickly. They can't throw lifelines to a generation of young men awash in smut and drowning in shame. Until we do this warrior's work of love and truth, we can't credibly witness the Father's saving power to a lost world.

We believe not because it's right, but because it's true—not because believing is the religiously correct thing to do, but because it accurately reflects reality.

As a matter of fact, pornograpy is a false substitute for intimacy. We're drawn to it, therefore, to the extent that we're afraid to get close to a real woman. In our masculine souls, we've known that fear ever since our first junior-high dance, and we're ashamed to admit it.

God proscribes pornography not only because it's immoral, ungodly, or unbiblical, but because it's *dishonest*. It undermines authentic manhood and disarms God's warriors. Indeed, it keeps a man from resolving his deeper sexual desires and fears. It therefore sabotages godly partnership with the woman—without which his armor is riddled with chinks and his destiny cut short (Gen. 2:18).

God hates pornography because it hurts us.

Kingdom warriors treat the wound that beckons the sin. By surrendering to Jesus and seeking the truth, we can explain to the sinner the genuinely destructive effects of his particular sin.

Speaking the Truth in Love

Talking to a brother about his sin is difficult for me—and all the men I know—largely because we've never let the Father teach us his transforming grace. We've never seen older men tell the truth in a way that prompted a sinner to change instead of to get defensive and angry. Often, in fact, we've been told the truth about our sin, but not with redeeming love, not by men who recognize it as their own.

Most men today, when they were boys, experienced either harsh, no-protest-allowed discipline from Dad, or none at all. Thus, we either lash the sinning brother with shame or avoid saying anything.

We don't know how to fight alongside a brother when he's under an attack that manifests in sinful behavior. Instead, we either condemn and destroy the brother ourselves, or abdicate, and let the Enemy do it.

When we sin ourselves, therefore, we don't readily receive correction; we either retaliate in anger or shrivel in shame.

We say, "When you tell another man something he's doing wrong, you touch a sore spot. I don't want to destroy the other guy—but I don't want him to retaliate and destroy me, either!"

The Destroyer, not the Creator, is running the show.

Kingdom warriors, however, seek to speak "the truth in a spirit of love," in order that we might "grow up in every way to Christ, who is the head" (Eph. 4:15). To avoid judging and shaming each other for a particular behavior, therefore, we first need to ask God why he doesn't want his children to do it. Then we're more likely to speak in love—that is, to promote the brother's own best interests, and not just mask our own sin.

This is frontier territory for men today, fraught with fears of the unknown—and sometimes, all too painfully known. Not every man will be happy when you broach the issue of his sin to him, even if you do it in the most loving spirit.

Men surrendered to the flesh will want to crucify you.

At the same time, if you don't respond to a brother's sin, the Enemy will—and the consequences will be far worse for him than if he'd taken it to the Father.

The consequences may also be worse for you. When I meet the Lord face-to-face, I don't want to hear him say, "I called you to reach out to your brother when he was slipping into the Enemy's hands. Why didn't you speak up?"

As God charged the prophet Ezekiel,

> I am making you a watchman for the nation of Israel. You will pass on to them the warnings I give you. If I announce that

an evil man is going to die but you do not warn him to change his ways *so that he can save his life*, he will die, still a sinner, but I will hold you responsible for his death. If you do warn an evil man and he doesn't stop sinning, he will die, still a sinner, but your life will be spared. (Ezek. 3:17-19, italics mine)

Significantly, the Father then calls his servant to address not only "evil men" who ignore him, but also sincere believers who are in danger of falling—that is, "a truly good man" who "starts doing evil" (Ezek. 3:20-21).

When a man doesn't know the Father loves him, he abandons other men to Law and shame, even as his father abandoned him. Nicely, he embraces love without truth—and withdraws from setting a brother right for fear of either shaming him or reaping his fury. Or ruthlessly, he embraces truth without love—lifting the sword to slash away.

As another has noted, "Love without power is sentimentality; power without love is demonic."

In either case, the Father loses at least two warriors—the "sinner," from the consequences of his sin, and the "whistle-blower," either for ignoring the brother's sin or condemning him.

I saw this diabolic scenario played out in a statewide Christian men's organization after the director had invited me to speak at their annual conference.

During our first long-distance conversation, he told me to expect 700 men. Nine months later, however, I found 150 men with their wives—and was welcomed by a different, "pro-tem" director.

"Where is the director I first talked to months ago?" I asked, confused.

"Oh . . . uh, didn't someone tell you?" he fumbled, lowering his eyes.

I hesitated as a deep minor chord sounded in my mind, like the organ music in a horror flick. *Oh Lord*, I thought, *not again!* I've heard this story so many times—with minor variations—that I can almost tell it myself without knowing the particular man's name. "Uh . . . , no," I said. "What happened?"

"Well, you know, we had some problems there," he began, hesitating. "He was married, with a family and all, and . . . well, he was caught with a prostitute a few months back."

In the embarrassed silence between us, my stomach began to churn with anger. *Just drop the whole thing*, I told myself. *Do your teaching tomorrow and go home.* But my heart began to thump—as when the Lord knocks on my door and I don't want to open it—and I knew I might as well push ahead and save myself a sleepless night.

Lord, help! I prayed quickly, *I don't want to shame this guy, but use me somehow to help them learn from all this.*

"In the world," I said finally, "men do autopsies—not to cause more destruction, but to avoid similar losses in the future. I want to know, so I can teach other men: What happened to the guy?"

My pro-tem host shifted uneasily and knit his brow. "Well, we did talk some, and he told us, you know, he'd gone to an X-rated movie, just to see what it was like. After that, he got some magazines."

"Did he give you any idea why he did all that?"

"Not really. I just remember he said that before long, he knew it was getting out of hand, but that if any of us in [the denominational organization] found out what was going on, we'd kick him out."

I sighed. "And what does that say about your organization?"

Confused, the pro-tem director shrugged and opened his hands. "I honestly don't know. But please, tell me—we really need some perspective on this whole thing. It's about torn us apart."

Feeling torn myself, I remembered when the leper begged Jesus for help, and Jesus "was filled with pity and anger" (Mark 1:41).

"The problem isn't just with your ex-director," I obliged, "but in your organization as well—and so you won't solve it just by kicking him out. That's why it's still 'torn apart' after he's gone and can't go on with business as usual.

"Apparently you see yourselves as an exclusive group, for men who don't sin. That's not the body of Christ, which Jesus designed for sinners. You guys are ashamed of what your director did, and that's entirely understandable. But instead of letting Jesus use the occasion to search your own hearts, you just kick him out of the organization so you can keep on looking good.

"You don't fool Jesus, though (Gal. 6:7). He knows if you kicked out every man who sinned you'd be out too, my brother; in fact, you wouldn't have any organization left. I can tell you, I'd be disqualified from speaking here.

"That's partly why your director fell in the first place. You guys are so afraid of your own sinful nature, so consumed by fear of punishment, that you can't hear the good news of mercy which the Father's brought you in Jesus. So you live in the darkness, filled with shame and quick to hide your own sinful thoughts and deeds—just as you did your director.

"But you don't get rid of your sin that way, any more than you heal your brother. You just hand it over to the Prince of Darkness—and he's having a field day with you."

My host nodded slowly.

"Falling to temptation," I explained, "means something's wrong in your life. Sure, there are consequences to pay. For starters, you can't continue in leadership because it's too dangerous for you as well as for the men you serve. A Christian leader is already in the Enemy's crosshairs, and you've stepped out from your covering and left him a clean shot.

"A leader battling temptation doesn't need other men to condemn and reject him; the fallen head of a Christian men's organization can do a great job at that all by himself. Instead, he needs other men he can feel safe with—fellow sinners in fact—to call and say, 'Help! I need you!'

"Without that, he has no resource but his own willpower, which is no match when the Enemy's found your weak spot."

I sighed again and hesitated. *Lord, get this operation over with! How much more do you want me to say?* "Before he fell," I said finally, "was your director in a small group with other men where they could pray and speak the truth to each other in love?"

The pro-tem director knit his brow. "Well, we did have our weekly staff meetings for business and all."

I shook my head. "Doesn't count," I said—then added, "... did it?"

He sighed. "No, I guess it didn't. He really didn't have any other men he was talking to about his personal life."

I left him with a simple question: "Do you?"

The Destructive Power of Shame

Holding each other accountable surfaces our shame more readily than any other warrior task. If the intensity of the battle indicates God's stake in its outcome, clearly this is a major theater for advancing God's Kingdom.

Why, then, do we men become so terrifed of shame that we would give up marriages, careers, even the Father's calling in order to avoid it?

What, in fact, is shame, where does it come from, and how does the Father God overcome it in us?

The Bible suggests first what it's not. In the Garden before the Fall, "the man and his wife were both naked, and they felt no shame" (Gen. 2:25, NIV). Shame requires a cover-up, a hiding—a darkness, in fact, that beckons the Enemy. It's overcome, therefore, by nakedness—by surrendering to the Father and facing squarely your need for him.

The self-striving of false religon, therefore, is rooted in the Snake's seductive lie that we can be like God—and the shame in the simple fact that we cannot.

The Snake suckered Adam and Eve by playing on their fear of lacking power alongside God. Biblical faith understands that shame is rooted in powerlessness—that is, "I don't have the power to measure up." All human efforts to overcome shame—from guns and money to drugs and promiscuous sex—therefore draw upon a false power, and beckon idolatry.

The more we try, the more we sin.

Sin doesn't breed shame; rather, shame breeds sin. To overcome sin, God needed first to overcome shame.

We can't measure up to God's standard. Since Adam's fall and until Jesus returns, shame is a given in our lives. The struggle is not how to eliminate it but rather how to manage it. When we discover we can't overcome shame thorugh our own efforts, however, we simply deny it and cover it up by fabricating our own dignity with a list of our accomplishments.

The Old Covenant Law plays into that charade by providing the correct list. And so at last, God offered us the New Covenant of grace:

> For we ourselves were once foolish, disobedient, and wrong. We were slaves to passions and pleasures of all kinds. . . . But when the kindness and love of God our Savior was revealed, he saved us. It was not because of any good deeds that we ourselves had done, but because of his own mercy that he saved us, through the Holy Spirit, who gives us new birth and new life by washing us. God poured out the Holy Spirit abundantly on us through Jesus Christ our Savior, so that by his grace we might be put right with God and come into possession of the eternal life we hope for. (Titus 3:3-7)

"This is a true saying," Titus adds.

Tragically, the vast majority of Christian men today—like those above who verbally punished the brother with sex magazines—are still trapped in the Old Covenant and don't believe that. Instead, they believe that shame overcomes sin. That is, "If you just make a man feel ashamed enough about what he's doing wrong, he'll stop."

But from a New Covenant perspective, that's like trying to put out a fire with kerosene. Shame doesn't cure lust; shame breeds lust. It's a man's hidden fears of sexual inadequacy that the Enemy manipulates with pornography. Thus, the apostle Paul spoke of those "who are burdened by the guilt of their sins and driven by all kinds of desires" (2 Tim. 3:6).

The New Covenant in Jesus proclaims that, even as "mercy triumphs over judgment" (James 2:13), grace has more power than shame to change a man. Even as Satan is a fallen angel, pornography is a counterfeit grace. The woman in the magazine or film accepts you as you are and, without judgment, freely and eagerly gives you what you want.

If you want to be free of lust, therefore, you need to soak in the Father's grace, to let him heal your sexual wounds and redeem your inadequacies.

Only Father God can overcome shame, with his grace: "Thanks be to God, who does this through our Lord Jesus Christ! . . . There is no condemnation now for those who live in union with Christ Jesus" (Rom. 7:25; 8:1).

An unfathered man, however, doesn't trust Father God's grace and tries to overcome his shame by himself—and always ends up only producing more shame. One cover-up leads to another. As Mark Twain put it, "It's easier to tell the truth—you don't have to remember so much."

Under the Old Covenant, my hope is in me, that I can perform correctly; my energies focus on the question, "Can I be obedient?" Under the New Covenant, my hope is in Jesus, that he's already done what's necessary; my energies focus on the question, "Can the Father be trusted?"

Shame, therefore, like disobedience, is fueled not by ignorance, but by distrust.

That's why it can be overcome only by restored relationship with Father God and not by mere striving after obedience. Trying harder to be righteous or godly can't overcome shame and restore you to your true self. In fact, when you're trying to do something humanly impossible, you only fail the more and increase your shame.

When Adam trusted God, he needed no protection. He was honest, open, vulnerable, and uncovered before the Father. Nothing about himself merited discomfort, hurt, or harm. But when he trusted the Enemy instead of the Father and decided to take his life into his own hands, he felt shame—and he and Eve covered themselves (Gen. 3:7).

"In the beginning," Adam knows who he is because he knows Whose he is: He's a beloved son walking in unbroken relationship with the Father. He knows that God loves him and wants the best for him. He therefore wants the best for himself, which the Father has given him in the Garden.

But he chooses not to be true to himself and instead acts falsely—as if he were not a beloved son, as if God could not be trusted. When he doesn't trust God, he can't trust that he's loved. He won't want the best for himself.

My grandmother would have told Adam, "Shame on you! You know better than to do that."

Shame comes from violating your own self, that is, from knowing what's best, but acting otherwise. It prompts a vicious circle, in which a man's sinful nature sparks him to do what's not best for himself; ashamed for violating his own best interest, he knows he doesn't deserve the best.

The apostle Paul portrayed the genesis of shame in three basic steps, which summarize the Old Covenant dilemma: (1) knowing the right thing to do, (2) knowing you can't do it, and (3) knowing the awful consequences for not doing it:

> We know that the Law is spiritual; but I am a mortal man, sold as a slave to sin. . . . For even though [1] the desire to do good is in me, [2] I am not able to do it. . . . What an unhappy man I am! Who will rescue me from [3] this body that is taking me to death? (Rom. 7:14, 18, 24)

Shame manifests itself, for example, in the victim of sexual molestation—who wants and knows the right thing to do (stay pure), knows he can't do it (because he's already been violated), and the awful consequences (shattered defenses and fear of intimacy). That's why the victim of sexual abuse often retreats and doesn't tell anyone, even keeps getting abused, and the abuser goes free.

It's also why you can't simply tell him when he later struggles as a consequence with impure sexual desires, "Just strive to act morally and you can overcome the effects of being molested." His root issue is not sin, but shame. It's not "Can I be sexually pure?" but "Can I trust God still to receive me as a son, tarnished as I am?" He no longer trusts his identity as the Father's beloved son, and therefore he often falls prey to sexual sin.

Adam defined sin not by disobeying the Law—Moses and the Law were yet thousands of years away. Rather, he distrusted God and thereby violated their perfect relationship. He didn't trust Whose he was, and therefore, he couldn't trust himself.

The world says, "When you can't trust yourself, it's time to try harder!"

God says, "It's time to trust your Father."

Biblical faith understands that shame is prompted by broken relationship with the Father—and overcome by Jesus, who restores that relationship.

And so, among men today, its sharpest hook is the father-wound. Every man knows in his masculine soul that he needs Dad's love to feel whole and manly. Without it, he knows he's male, but not that he's a man. He distrusts his masculinity and can't move in the uplifting strength his wife, children, and society need from him.

He feels shame—not because he's done something wrong, but because he *is* someone wrong. Hence, a generation of men readily capitulated to the politically correct message of the sixties, "It's shameful to be male."

The wound of absence beckons shame. In the unfathered boy, it says, "I don't have enough marbles to play with the other boys." In the man it says, "I don't have what it takes to be a man among men."

Jesus, therefore, is good news: you don't have to be ashamed for not getting what you needed from your earthly father. Your heavenly Father has come to provide it.

Shame and Guilt

Shame is endemic to human nature itself, as abiding and terminal as sin and our inability to save ourselves from its effects.

It's one thing to make a mistake, even choose to do something wrong when you could choose to do it right. That prompts guilt, which goes away when you make amends and do it right next time.

But when you're incapable of doing it right, when the more

you try, the more wrong you get it, the gap between what you "should be" and what you "are" fills you with shame.

Guilt comes from violating a social/legal standard; shame comes from violating your own standard. Guilt comes from breaking the law; shame comes from breaking relationship, even with yourself. As others have noted, guilt focuses on what you've done; shame, on who you are.

Guilt asks, "What do I have to do to make amends?" and dissipates when you do it.

Shame asks, "How can I ever forgive myself?" and can't be amended any more than your inborn sin-nature.

Shame prompts the debilitating sense of not measuring up—to yourself, to others, and to God. Of course we never measure up to God; but then God doesn't expect us to measure up to him. The people who expect us to measure up are other Christians.

Because our human nature is thereby trapped in terminal shame, any hint of it in our daily lives taps on the dam that holds it back—and threatens us unto death. That's why all of us, from president and pastor to schoolboy, are so anxious to hide our shortcomings.

And that's why shame is such a cheap, crippling weapon among Christians. It's hard to overestimate the power of shame to cripple men and sabotage Kingdom warriors.

In religion that focuses on shame, the goal is to be right. The truth encounter alone won't free a man trapped in shame-based religion because he can only seize upon any new truth as yet another "right answer" to which he must agree in order not to be shamed. He merely trades off one list of right answers for another, one collection of Christian character traits for another, one set of rules for another.

Shame breeds its own closed system. Some men will even say, "I was wrong before in believing God loved me conditionally, but now at last I'm really right, so now he must really love me."

As one Christian writer noted,

> I have never met a Christian who admits to being a legalist.
> I know Christians who admit to lying, stealing, envy, lust,

adultery, and murder—but none who admits to legalism. Legalism is always an accusation against someone else. My list of rules always seems legitimate, reasonable, and spiritual, while the other Christian's rules are strict, self-righteous, and carnal.[1]

Another word for shame is *disgrace*. God's antidote to shame—or *dis*grace—is grace. Grace is not a doctrine. It's a relationship. It's not what you believe, but whom you receive.

You can't exhort a man into grace. You can only invite him to receive it. Only open, honest, and trusting relationship with Father God can overcome the shame that fuels performance-oriented religion. Without that relationship, a Christian can righteously denounce "legalism"—and in the same breath command crippled men to "obedience" and exhort them to "biblical principles of manhood."

It's a tricky path that only the man humbly surrendered to the Father can walk. You can't reject his grace and strive to perform your way into his heart, but neither can you reject his grace for others by righteously condemning them when they're trapped in performance religion. You can only confess your own susceptibility to that very sin, and thereby learn to speak the truth with love (Eph. 4:15).

The Father God saves us from shame by calling us to the Cross—to confess and surrender our terminal inadequacy, die to our pride, and trust the Father to resurrect us in his image.

False Manhood

False religion purports to save us from shame by covering up our inadequacies—reassuring us that we are basically OK, exhorting us to try harder at pursuing such admirable goals as "excellence" and "integrity." Like the world's advertising, it promises all the glorious benefits of desirable character traits, without the fearful truth-telling required to develop them genuinely.

A story in a best-selling Christian book for men demonstrates graphically this worldly root of crippling shame in men—indeed, where we first learned the lie that shame overcomes sin.

The writer's twelve-month-old son has been wrestling with his father (the boy's grandfather) on the carpet at his house.

At one point, he writes, the little boy's finger inadvertently scratched the grandfather's eye:

> It didn't hurt much, but dad decided to take advantage of the situation and tease this little one.
>
> Down on his knees, granddad dropped his head to the floor and buried his face in the carpet. He covered the sides of his face with his hands and began howling and carrying on, as if in great distress.
>
> But little Kent had already picked up a few things about life. In a life span of twelve months, he'd begun to learn something about grandpas—and men. So he got down on the carpet as close as he could to his grandpa's face.
>
> "Aw, Bompa," he said. "Be a big Bompa."
>
> Kent knew something about Bompas. About big men. About strong men. His grandpa was a grown man, and Kent was expecting something of him. My little guy was already becoming alert to the masculine qualities of strength and courage. And in his one-year-old owning of this thing called "masculinity," he was trying to impart courage to another human being.[2]

Ironically, the writer adds that "Jesus Christ is the ultimate man. A perfect model."

Let it be known: Christians serve a different kingdom than Hollywood with its macho fantasy heroes. Jesus did not come simply to exhort us, "Buck up, pretend you're OK, and push ahead like a man!" In fact, the Scriptures are clear: Jesus himself did not act like a "big Bompa" when afflicted. He sweat as with "drops of blood" (Luke 22:44) before dying and with "loud cries and tears" (Heb. 5:7) begged the Father to spare him on the cross.

That may not be "religiously correct." But it's real.

And therefore, that's my kind of Savior—because I, too, am dying and can't save myself. I, too, get scared and angry, and I need a Father who can accept and love me as I am, not just when I'm tough and resolute.

As a young man, I allowed older men to shame me into pretending I was "big" and "strong" like them. I stuffed my pain—and it ate me up inside.

I never cried. I just popped Di-Gels—and agonized over why I felt so bound up and unable to get moving in my godly destiny.

When I finally decided that holding on to my pain was killing me, I gave up and let the tears of real life flow. In time, I discovered that the old men were just ashamed of their pain. They either didn't know they had a Father who had come in Jesus to bear it, or were too proud to let him.

"Be a man and don't cry" is a false gospel because it bespeaks a false Father, whose heart is not connected to his children. It's good news to men striving to be right, but it's death to those who long to be real.

The Cross says that pain is an occasion to trust and know your true and compassionate Father God. Ignoring your wound doesn't make it go away; hiding it with cosmetic bandages only ensures it will get infected and destroy your whole body. Teaching men to ignore their wounds fosters self-deception and opens us up to the Father of Lies.

On the cross, however, the Father of Truth has said, "The brokenness of the world is in all men. As you surrender your wounds to me, you enter into eternal fellowship as my sons."

Exhorting men to hide their wounds imparts shame, not courage. Indeed, it says only that the speaker is afraid of my wounds because they remind him of his own, and he doesn't trust in a Savior for either of us.

Sadly, even before his first birthday, that little boy had indeed "learned something profound about men": We're ashamed of our wounds because dad hasn't stood with us in our pain. He's internalized the crippling message men have received from their fathers for generations: Your wounds disqualify you from the company of men.

This is not the Good News of Jesus Christ, who says on the cross that a man's wounds, when surrendered to Father God, are the avenue to fellowship in his family. It's a seductive lie that later sabotages a mature faith in the Father God and compels a man instead to hide his wounds behind performance-oriented religion—and ultimately, other compulsive-addictive behaviors.

Owner of a Broken Heart

The powers of the world and the pride of the flesh sucker us into believing that real men don't have wounds—therefore, if you want people to think you're a man, you'd better cover them up. A man who's ashamed of his wounds, however, will shun the doctor—and die. He won't cry out for a Savior, and therefore, won't know the Father.

The Enemy can pick him off anytime.

Furthermore, a man who hides from his wounds ensures not only infection, but contagion. Unwilling to face his own pain, he desensitizes himself to where he can't recognize someone else's pain either.

Like any other addict, he doesn't care who suffers the effects of his behavior, even those closest to him, as long as he can avoid facing his own pain. He thereby becomes not just a casualty, but a destroyer, and joins the Enemy's forces.

Women, especially, have much to fear from boys reared like this, who will resent the woman when her mere presence reveals their weakness before the awesome mystery and power of sexual attraction. Thus the cooties that hide a third-grader's insecurity evolve into an adult misogyny (see my chapter "Beyond Fig Leaves and Cooties: Loving a Woman" in *Father & Son*).

Worst of all—and this is something genuinely to cry about—teaching a boy to deny his pain disqualifies him from ever receiving the Father's heart as a man and, thereby, from becoming a Kingdom warrior.

Because he'll never know what a broken heart feels like.

Healing your father-wound requires you to ask the Father God to give you his heart for your dad—that is, to pray, "Jesus, show me how you're praying for Dad" (Rom. 8:34). The Father sent Jesus to die for your dad. How do you think he feels to see your dad being hurt by your granddad and turning from his destiny to hurt you the same way?

The Father's heart is broken for your dad.

In order to receive his heart for your dad and be healed, you must prove to him that you can deal with a broken heart. Most men get this opportunity in times of great loss, such as the divorce or death of someone close.

If you've learned to be ashamed of your pain and stuffed it, you won't even know when your heart is broken. When the pain threatens to surface, you'll turn to compulsive behaviors to save you from it, instead of Jesus, to save you through it.

The Father won't give his heart to you any more than cast pearls before swine. You're not capable of appreciating its value.

But the man who's learned to take his broken heart to Jesus—indeed, to weep with Jesus for his brokenness—has proved himself worthy to receive the Father's heart. It's like the worldly warrior's Purple Heart for being wounded in battle—but so much more. It's the license and power to move in victory against the Enemy of life.

Lest any man think here that I'm giving men a license to be "crybabies": It's one thing to cry in a corner, alone and unheard; it's another to cry in your Father's lap. If you don't know what I mean, try it—and you will.

Indeed, like that little one-year-old, every boy has a right to "expect something of grown men": not a tough-guy charade, but self-honesty, and thereby, permission to be real.

The Enemy seeks above all to cut men off from Jesus. He therefore delights to see fathers training sons to hide their pain. A man who's ashamed of woundedness will be ashamed of Jesus. He'll stay away from any organization that proclaims a founder and leader who was wounded unto death on the cross.

That's why many men don't come to church.

I don't want my son to be ashamed of his wounds. I've wasted far too much of my own adult energies struggling to be free of just that emotional and spiritual bondage. I want him to know that when he's wounded, his daddy stands with him—unto his heavenly Daddy.

I want my son to declare, like the apostle Paul, "I am not ashamed of the gospel" (Rom. 1:16, RSV). Among the first words I taught him, therefore, were *owwy* and *scared*. I want him to know when he feels pain and fear, and to take it boldly and hopefully to Jesus—not to cover it up shamefully, and thereby let the Prince of Darkness use it to destroy him.

I want my son to be a Kingdom warrior. If he doesn't learn how to surrender his own brokenness to the Father God, he'll cower before its destructive power—and won't dare stand with other men in their brokenness. I want him to be able to "rejoice with those who rejoice, weep with those who weep" (Rom. 12:15, RSV).

I want him not to shame his wounded brothers, but rather, to stand with and comfort them in their pain even as he speaks the truth that would set them free—and thereby to show them the courage that Jesus gives a man who takes his wounds to him.

I want my son to fulfill his destiny in the Father God. When he eventually comes face-up against his own hopelessly sinful condition, I want him to cry out to Jesus instead of pretending to be OK "like a big Bompa" and then falling like all the "big men" who live such a lie.

And so today, when he's hurt, I don't tell him, "Be a big boy and stop crying." Rather, I hold him as he cries, lay my hand on the bruise, and pray out loud to Jesus to come and heal him. When he's hurt, he now comes running to me crying, "Daddy, pray to Jesus!"

His wounds have been occasions for me to lead him to Jesus—indeed, the most real and appropriate occasions to do so.

The Enemy proclaims his own competing image of saving power. He has seduced generations of boys—who struggle with insecurity of smallness—with "superheroes," from Superman to Power Rangers, who promise, "We will save you from the shame of your weakness and, thereby, make you acceptable among men."

The crucified Lord, however, proclaims, "My grace is all you need, for my power is greatest when you are weak" (2 Cor. 12:9).

We're not trapped in shame because we keep falling. We keep

falling because we're trapped in shame. Grace frees you from the fear of making mistakes, and thereby gives you courage to take risks. Grace is essential to the Kingdom warror.

May we dare take our weakness to Jesus, so he can free us from our crippling shame with the Father's grace.

We'll be ready, then, to appreciate at last the primary weapon of Kingdom warriors—our most powerful weapon, in fact, against the shame that fosters sin.

SEVEN

Truth:
The Number One Weapon

So put on God's armor now! Then when the evil day comes,
you will be able to resist the enemy's attacks; and after fighting to the
end, you will still hold your ground. So stand ready, with truth as a
belt tight around your waist. Ephesians 6:13-14a

Jesus answered him, "I am the way, the truth
and the life." John 14:6

"His truth is marching on. Glory, glory, hallelujah!"
"Battle Hymn of the Republic"

THE FATHER God's victory over the world depends upon our readiness as his warriors to wear the "belt of truth." In the ancient soldier's uniform, in fact, the belt was the foundational garment that held up all the others and carried your sword.

Thus, the Kingdom warrior can bear the sword of God's living Word (Eph. 6:17) only insofar as he walks in the truth. The man who doesn't, who seeks to hide from the shameful truth about himself, wields God's Word destructively, to defend his pride. Often he fabricates an insulated system whereby he can appear unassailable; dissenters are reproached and made to bear his shame. In extreme forms, this mentality breeds cults.

Among liberal/universalists, the system is called "politically correct"; among conservative/fundamentalists, it might be called "religiously correct."

The entire "politically correct" movement, for example, is a shame-based religion, complete with its own "inclusive spirituality" and standards by which the "who's in" and "who's out" are clearly defined—and by which Father God and masculinity, by no coincidence, are out. It's no different in God's eyes than its performance-oriented counterpart in the church—which largely spawned it as a negative reaction.

In effect, everyone dumps their shame onto others because they don't trust the Father enough to take it to Jesus.

The Kingdom warrior, however, wants to trust the Father's mercy and grace and therefore wants to know the truth even as a sick man wants a doctor.

The more intense the battle, the more important it becomes to raise the Father God's standard of truth lest people follow the world's standard of face-saving deception into the Enemy's hand.

Armies of the world are designed at best to preserve life, not to enhance it; soldiers are trained to kill, not to bring the Kingdom of God-Who-Is-Life. In this broken world, such killing may at times be necessary to defend and preserve lives, but it is yet to be atoned, and never celebrated. Killing can't bring the Kingdom of God because it reflects the image of the Destroyer and not the Creator.

Thus, the great warrior King David was honored by God and his people but disqualified from building his temple for having shed blood (1 Chron. 28:3). Under the New Covenant, the temple of the new kingdom is Jesus' body, the church. Kingdom warriors are called to build God's temple among us today in the body of Christ and, therefore, do not kill.

At their finest, armies of the world protect a people from external forces so they can surrender freely to God (1 Tim. 2:1-2)—and thereby manifest the fullness of his power and put the army of the flesh out of business. If the people abuse the freedom that their armies secure by using it merely to pursue their own selfish pleasures, the soldiers are wasting their time and lives, for the Enemy will destroy them all from within.

In that sense, Kingdom warriors are indebted to the world's armies.

We may justly honor, for example, those soldiers who some 130-odd years ago fought and died to free the slaves and preserve the Union. To honor them truly, however, we must proceed on God's mission from the beachhead they died to establish. We must dare face the powers of death in our own time, surrender our pride, and battle for forgiveness and reconciliation—lest we simply pass the deadly burden of racism yet another generation to our sons.

Nevertheless, even as they fought the Confederate slave owners, Union soldiers were themselves infected with racism; in his 1866 letters from the Philadelphia Marine Regiment—found in my late aunt's family Bible—my great-grandfather freely used racial slurs in reference to the slaves and resented their social advancement.

Certainly, the Supreme Court school desegregation decision of 1956 and the Civil Rights Act of 1964 were modern strikes at this stronghold of the Enemy among us. Like my great-grandfather, those who worked for such freedom, whether Supreme Court justice or senator, grunt marine or general, may not have known Jesus. But Jesus knows his people, and he hears their cries for deliverance—and works through even reluctant pharaohs, Supreme Court justices, or marine privates, to set them free.

Meanwhile, those of us who do know Jesus and God's written Word through history can recognize his hand at work in such acts of deliverance. Indeed, the Father God is banking on us to discern and proclaim his hand at work, wherever he chooses to extend it, lest his glory be wrested away by the powers of the world.

Similarly, I honor my father's generation for fighting World War II to preserve my generation from German and Japanese imperialism. Indeed, I'm committed to building a different force of men today precisely out of honor for those valiant soldiers. I don't want them to have died simply so my generation could enjoy business as usual.

Perhaps our national unwillingness after World War II to repent of our killing, and our compulsion instead to embrace the economic consumerism of the fifties, led us so rashly into—and so ignominously out of—Vietnam.

During that war, many in our country did cry out against the killing, even as the TV news body counts invariably reflected more Vietcong than American dead. Throughout the conflict, in fact, the nation battled within after a deeper truth. As one couplet circulated among the antiwar movement cynically noted,

> *American men are not like others;*
> *Only American men have mothers.*

Yes, Christians must repent for killing even soldiers sworn to destroy you. Otherwise, you forget your connection to the Father's human creation and have surrendered to his Enemy.

The apostle Paul declared that "the weapons we use in our fight are not the world's weapons but God's powerful weapons, which we use to destroy strongholds." We must "destroy false arguments" and "pull down every proud obstacle that is raised against the knowledge of God"—looking honestly in ourselves to "take every thought captive and make it obey Christ" (2 Cor. 10:4-5).

Racism, for example, has polluted our country at large through its European roots, from the decimation of Native Americans to slavery of Africans and exploitation of Asian and Latin American labor. At the same time, the Enemy is an equal-opportunity destroyer and no respecter of persons. In my own generation, I've seen racism among African Americans, Asians, Latinos, and Americans of all colors.

Comedian Woody Allen offers his inimitably humorous view of this truth in noting, "As a kid, my parents sent me one summer to an Interfaith Camp—where I was sadistically beaten, mugged, and spat upon by boys of all races, creeds, and colors."[1]

Even as an abused child is statistically more likely to grow up and abuse his own children as a parent, so a man subjected to racism is himself entirely susceptible to internalizing and manifesting it against others. If he doesn't stay surrendered to Jesus as it strikes, it will invade and oppress him.

The Enemy, after all, invades in order to destroy. If he can't make the victims of racism turn against God for allowing its destructive effects, he'll destroy their souls by manifesting racism through them in turn.

Ironically, the Black Muslims offer a striking case in point. Quick to renounce any white cultural or spiritual/religious influence among them, their "white devil" doctrine nevertheless manifests precisely the spirit of racism that whites have borne them—even in blatant disregard for Islamic principles of brotherhood.

Indeed, their readiness to embrace Islam's rigidly enforced, shame-based behavior codes and family role structures suggests the old familiar legalism that white evangelicalism often bore their parents.

Again, whites who have been economically and socially discriminated against often are the quickest to discriminate similarly against nonwhites. Historically, for example, the Southern white aristocracy maintained their privileged station by whipping up racial hatred among working-class whites to distract them from their own low wages, poor working conditions, and lack of unions. Treated unjustly themselves, the working-class whites succumbed to the Enemy and in turn treated blacks unjustly—instead of battling together with black workers for God's justice.

When men suppress the truth, they become oppressed by lies. Energy given us by God to battle for the truth is wasted oppressing other men.

Thus, racism becomes an increasingly vicious cycle, as the Enemy seduces us into doing his destructive work for him.

Truth Overcomes Shame

The greatest damage that can be done to a man is the eternal loss of cutting him off from the Father God—and thereby leaving him defenseless before the Destroyer. If the avenue to restored and fulfilled relationship with the Father God begins at the Cross, where all truth about us is revealed, then racism destroys both perpetrator and victim. It not only condemns the former for his sin, but also allows the victim to circumvent the Cross by focusing on the oppressor's sin and denying his own.

That's why the Jewish calendar begins with Yom Kippur, the Day of Atonement (Lev. 23:26ff.). Indeed, knowing full well that his people would be viciously persecuted, God instituted that foundational season of searching their own hearts and seeking forgiveness in order not to ignore their own sin and thereby abandon themselves to the authentic Enemy.

As a Christian, I say, let the scalpel of God's truth fall on men of all colors, unto life eternal—lest the Enemy's sword slash and unite us unto death eternal. As a white man, even a Gentile, I say, Let it fall on me. I want the Father's blessing of healing and the joy of minstering it to others.

In child parlance, "Last one to the cross is a rotten egg!"

Again, truth is a double-edged sword (Heb. 4:12). A man's only license to speak the word of truth to another is his determination to hear it spoken to himself.

As Andy Comiskey, director of the Christian homosexual outreach Desert Stream Ministries, pleaded at a Christian leaders' conference, "There's plenty of other sins besides homosexuality to repent of. Please don't presume to tell men trapped in homosexuality about their sin until you've let the Lord reveal your own, hopelessly sinful condition to you first. We need brothers walking alongside of us, not judges standing over us."

Certainly, Scripture enjoins us to cooperate with God in overturning unjust and oppressive political structures that the Enemy has erected among us (Isaiah 58:6-7). Before the modern civil rights movement, segregation allowed white Americans to deny racism as an occasion to seek God's deliverance and healing. We thus surrendered the soul of our nation to the Enemy.

The segregationists were right in declaring that legislation can't change hearts. But, like the world's armies, it can enforce enough boundaries on destructive behavior long enough to protect the victims and to establish a beachhead for God's truth among honest men.

At the same time, efforts to achieve "social justice" become self-centered, lack redemptive power, and ultimately serve the Enemy if divorced from Jesus, because they lack the compassion that can come only through a truthful view of one's own sinful nature and God's mercy.

Sadly, many Christians have used that fact to hide from accountability, saying, "It's wrong to work politically for social justice. We should wait for Jesus to change people's hearts." But if we are genuinely born-again Christians, Jesus has already changed our hearts and is waiting for us to act like it—both socially and politically.

Yet the secular liberals often are no quicker to face the truth and serve the needs of oppressed people.

For example, white activists in the university town where I lived in the sixties organized a "free university" with courses in "sensory awareness" and "confrontation." In the black community nearby, meanwhile, fully sensitized and overconfronted eighth graders had not been taught to read.

Again, the use of drugs became an indispensable credential for white activists. The history of the black community, however, has been stained with tragic drug abuse—not as an effort toward "recreation" and "mind-expansion," but as a desperate, suicidal attempt to escape the pain of racism.

The white liberal/universalist movement has attacked beauty contests, the family, and the aggression syndrome in war and athletics. Yet, except for having children, these popular arenas of esteem in America have only recently been opened to nonwhites. A fully integrated military, for example, came only in time for the antiwar movement, and black Miss America contestants arrived only in time to face white "women's liberation" pickets.

Historically, whites have granted others a rung on the national ladder of esteem only after exploiting it themselves and then scorning it as lower.

The Kingdom warrior, meanwhile, knows that without God's truth our human nature will lead us into the Father of Lies' embrace. He is thereby ordained to minister truth that sets others free—not just from racism, but wherever the Enemy has separated us from each other in shame.

I once pastored a church of several hundred members, of which 80 percent were single adults. When I arrived, I found that many men there had variously dated and broken off relationships within the congregation, causing a painful, often angry division between the men and the women. After some months of preaching on sexuality and ministering to deep sexual woundedness both individually and through groups, I sensed the body had been readied for a bold truth-teller to raise the sword and excise this cancer.

I approached one man I'd ministered to, who was about to be married and had experienced considerable healing from sexual addiction—which he had years earlier manifested among several women at the church. Gingerly, I asked him if he'd consider coming to the pulpit one Sunday to confess how he had mistreated women and on behalf of the men there ask the women's forgiveness.

"Wow!" he said, taken aback. "That . . . would be tough." He thought for a minute, and then added, "But you know, it would really set me free from whatever guilt or shame I might still be carrying—and I want to put that behind me in my marriage."

He paused again, knit his brow, and then smiled. "I'll do it."

I was genuinely impressed. "You're a real warrior," I told him.

As the pastoral staff planned the event, we decided to invite a woman, essentially to make her own confession in turn and similarly ask the men's forgiveness.

That Sunday, both the man and the woman spoke truthfully of their sin and God's grace. Shame fled, and others in the congregation rose up in tears to confess how they, too, had sinned against those of the opposite sex and asked forgiveness.

Everyone there sensed a distinct cleansing in the body, that we'd turned a corner, never to turn back.

Again, Kingdom warriors can raise the sword of truth to battle for reconciliation among churches.

I was ordained by an old-line denomination whose mainstream believes neither in the supernatural workings of the Holy Spirit nor the Lordship and saving work of Jesus. Some years after I had come to experience and therefore believe in these myself, I attended a weeklong spiritual renewal retreat at a charismatic Catholic monastery.

At lunch one day I sat next to a resident initiate in her mid-twenties. After we had laughed and shared uplifting stories about how Jesus had gotten our attention and won us to himself, she happened to mention that she had been raised in an old-line Protestant denomination. To my surprise, it was the one in which I was ordained.

"That's amazing!" I exclaimed. "I'm a minister in that denomination!"

Immediately her face clouded over, her face dropped, and an invisible wall fell between us.

Puzzled, I waited a moment. "Is something wrong?" I asked finally.

She sighed. "Well, I . . . they didn't . . . I mean, I guess they couldn't understand what really was happening in my life."

A deep sadness had taken over, and in my heart, I took my shoes off. *Lord, how do you want me to proceed?* I prayed quietly. Clearly, it was too late to turn back. "Was it painful?" I asked.

Nodding, she turned away as tears came to her eyes. "The pastor . . . I mean, he'd been my pastor all through my growing up, and I looked up to him so much. When I knew Jesus was real and had experienced the Holy Spirit, I couldn't wait to tell him about it. I made an appointment, and kind of burst excitedly into his office. I hardly let him say hello before I'd told him the whole story."

She dropped her head.

Again, I waited, prayed. "And . . . what did he say?"

"He looked down his nose at me and said, 'Oh, Sally, how can you possibly believe all that evangelical nonsense? I thought you were more intelligent than that, after all the years I taught you here.'

"I couldn't believe it. I was shocked. I thought, *Maybe he's just kidding*. But he wasn't. He . . . he meant it.

"I . . . didn't know what to do. It was like he'd stuck a knife in my heart. I tried to explain it wasn't like he thought, but he just kept putting me down and wouldn't listen. Finally, I managed to pull myself together and leave, and I never, ever went back—not there or to any other denominational church like it."

Sitting across the table as this woman poured out her pain from a fellow clergyman, I prayed quietly—and desperately. "Jesus, help! How do you want to use me to help this woman?"

In the holy quiet of her tears and my surrender, I felt a strange nudging. I waited, and it persisted—so I stepped out in faith.

Reaching across the table, I took her hand. "Sally, I want to speak to you as a [denomination] minister. I want you to know I'm sorry for what he did to you." I paused, and an unsettling thought struck me: *No, that won't do it. The truth is, you've been where that guy is yourself, before you met Jesus. You'd have put her down back then the same way he did.*

I wondered: How many people—how many Sallys—did I wound then without knowing it, because they never told me?

"I'm sorry for what I did to you, Sally." The words flowed suddenly, freely, and I felt tears come to my own eyes.

Sally looked up at me, riveting her eyes on mine.

"You came to me excited about meeting Jesus," I continued. "What could be more exciting than that?

"But I was scared. I was too proud to admit it, but I needed to meet Jesus, too. You were like a part of myself I hadn't dared to accept and listen to. And so I put you down the same way I've put down that part of myself. I'd tried so hard to prove I was competent and in control of everything and didn't need to be saved from anything. But in my heart I was lying to myself and everyone else in the church.

"I sacrificed your beautiful joy to my awful pride, Sally. I'm so sorry—can you ever forgive me?"

Tears streaming down her face, Sally smiled radiantly, and put her other hand on top of mine. "Oh, yes, Reverend, I understand now and I do forgive you. I thank you for all the time you spent teaching me when I was younger, and I just hope someday you'll know the joy of meeting Jesus yourself."

Our speaking the truth opens us to receive God's grace. Shame flees, and we are reconciled to him and to one another.

The Price of Falsehood

In *Healing the Masculine Soul,* I noted Christian author Leanne Payne's remarkable statement, "The power to honor the truth—to speak it and be it—is at the heart of true masculinity."[2] Hence, the great and eternal contest among men: Who among us can claim the most genuine grasp on truth?

The world's counterfeit, for example, is manifested in the angry youth idol, whose slouchy, disengaged posture draws those seeking a cover-up for their lack of authentic life experience. It sneers, "I'm in touch with a deeper truth than others, a more authentic reality."

In fact, a young man's defiant "cool and hip" stance, like its "mature" counterpart *sophistication,* only masks the painful reality of his own unmet needs. It feeds on the shame of not being mature and authentic enough to face those needs.

Often it emanates from those who have been marginalized by the larger society and who feel compelled to fabricate their own authenticity. Without old men to reassure these young men in their struggle for identity and destiny, that shame festers—and the young men embrace instead the Father of Lies.

Clearly, the exclusionary "cool and hip" posture can't accommodate Jesus on the cross: at one with the Father, with no need therefore to mask any inadequacy, and therefore, freely pouring out his life for others.

The rebellious youth smirks, "I'm into something more real than you"; the crucified Jesus proclaims, "Someone more real than anyone is into you."

If indeed manhood requires the truth, then the warrior requires the truth.

Thus, the author of Hebrews uses the military image of a sword to describe the Word of God—which, as a surgeon's scalpel seeks the cancer, cuts deeply through a man's defenses and exposes his hidden sin:

The word of God is alive and active, sharper than any double-edged sword. It cuts all the way through, to where soul and spirit meet, to where joints and marrow come together. It judges the desires and thoughts of man's heart. There is nothing that can be hid from God; everything in all creation is exposed and lies open before his eyes. And it is to him that we must all give account of ourselves. (Heb. 4:12-13)

Significantly, this sword is "double-edged," that is, it cuts both outwardly, to reveal the sin of others, and inwardly, to reveal a man's own sin.

A man who hides from the truth of his sinful nature skirts authentic manhood. He may spend energy, time, and money erecting defenses and facades to keep others, and even himself, from seeing that truth. But the more he hides his brokenness, the more he feeds the cancer, and the more radical the surgery required later to remove it.

That's why Jesus said the prostitutes and tax collectors would enter the Kingdom of God before the clergy and seminary professors: The former know they have nothing to lose but their condemnation in surrendering to him.

As authentic men, Kingdom warriors teach their community or society by example to honor the truth. Conversely, where men choose not to be authentic as Kingdom warriors, falsehood reigns.

Where politicians renege on campaign promises, advertisers disguise product flaws, suitors sweet-talk the woman into compliance, ministries refuse financial disclosure, citizens lie on tax returns, molested boys parade as men for "gay pride," people spend more money on cosmetics than on education, and more time watching actors than talking honestly together—there, the men have abdicated.

What, indeed, makes falsehood so attractive? Why does a man lie?

Because he fears the truth.

But why would a man fear the truth?

Because its consequences are often painful.

But aren't men supposed to be able to bear pain? Why would a man withdraw from the pain of the truth?

Because he doesn't know his Father stands with him in it.

As a child who fears punishment concocts excuses, we lie in order to protect ourselves from pain. We don't know the Father—that he loves us, wants to fulfill us, and uses the sharp pain of his truth as a scalpel to heal and restore us to our true destiny as his sons.

"If you obey my teaching," Jesus promised—if you step out as I've called you—"you will know the truth"—you'll realize it's more than you can do yourself—"and the truth will make you free"—to let the Father do it in you (John 8:32).

The man who doesn't trust the Father with his neediness invites the Enemy to blackmail him, saying, "If the truth about you came out, you'd be rejected, scorned, abandoned by everyone you care about and kicked out in the cold." In return for hiding our sin—as with racism, pride, or condemnation—the Enemy asks simply that we not oppose him. That is, we must get off the battlefield—abdicate our calling as warriors, withdraw from our destiny, and turn the world and everyone else in it over to him.

On paper, it looks simple to choose. But it's not easy for a generation of fatherless men, who hunger for acceptance and approval, have little sense of their destiny anyhow, and therefore lack confidence to take responsibility for their world.

The Enemy goes for your weak spot. That's why we call him the Enemy. He's there for you when you want to run from the truth: A teenager fears the truth of his immaturity, and the gang promises a place to deny it in exchange for affirmation and belonging. A suitor fears his inadequacies with the woman and can't commit to marriage. A middle-aged man fears his need for others and retreats to the TV.

Certainly, those blinded by their own fear of the truth may very well reject you as you disclose your brokenness and need— even as Sally's old-line pastor. But, like Jesus, a Kingdom warrior is willing to pay the price of the world's rejection in order to become his true self in the Father's destiny. Thus, Sally left her childhood church and sought others who could affirm Father God's work in her.

All human fabrications designed to protect us from the truth tremble in the presence of the Truth-teller; hence, the myth of conservative versus liberal Christians. Indeed, the Kingdom truth-teller gets attacked from all sides of the political spectrum: "How terrible when all people speak well of you; their ancestors said the very same things about the false prophets" (Luke 6:26).

The truth-teller is by definition a warrior, because the powers of the flesh fight against any truth that threatens our pride (Rom. 7:23).

Humility before the truth, trust in the Father God's mercy, and a longing to fulfill his calling, lower the drawbridge to a man's heart so the Commander of the Lord's army can enter.

From a military/strategic view, the Destroyer calls us to retreat from the truth and the Creator calls us to surrender to it. In fact, the destructive effects of the former were seen graphically in the Vietnam war.

In a 1993 *Newsweek* feature, for example, America's most decorated living veteran, David Hackworth, returned to meet the Vietnamese commanders who had opposed him twenty-five years earlier. He noted to his hosts that their rice-paddy terrain had forced Americans to fight "like fish out of water."

"Yes," one former Vietcong leader nodded, "your army acted like the British fish during your own war for independence. America lost here because its commanders didn't understand the people's cause, the terrain, or the nature of the war."

"He was right," Hackworth declared. "The U.S. military fought an unconventional enemy with conventional tactics."

Indeed, as we shall see, this is the very downfall of Christian men today as we struggle in life's battles, namely, that—like British redcoats in the colonial forest—we try to fight our spiritual enemy with weapons of the flesh (2 Cor. 10:3-5).

The Enemy of God is unconventional by any human standard and can't be either seen or overcome by any power humans amass.

"We were a superpower," Hackworth continued. "How could you stand up against a force that filled the sky with aircraft and could fire more artillery rounds in one engagement than your side used in one year?"

"Yes, we were weaker materially," his host declared, "but our spirit and will were stronger than yours. Our war was just; yours was not. Your brave soldiers knew this, as did the American people."

Hackworth concludes by castigating a proud American military leadership for not facing the truth of their mistakes and therefore not learning the lessons that would insure against such a "tragedy" again:

> For almost two decades, service schools avoided teaching the lessons of Vietnam and trained primarily for the pleasantly familiar "big battle war" on the plains of Europe. To this day, there hasn't been a real postmortem on the tactical and strategic mistakes of that misadventure. Instead of searching for the truth, which could still save lives in the Balkans and Somalia, there has been a full-blown campaign to rewrite the history of the war.

Hackworth caricatures this military rewrite as cosmetic; "America won the war tactically. We just happened to lose it strategically."

He concludes,

> But to close the books on Vietnam, we must understand that America lost on the battlefield not because of peace protests at Berkeley or failures of nerve in the Congress, but because our military leadership thought bombs could beat a people's hunger for independence. The price for that lack of moral courage to tell the politicians that it was a bad war fought with a flawed strategy was death for thousands of young Americans.[3]

When a man withdraws from the truth, others pay the price.

In Vietnam, our animal "fight or flight" power model allowed us no options but to dump huge tonnage of bombs—and when that failed, to retreat in defeat.

The "fight" option was lost twenty-five years ago. Today, Hackworth suggests, our myopia dictates the only remaining option—to persist in emotional "flight": "After the war, U.S. military leadership, humiliated by defeat, simply buried the experience."

Shame keeps us from learning from our mistakes.

Hiding behind Religious Systems

Pride is the world's narcotic remedy for shame. When a system or standard is recognized as absolute truth, honest men will be on their faces before it. Proud men, on the other hand, presume to embrace it—and very quickly alter it to fit the contours of their own brokenness.

Thus, everyone wants to be known as a "Christian" or "godly man" but few want to pay its price of transparency before the Father and other men.

I once ministered to a new Christian in her mid-thirties who had a gift for asking those clean, utterly naive questions that blast the foundations of false religion.

She had talked with another woman member of an old-line denomination and was surprised that the other's church rejected the divinity of Jesus, the authority of the Bible, and virtually all other tenets of orthodox Christian faith. "Why do those people call themselves 'Christians'?" Alice asked matter-of-factly. "I mean, they could just as well start their own religious groups with those beliefs, build their buildings, and worship as they please."

Certainly, various cultural groups can find richly unique ways to worship and express their surrender to Jesus. But someone who thinks all that fuss about Jesus is "too narrow," smacks of "intolerance," and truncates your "freedom" could, for example, simply join Baha'i—a designer religion that affirms and blends virtually all major world faiths.

The answer to the woman's question, I suspect, lies in our common human fear of shame and the longing after unassailable *right*ness. We all want to overcome the messy brokenness deep in our souls and appear clean, good, and right. The child in us still wants Daddy's approval and love.

In their hearts, those who reject Jesus as sole Lord and Savior yet still call themselves "Christian" likely would feel ashamed to say they were not Christian. They lack the courage to walk the talk—that is, to break loose from the socially protective umbrella of "the Christian church," follow what they purport to believe, and begin to experience fully its effects.

It's like the adolescent who rejects his parents—but insists on living at home and not paying rent.

In churches, it's the businessman who says God overlooks his shady tactics, the homosexual who says God blesses his lifestyle, the abortionist who says God has no problem with killing "unwanted" babies, the pastor who uses Scripture to shame church members into submission, the unmarried couple living together who say God would rather they "get to know each other better" before marrying.

I have little respect for those who hide behind Mother Church's skirts, appropriating her blessing for their own, self-centered lifestyle.

The truth, as another has paraphrased, will set you free—but first, it'll hurt like the dickens. When a man commits to the truth about himself, however—through death unto new life—the Father will bring him into the deepest truth that sustains the Kingdom warrior.

Dave, for example, a junior executive in his early thirties, came to me when his marriage and job were falling apart.

"I'm fed up with the way my life's going," he declared. "I'm so tied up inside I've built defenses and fantasies to the point where I don't know the truth from the lies anymore. I've got to get free. Whatever it takes, whatever I have to see about myself—bring it on!"

"Are you ready to tell Jesus that?" I asked. "If you are, he'll show you what you need to face—but it's likely to hurt."

"It can't hurt any worse than what's going on in me now," Dave sighed, dropping his head and closing his eyes. "Oh, Jesus, come please, and show me the truth about myself."

For the next hour and a half, Jesus answered Dave's prayer. It was a battle, painful but exhilarating, as rationalizations, fantasies, lies, and buried memories literally lined up to be brought into the light. Exhausted from listening, confessing, crying, and begging Jesus to keep going, Dave slumped finally in the chair and fell quiet.

"Lord, where are we?" I prayed hesitantly. "Is that all, or . . . is there still more?"

To my dismay I heard, *There's one more thing.*

Looking at Dave crumpled across from me, I took a deep breath. "Well, Dave, you've really been through it," I noted. "I, uh, sense though, that there's still something else the Lord wants to deal with. What do you say? Shall we close up for today, or do you want to keep going?"

Dave sat quietly, then sighed. "I'm wiped out. But we've come this far—let's go another round, if you're willing to hang in there with me." With some effort, he sat up in the chair and took a deep breath, waiting.

"Sure," I said—then prayed that Jesus would honor Dave's longing for the truth and trust in him to surface it. "Do you want to go ahead and tell Jesus you want him to keep going?"

Dave thanked Jesus profusely for bringing him into so much truth and freedom, then said, "Keep going, Jesus. I want everything you died to give me. If there's more truth I need to face, show me."

"Yes, Lord," I prayed, "please show us whatever truth Dave needs to see."

Throughout our time together, I had received many words and images from the Lord in answer to that prayer—but now I heard nothing, saw nothing. After a few minutes of silence, I wondered: Did I miss it? Maybe the Lord had surfaced all the truth necessary for Dave's freedom at this point. Or maybe . . .

My thoughts were interrupted by Dave's laughter.

Puzzled, I waited, then looked up.

To my surprise, Dave had a peaceful, happy grin on his face.

"He said, *You're my son and I love you.*"

And that, at last, is the foundational truth that sets you free—to be a brother among brothers, a man among men, and a warrior among warriors in the Kingdom of God.

Glory, glory, hallelujah!

EIGHT

Victory over Racism

*With his own body [Christ] broke down the wall that separated them
and kept them enemies. He abolished the Jewish Law with its
commandments and rules, in order to create out of the two races one
new people in union with himself, in this way making peace. By his
death on the cross Christ destroyed their enmity; by means of the cross
he united both races into one body and brought them back to God.*
Ephesians 2:14-16

PALM trees stirred above the roaring chatter of the village market
late that summer in 1965 as I walked home from the Nigerian
school where I had come as a Peace Corps teacher earlier in the
year.

"Mr. America!" a voice suddenly called out. "Come now, and
tell us, what is this?"

I turned to see a young man emerging from a group of others,
his brow knit and waving a crumpled newspaper sheet. As the
only white man and the only American most in the village had
ever known, I often heard animated questions about "American
wonders" from Elvis to freeways; I smiled expectantly and
reached out to look at the paper.

"THIRTY AMERICANS KILLED IN LOS ANGELES RIOTING"

Emblazoned in large back type across the front page, the words leapt out, arrested, and clubbed me.

Riot? Killings?—not in America! I thought, stunned. *In Los Angeles? Impossible!*

I'd just done my three-month's Peace Corps training right there at UCLA. I knew Los Angeles!

Didn't I . . . ?

Anxious to hear my explanation, the group of men got up to join their friend and gathered around me as I grasped the paper in disbelief. Horrified, I raced through the article.

It was true. Thirty people had been killed in a riot in my country just a week earlier! I held my breath. Yes, the reporter declared, in America, in Los Angeles, thirty people had been killed, "all of them Negroes."

Suddenly, an ever-so-slight sigh of relief escaped my lips.

In the quick of a gasp, it was gone. Like the fast-speed shutter of a camera, the lens of my soul blinked and photographed a terrifying monster within. Bewildered, frightened, I immediately shoved it back as the dark faces clustered around me. "I . . . I don't know . . . how this could happen," I stammered.

I didn't dare.

The same voice that would not allow me to face the rioting and killing in my country would not allow me to face the racism in my soul.

Compensating for the Racism Within

I had come as a white American to black Africa precisely in order to demonstrate that not all white people are racist. I had invested two years of my life into being a redeeming model of interracial brotherhood, to prove that I was different from the European colonizers, even my own forefathers. I came with the Peace Corps, to renounce the old way of battling over differences and demonstrate instead a new and righteous America.

My country was depending on me. Imagine the shame if . . .

I just couldn't because I didn't know the truth—neither of my own brokenness and the Enemy who had taken advantage of it, nor of Jesus' redemption. And so, I succumbed to the very shame-based, rigid, fear-ridden mentality that I had ostensibly dedicated myself to overcome—albeit on the other end of the political spectrum.

But a demon shunned is a demon unleashed; consigning it to the darkness is like tossing Brer Rabbit into the briar patch. Shame wears many disguises, accommodates every human enterprise but the truth.

For years thereafter, I tried desperately to exorcise myself by dissociating from my European cultural heritage. Traveling six thousand miles and spending two years among black Africans had not done the job, so I tried harder. I scorned my white parents mercilessly, moved to a black neighborhood, espoused radical politics, worked in civil rights programs, listened only to soul music.

The "civil-rights" movement, meanwhile, was being transformed into a cry for "black power." Black people were taking care of their own business and were no longer willing to protect me from mine.

At my liberal seminary, however, I found many others to hide with me from the truth, and I joined a liberal denomination that afforded similar protection. As long as everyone in my church is preaching "racial justice," I reasoned, I could be seen as righteous myself. Who needed black people sitting beside us in the pews? After all, we had the correct doctrine—and a black denominational executive to prove it.

Heartfelt repentance, we activists presumed, was something other people needed, especially those awful Southern rednecks. It never occurred to us that, in order to lead others into the truth, we needed to walk in it ourselves.

On graduating from seminary I was offered a job at a racially mixed showcase church in a largely black community, but I turned it down. A previous "civil rights information internship" in a white suburb had convinced me that integration depended upon changing whites, who held the political and economical power. "We had the Jackie Robinsons for years," as one black community organizer told us; "we just didn't have the Branch Rickeys."

At my young age, meanwhile, I held no worldly power. As long as racism was seen as a political-economic issue, I shared no guilt.

And so, ten years after returning from Nigeria, I began pastoring a small church in an entirely white, middle-class neighborhood, many residents of which had fled the advancing black population further north. Determined to rally the congregation to social justice issues, I was dismayed as my many articulate sermons on racism, sexism, disarmament, and poverty only made people angry.

Amazing as it seems to me now, I was an ordained pastor with three years of seminary training, but I had no personal relationship with Jesus. Two years into my pastorate, I gave my life to Jesus, and in a renewed burst of righteousness, determined to rally the congregation to evangelism and healing ministries. Naively, I assumed those who opposed my previous liberal theology would now rush to embrace my new orthodox theology— which I nevertheless preached out of the same old shame-base: "If you do it my [right] way, you're a certified Christian."

To my surprise, my detractors accused me of "upsetting the church in one way after another" and formed a vigilante committee to oust me. Reeling, I became extremely cautious in my conversations. And then, at a deacon's meeting, one of the dissenters "shared" her "deep concern" that I had not visited a widowed parishioner in the hospital.

I panicked as, in a flash, I realized she was right. I'd absolutely forgotten to make that pastoral call! Flushed with shame, I stammered my way desperately through a defense. As if caught naked, I struggled through the rest of the meeting and drove home feeling as if I had a bowling ball in my stomach.

At home, I raced into the bedroom and fell on my face. "Lord Jesus!" I fumed. "I thought you wanted me to succeed at this church! Why did you let me get dumped on like that, when I'm trying so hard to get these people to open up to you?"

For some time I poured out my feelings, and when at last I lay exasperated but quiet, I sensed the Father's saying, *Why didn't you come to me first?*

Confused and angry, I shifted on the floor. "What do you mean?" I demanded.

Why didn't you ask me if you had made any mistakes, if there were any chinks in your armor? I wanted to show you myself, so you could make amends and be restored to relationship under the umbrella of my mercy and grace. When you didn't ask me, I had to allow the Enemy to show you.

I want them to open up to me more than you do. Stop trying to run the show. Let go of them, and let me work in you.

I lay quietly for a long, long time.

It was a tough lesson, but essential for the warrior.

If Satan can cite Scripture (Matt. 4:6), he can speak the truth. Therefore, if he can't get us to embrace a lie outright, he'll hit us so ungraciously with the truth that we feel justified in rejecting it—and remain broken and dishonest in his grip.

The hardest time to walk in the truth is when it's wielded against you with malice. But the Father will allow such occasions to test you appropriately as his warrior: Are you fighting for the truth or for your own pride?

The Enemy suckers shame-based men into the battle on his terms, so you defend or counterattack too quickly.

Suppose, for example, I had replied instead to my accusing deacon, "You're right. I forgot to visit Mrs. Jones, and didn't do my job. I know that must have hurt her, and I need to ask her forgiveness—and yours. Thank you for bringing this to my attention." That kind of truth-telling would have secured me in the Father's hand of grace and disarmed my detractors. Trying to defend myself only cut me off from the Father and left me defenseless—and therefore incited them.

If someone is attacking you with lies, be prepared to stand and speak the truth as the Spirit leads. But if they slash you with the truth, no matter how viciously, own up to it quickly. Let Jesus deal with them for their unmerciful attitude or spirit of vengeance.

You can say, "It's hard for me to listen to you when I'm

spending so much energy defending myself—I'd rather spend that energy opening up and getting to the truth together." But even if your accuser refuses to respect your honesty, the long-run consequences of denying the truth will harm you far more than any shame the other may inflict.

As Jesus urged his disciples,

> Settle matters quickly with your adversary who is taking you to court. Do it while you are still with him on the way, or he may hand you over to the judge, and the judge may hand you over to the officer, and you may be thrown into prison. I tell you the truth, you will not get out until you have paid the last penny. (Matt. 5:25-26, NIV)[1]

At that deacon's meeting, I did not settle the matter quickly with the truth—and was thereby handed over to the harsh judgment of the church.

As the Adversary-Accuser, the Enemy knows our sin quite well. His strategy is always to get us in an undefendable position, and our sin-nature puts us right there. He doesn't often waste time hurling false accusations that we can easily refute. Telling the truth with a vengeance can be far more destructive than telling a lie—especially among men who are bound by shame and therefore fear the truth.

The saying, "Only a fool has himself as a lawyer," is apt in the heavenly court. That is, the Enemy seizes upon and hounds us with our genuine sin, our true and demonstrated brokenness, in order to convince us it's terminal, that nowhere can we find love and grace after what we've done. If we agree with that lie and don't surrender to Jesus, shame takes over and dictates our options: either defend yourself and sacrifice your integrity, or surrender to the Enemy and sacrifice your destiny—that is, for me in this case, either make excuses or resign.

Thus, my deacon-detractor at church rightly accused me of faulty pastoring—not so much for forgetting to visit a parishioner in the hospital, but for defending myself against the truth, and thereby, modeling shameful pride instead of graceful humility.

I didn't trust the Father's mercy, and thought I had to be perfect for him to accept me. My brokenness thereby prompted shame—a wide avenue beckoning the Enemy, instead of a humble path to the Father's heart.

The good news in Jesus, meanwhile, is not that you have to be right, but that you get to be real. Guilt-ridden by my oversight, ashamed for violating my own pastoral care standards, defenseless before my accusers, I realized that my only hope for freedom was to bring any and all of my sin out into the light. Praying alone and with other brothers, I begged Jesus to show me whatever he wanted to clean out of me. A number of issues surfaced. Terrified but determined, I visited the vigilante committee members one-by-one at their homes to confess my sin of not trusting the Lord and to ask their forgiveness.

Racism, Right and Left
Having experienced its destruction, I became determined to smoke out all shame within me. Eventually, I remembered at last my sigh of relief in the Nigerian market fifteen years earlier.

True, I had never used racial slurs or acted out racism. Working hard to attain liberal politics, universalistic theology, and courteous behavior toward those of all races made me feel "right"—or, at least, "right*er*" than those working for conservative politics, fundamentalist theology, and elitist behavior.

I saw this mentality reflected in 1992 when I told my humbling Nigerian marketplace story in the *Returned Peace Corps Volunteer Writers* magazine. My fellow returned volunteers in the subsequent "Letters to the Editor" column lashed me mercilessly for suggesting that they might benefit from a similar self-examination.

That stung. But it forced me at last to realize that the Peace Corps fraternity of my idealistic youth, though used by the Father God to further his peace agenda, was not surrendered to Jesus—and therefore, could not be trusted to embrace me in ultimate truth.

Indeed, even as I grieved that loss, I remembered my own youthful season of righteous universalism, in which my underlying shame led me simply to exchange one hypocrisy for another: I bowed respectfully for native African rituals while scoffing at church sacraments, exalted the "mantra" chants of Eastern religions while ridiculing Christian glossolalia, and boogalooed to the black spiritual "O Happy Day" while scorning the Scottish hymn "Amazing Grace."

I knew how to be right, but not how to be real.

I didn't know Jesus, and I was therefore ashamed to know the truth.

The apostle Paul knew such shame—but he also knew Jesus:

> As far as a person can be righteous by obeying the commands of the Law, I was without fault. But all those things that I might count as profit I now reckon as loss for Christ's sake. Not only those things; I reckon everything as complete loss for the sake of what is so much more valuable, the knowledge of Christ Jesus my Lord. For his sake I have thrown everything away; I consider it all as mere garbage, so that I may gain Christ and be completely united with him. I no longer have a righteousness of my own, the kind that is gained by obeying the Law. I now have the righteousness that is given through faith in Christ, the righteousness that comes from God and is based on faith. All I want is to know Christ and to experience the power of his resurrection, to share in his sufferings and become like him in his death, in the hope that I myself will be raised from death to life. (Phil. 3:6-11)

In pursuing the politically correct agenda, I had sought to conjure "a righteousness of my own." This effort only hid my brokenness and kept me from getting free of my shame and from helping others get free.

A classic example of this myopia and its destructive potential to others surfaced at a Nigerian high school where a fellow Peace Corps volunteer was sent. Nigeria's national and regional boundaries—established by European colonists who did not respect the integrity of indigenous tribes—include and variously bisect some two hundred separate cultural/linguistic peoples, each of whom must contend for a voice in national policy. Hence, bloody civil conflict often flares up among ethnic groups—as in our own "American tribal warfare," as my Nigerian friends used to say.

Upon arriving at his school, the volunteer was outraged to find a rigidly enforced policy that only English, and no indigenous languages, were to be spoken on campus. Within weeks, this American liberal universalist had begun stirring students against the school administration for what he perceived as "latent colonialism" and discrimination against "Nigeria's own rich, cultural heritage."

The principal however, a Nigerian himself, saw otherwise. To choose any indigenous Nigerian language as a *lingua franca* would incite tribal warfare and bloodshed on campus. Since all students spoke English regardless of their ethnic/linguistic background, and none were of English ancestry themselves, English was the obvious choice. The principal therefore threatened to fire the volunteer and protest to American authorities if he persisted thus in imposing his "American perspective."

Universalism is no substitute for authentic relationship—either with God or one another.

However righteous my liberalism made me feel, I had never dared get close enough to be a true friend with any black person because I feared the shame if something racist inadvertently slipped out of my mouth. That is, I lacked freedom in relationships with nonwhites because I lacked the truth about myself and about God. I feared nonwhites because their mere presence could expose my shameful secret.

Neither, therefore, was I effective in combating the spirit of racism in society. Only white persons came to my church—in spite of our denomination's desperation to foster a more ethnically diverse image. The great civil-rights rallies of the sixties were gone, as was the clear-cut mandate for "integration"; apart from a yearly sermon on World Communion Sunday, my witness to "racial justice" was nil.

Integration, I realized, is a Christian concept based upon

relationship with the Father God. He alone makes us sons and daughters in Jesus, and thereby brothers and sisters. The integration he seeks can't, therefore, be accomplished simply by human power, which is hopelessly geared to "me and mine."

As long as the racial justice movement was being spearheaded by Christians like Rev. Martin Luther King, Jr., civil rights were not an end in themselves, but rather, a means to God's larger goal to confer the dignity of sonship and daughtership in Jesus.

But in those days, I never met a white activist—even among us pastors—who was publicly surrendered to Jesus. Sadly, the evangelicals I met either defended segregation or ignored the racial issue.

We liberals, therefore, were anxious to join hands and sing "We Shall Overcome," but were nevertheless embarrassed by a black chorus of "King Jesus Is a-Listenin' All Day Long."

True, we could accept such graphic and unseemly devotion to "Jesus" among blacks, but only because to criticize it might sound racist—even though we'd never countenance such a thing in our own, more sophisticated churches. We therefore had to dignify spirituals because they were black—not because they dignified Jesus.

Indeed, since their content embarrassed us, we reframed them not as worship to Jesus, but rather, an American art form, like the Christmas crèche scene at shopping malls. We all knew blacks just hadn't been afforded the education we had and were thus vulnerable to such simplistic thinking. After all, wasn't the whole struggle about equal education and advancement?

Certainly it was to us educated and advanced white people.

When the courts finally outlawed racial discrimination and thereby paved the way for God's larger agenda, the liberal church essentially abdicated, as if the job had been completed. In fact, however, the liberal church had become smug with its "prophetic social justice" and increasingly fearful as the double-edged prophetic sword inevitably turned back upon themselves.

I myself had not dared to continue holding that sword of truth as it swung back toward me. But the Nigerian market scene was branded on my memory, and its painful truth had not left, no matter how desperately I ran from it.

And so at last, drowning in shame, I surrendered. I fell on my face before Jesus and asked him to forgive me for not trusting him with my brokenness and thereby yielding to the Enemy. I wept for the energy I'd wasted hiding from the truth. I told Jesus how much I hated the racism in me and in his name cast that spirit out of me. I then asked Jesus to replace it with his spirit of true brotherhood, keep me vigilant against its return, and use me to overcome it in the world.

In this process, I realized how the Enemy uses shame to bind us in racism. We like to think we're righteous men of integrity. But the presence of persons of different races often stirs a natural uncertainty and fear. We are ashamed of that fear, because it reminds us we are not all-powerful, perfectly accepting, color-blind gods ourselves; if we don't take it to the Father to reassure us of his purposes in making us different, ultimately we seek to justify it with negative stereotypes.

When you don't take your shame to Jesus, you cast it upon others.

Most often racism suggests itself among men who feel inferior or inadequate in endeavors that they value. Where shame rules, those men will seek others to view as superior performers and thus whom they can resent and dump their self-judgment on.

"I don't like feeling bad about myself," goes the reasoning, "so I'll portray you in a way that justifies my feeling bad about you instead."

Schoolboys, for example, wield "cootie bugs"—a cruel attack on feminine dignity—when they feel they lack the social and intellectual maturity of girls their age. (See my chapter "Beyond Fig Leaves and Cooties: Loving a Woman" in *Father & Son*.)

Similarly, German anti-Semitism was largely fueled by the shame of feeling out-performed by Jews—such as Einstein—in the very professions that defined German self-esteem: science, music, philosophy, theology, business. Similarly, many white males judge their self-worth by sexual performance, athletic ability, or "hip" trend setting. When they rate themselves low

and feel ashamed, they project a high rating of those charac-
teristics onto nonwhite males and dump their shame through
racism.

Truth is the first casualty when men try to cover their shame—
and others soon suffer the effects. Ultimately, the legal and social
systems that we erect against others to hide our shame become
riddled with hypocrisy and deception—from Jim Crow legislation by whites to the "white devil" image among Black Muslims.

Here the distinction between shame and guilt becomes
graphic.

Since shame grows out of who you are instead of what you do,
no one could be made to feel guilty for not being a certain race.
You didn't do anything, right or wrong, to be born a particular
race; therefore, it bears neither shame nor pride.

But those of us who are white have used our superior worldly
power in guns and money to cover our shame and communicate
to others, "You should be ashamed for not being white."

Because shame is intrinsic to human life, nonwhites who have
not surrendered to Jesus are vulnerable to believing this lie,
especially when immersed in a dominant white culture that
reinforces it. Hence, a multimillionaire African American pop
idol like Michael Jackson straightens his hair and gets plastic
surgery to narrow his nose. Only deep shame could drive such a
flight from oneself—the kind likely beckoned by Jackson's childhood abuse.

Within such a toxic system, white activists battling racism
often become infected themselves by virtue of their own innate
susceptability and feel ashamed for being white. The old segre-
gationist dispensation masked the truth of whites' sinful nature
and thereby served their shame; the new, politically correct
dispensation serves black shame similarly, affording African
Americans a way to avoid facing the truth of their own sinful
condition.

I realized that my liberal theological training had truncated
the truth and tailored eternal faith to fit a temporal political
agenda, preaching unity by virtue of our humanity alone.
Whether in advocating disarmament or women's rights, I had

heard invoked as a mantra, "neither Jew nor Greek, slave nor free, male or female"—the added assumption being "in union with one another."

I never heard the authentic biblical condition of that promise, "in union with Christ" because none of us had surrendered to Jesus deeply enough to discover whether he truly can unite us. Therefore, we could only try desperately to believe that human willpower could do it.

On the other hand, the evangelical churches I knew had jettisoned their rich heritage of spearheading the antislavery movement a century earlier and now denied that any racial problems existed. Both the liberal/universalists and the evangelical/fundamentalists were equally anxious to cover the shame of their largely white constituency—the former, by recruiting racial/ethnic minorities; the latter, by ignoring them.

The most racially integrated congregations, meanwhile, I found in the Pentecostal churches—which neither recruit nor exclude racial groups, but attempt simply to proclaim the truth of who Jesus is and surrender to his Spirit.

In the town where I live, the Church of God—rooted in the Azusa Street Pentecostal revival at the turn of the century—has nearly as many whites as blacks, and a fair proportion of Latinos and Asians. The historic "mainline" churches in town, for all their denominational boards of racial justice and the like, are virtually all white—as are the evangelical/fundamentalists.

Healing the Wounds of Racism

Where shame is served, truth starves and manhood flees. Terminal condemnation threatens, and we run for cover—usually behind either renewed racist attacks or moral abdication that says to the other, "Do whatever you like; I'm so guilty I have no right to hold you accountable, even to common standards of decency and respect."

The Father of Lies prompts us to say, "Forgive me for being black" or, "Forgive me for being white," in order to sabotage our true destiny in the Father God—who made us all the way we are and loves us all as his children. When we speak the truth to a situation, however—when indeed, we beg Jesus to show us the truth lest the Father of Lies destroy us—we become ready and able to enjoy the fellowship that the Father God gives his sons and daughters.

We can't overcome shame by our own efforts. That's why Jesus came. But we can surrender to him and put ourselves where he can restore us as his sons, and thereby, as brothers together.

When a bone is broken, for example, no human power can force the broken edges of bone to reknit. But a doctor can put the pieces back together, put a splint over the break, and trust in the body's healing power. As any man who's broken a bone can testify, resetting it can be awfully painful—but doing nothing allows the brokenness to become infected and then destroy the entire body.

We don't have to let shame overshadow and preempt the manageable issue of guilt for harming those of other races. We can't heal ourselves, but we can get up on the operating table where the Father can heal us. We can come together as different races—as broken bones in the body of Christ—and confess our sins against each other, ask forgiveness, and unite as Kingdom warriors to overcome strongholds of racism in our society.

To the man enslaved to shame, that's just an idealistic pipe dream. To the Kingdom warrior, that's precisely the victory Jesus died to win, and thereby, our turf to occupy.

Leaders, again, go first.

New Zealander John Dawson, director of urban missions for Youth With A Mission and twenty-year resident of Los Angeles, reports the amazing effects of such "stark honesty." After confessing his own boyhood racism to a large interracial gathering in New Zealand, Dawson witnessed a powerful outpouring of reconciliation.

Could this take place in the cities of America? he asked himself. He decided to find out when he returned to California and visited Bakersfield. In *Healing America's Wounds* he writes:

A large group of pastors was gathered in one of the historic black churches downtown. I noticed as they took their seats that the black pastors tended to sit to my right and the whites to my left; I thought it unusual to see such separation in a California city.

My heart was full of faith because of what I had experienced in New Zealand. . . . I gave them a report on what I had seen with my own eyes: auditoriums filled with weeping people; national wounds healed; the missing key to revival beginning to turn an ancient, rusted lock.

I felt the Spirit of God asking me to give him room, so I asked him to move upon us and knelt down behind the wooden podium to wait. The silence was awful. Nothing happened. *It's not going to work here,* I thought as I eyed the exit longingly.

Then it happened. A man began weeping on the left side of the room. I peeked around the podium and I saw a well-dressed man with his head in his hands sobbing, "Oh God, forgive us" many times. There was no tension or stridency; there seemed to be a united understanding of what was happening.

"Lord, I want to represent my vocation," he prayed. "We as the city police department have historically been such an instrument of rejection and injustice in our dealings with the black community. We have caused such woundings, such sorrow, please forgive me, please forgive us." And then to the black pastors: "I want to humble myself as a part of the police department. You have endured so much and, as a police officer who is a fellow believer, I want to ask your forgiveness."

"We forgive you," came the gracious chorus of voices from all sides. Tears were flowing now. The sense of God's presence was palpable. It was such a simple thing to do, to say, yet foundational stones were moving in the heavenlies. You could feel it.

Since that day, I have seen and heard such things countless times. Pagan Americans are hopelessly trapped in old patterns of fear and distrust, but God's people are experiencing a season of grace for repentance and healing. This comes in the form of "godly sorrow" (2 Cor. 7:10).[2]

Such "godly sorrow" shapes the Kingdom warrior.

Yet the Father had more to teach me beyond my sorrow.

As I begged Jesus to heal not only my shame, but the racism it fostered, I read Alex Haley's *Roots* and determined like him to discover and embrace my own ethnic heritage. While in Nigeria years before, in fact, I had met a Norwegian missionary who told me the Dalbey name originated in Norway.

I began taking a Norwegian language course in 1984 and eventually, through a series of Lutheran connections, went to live for several weeks at a Christian retreat center outside Oslo.

I had previously studied Spanish in Mexico and Igbo in Nigeria. In both countries, my blond hair and pale skin marked me as a foreigner, and local folks hospitably cut me plenty of slack before I opened my mouth. But in Norway, no such grace was afforded; as soon as I walked into a store, clerks immediately spoke rapid-fire Norwegian to me, and assumed I would respond in kind. Often overwhelmed, I nevertheless took it more as an honor than a burden, as if being accepted as family.

Before long, I recognized among Norwegians many familiar cultural cognates from my upbringing: order, moral uprightness, thrift and simplicity, emotional reserve, and discomfort with physical affection.

All this was heady stuff to an American longing for roots, and soon I was asking the Lord, "Do you want me to leave the U.S. and relocate to Norway?"

One evening, the community of staff and residents shared in their monthly agape meal—complete with bananas and oranges, an imported wintertime delicacy in Norway. Afterward, we prayed for each other, and when several laid hands on me, I was altogether ready for the Father to answer The Question.

Excitedly, I listened to the various prayers offered over me. *Styrke* (strength) and *kraft* (power) were invoked often, confirming my warrior calling even then—but nothing was said about any future move. As the voices trailed off, I sighed in disappointment.

And then it came.

You have found your home.

My eyes burst open as the words broke forth in my mind. Glancing at the others still closed-eyed around me, I closed my eyes again quickly. "Lord, is that you?" I prayed excitedly. "What do you mean? Do you want me to pick up and move to Norway? It's OK—just tell me, and I'm ready, Father!"

You have found your home, I heard again. And then, *Wherever people gather who love and serve me, there is your home.*

Awed, humbled, silenced beyond voice, I sat there—thousands of miles from California—among my Christian brothers and sisters.

At home.

And yet, forever catapulted far beyond America and Norway, broken open to the Truth that freed me beyond measure—a revelation, in fact, reserved for the end of my "ethnic journey" in this world.

Jesus had freed me not only from racism against others, but also from any ethnic pride that might beckon it.

Like old buildings that are razed for newer and more promising structures, something exploded and crumbled in my soul—even as foundations both new and ancient broke forth.

I thought at once of the biblical patriarchs, who

> admitted openly that they were foreigners and refugees on earth. Those who say such things make it clear that they are looking for a country of their own. They did not keep thinking about the country they had left; if they had, they would have had the chance to return. Instead, it was a better country they longed for, the heavenly country. And so God is not ashamed for them to call him their God, because he has prepared a city for them (Heb. 11:13-16).

As the apostle Paul framed it,

> It is through faith that all of you are God's sons in union with Christ Jesus. You were baptized into union with Christ, and

now you are clothed, so to speak, with the life of Christ himself. So there is no difference between Jews and Gentiles, between slaves and free men, between men and women; you are all one in union with Christ Jesus. If you belong to Christ, then you are the descendants of Abraham and will receive what God has promised. (Gal. 3:26-29)

Oneness in Christ

In this broken world where racism still has considerable rein, I will always be subject to its attack. But God freed me from its power to shame me into withdrawal when I discovered at last I can go to Jesus when it attacks.

We learn to honor the truth by submitting to it—and experiencing the freedom it bears.

When I finally let Jesus show me my own sinful nature, I became neither an angel nor a devil, but something better, namely, a son of the Father. This has allowed me to see other Christians as my brothers and sisters, no matter what their color.

Often, another sigh now escapes my lips—this time, a deep relief that I can be broken and still loved, that I can bring forth my deepest, darkest sin, and Jesus will not only still love me but also set me free from its effects.

Certainly, I'm a fellow human being with those of all races, respecting their rights and sharing with them a common need for food, shelter, love, and purposefulness. But I share only with Christians my sense of where our rights originate and how our human needs are met.

Our emotional, physical, and spiritual makeup is essentially the same as human beings. I'm no more adequate in my own human ability to be upright than any other person. But I am accountable to the same Father God and, thereby, share a common destiny only with those surrendered to Jesus. I've felt more at home, for example, with Christian Europeans than with non-Christian Americans.

I once heard an American preacher say that he visited Europe and was shocked to see so many McDonald's hamburger stands there. In fact, Americans visiting Europe flock to them in an effort to feel more at home in a strange culture. Christians, he said, should regard churches around the world like that, as touchstones of their deepest identity, no matter where they travel.

When you're traveling outside the U.S., he challenged his congregation, do you feel more at home at a McDonald's or at an indigenous church?

Again, I've come to feel safer dropping my emotional guard with a nonwhite Christian than with a white nonbeliever.

I witnessed this principle once while ministering with several others to a woman who had been divorced by her first husband, who shared her ethnic background, when neither were Christian. She later became a believer and sought my counsel and prayer when she became engaged again to a man who was a Christian but of a different ethnic background.

As she talked, the two sounded like a good match. Each had a long and solid relationship with the Lord and shared similar values, education, and life goals. "Frankly," she said, "everything is just so good, I want to be sure the ethnic thing won't be a big problem."

We prayed on several occasions, and eventually one person began to prophesy over her, saying, "Your first husband was the foreigner."

That word of truth freed her to discuss openly with her fiancé their different heritages and thereby removed any hooks the Enemy might have otherwise seized in this area of their relationship.

Even as Jesus shapes this new identity in me, however, the unregenerate "old Adam" occasionally rears his head to remind me I'll always need the Holy Spirit to keep freeing me from shame.

Soon after *Father & Son* was published, for example, the associate pastor of an African American church in another state called and asked if I would teach at their men's retreat.

"I'd be delighted," I said excitedly, and we talked for a good while getting to know each other and setting up the date. After we hung up, I thanked the Father for healing me and bringing me to that point of ministry to men of all colors.

Within moments, however, shame-full fears and self-doubts assaulted me. After all, how could I—a middle-class white male—presume to speak with authority to the very black men who had suffered so much at the hands of others like me? What if I said something that got misinterpreted as racist? Suppose . . .

Overwhelmed, I fell quickly to my knees and surrendered all questions to Jesus. "You brought me here by grace," I said. "If you want me to bring your word to those men, you're going to have to lead me through this by more grace."

Much of the time leading up to and during that retreat I spent on my knees. The battle was heavy, and the morning of my second day among the men, flu symptoms overcame me. Nauseated, head aching, and fearful of doing something "wrong," I girded myself and stood up to speak.

Ten minutes later, as sweat rolled down my back, I felt my knees buckling, and asked for a chair and a glass of water. With as much grace as I could muster, I took the microphone off the stand and finished my teaching seated onstage—pausing often in my delivery just to pray quietly, "Jesus! Help! Surely you didn't send me these three thousand miles just to keel over up here in front of everybody!"

By that evening I was feeling better, and when the conference ended two days later, one of the men pulled me aside. "You know, I need to confess something to you, brother," he said. "At first, I didn't think you could, you know, really speak to us. But . . . well, you did. I mean, the Lord really used you to hit us where we need it—and I thank you."

We hugged, and as we parted, I smiled. "Well, brother, let me make a confession myself. It got pretty clear there at the beginning that I couldn't do it! I just appreciate your talking to me honestly like this—and I'm thankful the Lord did it through me."

Just because you've been through the Father's boot camp doesn't mean the battle will be easy.

As the apostle Paul declared to the Ephesians, the Law sets us up to be enemies, with performance standards that allow a man to hide his shame by thinking he's better than another. On the cross, however, Jesus said, "Dump your shame on me instead of each other, and I'll show you the Father's grace. He'll make you his sons and, thereby, brothers."

Let it be.

NINE

Battling Addiction

We were slaves to passions and pleasures of all kinds. Titus 3:3

*Do not get drunk with wine, which will only ruin you;
instead, be filled with the Spirit.* Ephesians 5:18

NOTHING unmasks performance-oriented religion more quickly than addictions, which thrive on shame and have therefore become a primary Enemy stronghold among men today.

Webster's dictionary notes that the word *addict* comes from two Latin roots, the preposition *ad*, meaning "toward," and the verb *dicere*, meaning "to speak." Hence, *addicere*, "to speak toward," or as in *Webster's*, "to give assent, to give [oneself] up to [a strong habit]."[1]

Clearly, the thrust here is to surrender.

The alcoholic, for example, has surrendered to alcohol, and his own willpower is no longer sufficient to stop himself from drinking.

From a spiritual perspective, it's like spilling glue. You can wipe it up easily if you act quickly, but if you let it sit, it hardens and you need special tools to remove it. If you sin once, you can stop from doing it again by your own willpower. But if you persist in that sin and thus give your will up to it, the Enemy seizes and consolidates it under his power.

The spilled glue has hardened, and the man's own hand no longer has the power to wipe it up. He needs special tools.

A man can choose to jump into a pit deeper than he's able to climb out. Once he's in, though, you can't hold him responsible for not climbing out himself. But you can and must hold him responsible for not recognizing his predicament and calling out for help. The man who does so is humbled and delivered; the man who refuses is humiliated and destroyed.

Weakness, even stupidity, may get a man into the pit, but it's pride that keeps him there. That's why addictions beckon a deeper healing than simply stopping the behavior.

You can't judge an alcoholic for desiring to drink, nor even for his drinking, since he literally has no power to stop himself. All exhortations for him to stop—no matter how biblical or righteously intended—not only fail, but fuel the very shame that drives his addiction, by telling him he should be doing something he can't.

Nevertheless—and here is the profound truth that only the Kingdom warrior can appropriate—he can and must be held responsible for the effects of his drinking. Responsibility requires choice, and he *can* choose to face his powerlessness and surrender to God, whose power alone can stop him.

If God can't overcome alcoholism and its effects, then the alcoholic ultimately has no recourse and can't be held responsible for his actions. But his drinking *does* harm others, even as he can kill someone while driving drunk. Similarly, secondhand smoke can cause cancer.

The addict is thereby trapped between the proverbial rock and a hard place—gripped by a destructive behavior pattern more powerful than his will, and yet fully accountable for its effects!

In fact, that's how the apostle Paul aptly describes life in this world: "When I want to do what is good, what is evil is the only choice I have. . . . What an unhappy man I am! Who will rescue me from this body that is taking me to death?" (Rom. 7:21, 24).

Significantly, the answer is not a substance, behavior, or human being, but rather, the Father-God himself: "Thanks be to God, who does this through our Lord Jesus Christ!" (Rom. 7:25).

The difference between powerlessness and hopelessness is Jesus.

Addictions, therefore, are not limited to alcoholism and drugs. While sadly true for some men, images of a man falling off a barstool or shooting a heroin needle can serve as distractions that safely distance others of us from the far broader notion of addiction required to recognize and overcome it, even in ourselves. It's like caricaturing the Enemy as a red-suited man with horns, tail, and pitchfork—as if he were foolish enough to be so readily spotted and monitored. The only men Jesus explicitly identified with the Enemy blended all too well into their society as respectable, well-dressed men with Bibles (John 8:44).

Other Addictions

Addiction has as many faces as men have ways to avoid surrendering to the Father God. Sexual activity, for example, beckons an altered spiritual state and becomes addictive—that is, supplants a man's will—outside God's intent (1 Cor. 6:15-17 and my chapter "From Love Bug to Faith: Sexuality & Spirituality" in *Healing the Masculine Soul*).

The ancient prophet Hosea spoke forthrightly about surrendering to such false cravings:

> They shall eat but never be satisfied, behave wantonly but their lust will never be overtaxed, for they have forsaken the Lord to give themselves to sacred prostitution. (Hos. 4:10-11, NEB)

The compulsive-addictive dimension of fornication or homosexuality, for example, is clear in the AIDS epidemic—a disease that is preventable by simply abstaining from sexual activity. Even when contracted otherwise, its source ultimately points back to sexual transmission; transfused infected blood often can be traced to someone infected through sexual contact. Nevertheless, men continue to engage in sexual activity and not only contract the disease and pass it on to others, but—in classic addictive denial—present themselves as heroic "victims."

In a further attempt to mask their denial, men who have given themselves up to homosexual acts cling doggedly to the claim that they can't change their behavior. And of course, that's quite true. They're addicted.

Much as they try, therefore, they can't dodge responsibility for their actions, if only because AIDS—and its incipient spread to non-homosexuals—demonstrates that homosexual behavior, like alcoholism, can indeed harm others. Ask any hemophiliac, many of whom in this country have contracted AIDS from tainted transfusions.

Indeed, the growing witness of many men today who have abandoned homosexual behavior testifies that, like alcoholics, they can surrender to the God who is able to change them. The man thus saved from homosexual addiction tears the mask off those who remain in denial. He witnesses to the Power who has overcome the world (1 John 4:4) and thereby threatens those who remain in its grip.

Most often, though, he's ignored or discounted by the world's media and scorned by those who practice homosexuality. He, and the growing number of others like him, are the truly heroic men to emerge from the homosexual epidemic—boldly facing the truth lesser men flee and pushing ahead in humble surrender to the Father God.

Like our inborn sin-nature, addictions can be recognized and overcome at their root only through surrender to Jesus and his truth. Thus, the apostle Paul doesn't command the Ephesians to abstain from alcohol—he even encourages his disciple Timothy to drink "a little wine to help your digestion" (1 Tim. 5:23). Rather, he exhorts them not to *surrender* to alcohol: "be filled instead with the Holy Spirit and controlled by him" (Eph. 5:18, TLB).

The archaic use of the word *spirits* for alcoholic beverages, for example, demonstrates graphically the counterfeit dimension of addictions. Christian musician Carman's 1993 concert tour title, "Addicted to Jesus," makes the counterpoint.

When we forget the Source and Focus of the true call to surrender, we give ourselves up to false calls, and addictions manifest.

Most Top 40 songs, for example, portray relationship addiction—that is, in which the man looks to the woman to save him from the truth. Thus, the addict croons to the woman, "If only I had your love, I could kick this habit." Country singer Willie Nelson cut the definitive anthem to addiction in 1978 with "I Can Get Off on You," in which having the woman's love at last assures him he can throw away his marijuana, cocaine, and pills.

That's idolatry. It's the classic addictive relationship, epidemic among a generation of men abandoned by their fathers to believe that "Mom [the woman] saves me." That is, the man uses the woman like a drug to avoid facing his deeper need for identity and destiny. Ironically, sadly—as in Willie Nelson's song—he hasn't overcome his addiction; he's merely exchanged one for another.

What, indeed, will happen when the woman has a bad day and gets irritable?

Any bartender knows.

Indeed, when enough people forget on whom their will to surrender was designed to focus, they become what Anne Schaef portrays in her book *When Society Becomes an Addict*—compulsively surrendering to a variety of behaviors that promise to fulfill needs, but are patently incapable of doing so.[2]

Too often the people of God would qualify thus. As the prophet Isaiah declared,

> Why spend money on what does not satisfy? Why spend your wages and still be hungry? Listen to me and do what I say, and you will enjoy the best food of all. (Isa. 55:2)

The Ultimate Addiction
Unable to provide for our deepest needs, we are creatures of surrender.

Jesus essentially asks us, "Will you yield to the authentic Source and Focus of your will to surrender? Or will you short-circuit the Father's call to himself and give assent instead to some false substitute?"

The ultimate addiction is sin itself—the proud compulsion to control your own life and thereby avoid the truth of our broken human condition and our need for God to save us from it. To "sin" means to "miss the mark"; we're hooked on sinning because our innate pride doesn't allow us to hit the mark, that is, to yield to the Father.

Furthermore, this Ultimate Addiction comes complete with its Ultimate Shame—knowing we are not capable of doing what God has called us to do. "When I want to do what is good, what is evil is the only choice I have," as the apostle Paul put it (Rom. 7:21).

In fact, the twelve-step program, which began with Alcoholics Anonymous, was explicitly based upon Romans 7:14-25, and may aptly be summarized, "Surrender to God and not alcohol": Step 1 is to confess you are powerless to change yourself; Step 2, to acknowledge that only a Power greater than you can do it; and Step 3, to surrender to that Power.

Secularized, however, the "twelve-step program" falls ominously short in failing to name Jesus as the only power able to save us from our sin-addiction. Consequently, participants ground their identity in their addictive behavior rather than in Jesus. The program teaches a man, for example, to present himself primarily as "an alcoholic" or "an overeater," instead of "a beloved son of the Father."

The overwhelming human urge to deny our addiction is rightly to be feared and confronted. But it can only be overcome by the full truth—namely, of who we are in Christ. The half-truth that we are addicts beckons its own ingrown "victim" spirit, which fosters resignation, blame, and denial.

Increasingly, Christian groups such as Overcomers Anonymous have restored the program to its biblical roots in Jesus as Higher Power. This recentering precludes both demonic, New

Age definitions of Higher Power and a "victim" mentality by restoring participants to their true identity and power in Christ.

We Christians, however, have no license to criticize AA as long as we continue to hide from our own sin-addiction behind self-righteous, performance-oriented religion—especially since the program's basic truths about compulsive behaviors are derived from a biblical understanding of sin.

Thus, we can't judge another man for desiring to sin, or even for sinning, because that's our inborn condition, the given state of our human nature as part of a fallen world. Nevertheless, we can and must hold each other responsible for the effects of our sin, because every man is able to confess he can't save himself from his sinful condition and surrender to Jesus, who can.

Furthermore, you can't make a man stop sinning—any more than stop an alcoholic from drinking—by commanding him to "obey God" or exhorting him to "do what the Bible says." Addictions, as with our proud human inclination to turn away from God, are rooted more deeply than in mere human will-power.

Indeed, that's why we sin-addicts need a Savior.

Exhorting Others to Change

Until we Christian men realize this—indeed, face it in ourselves—we'll only push each other deeper into our addictions. Like the Pharisees, we'll heap burdens on others without lifting a finger to help them (Luke 11:46).

The more diligently a man hides from the truth, the harder he'll judge those who are exposed. In the spring of 1994, Dodger outfielder Darryl Strawberry was fired for repeated drug offenses. "I can't comprehend," said manager Tommy LaSorda, who has struggled with an eating problem for years, "how a man could be dumb enough or weak enough to take drugs."[3]

Exhorting an addict to stop only increases the very sense of shame that fuels his addiction. Precisely at that point of unmitigated shame—overwhelmed by his inadequacies before an exacting, punishing God—a man begins to seek saving power in a martini, an illicit sexual encounter, a workaholic twelve-hour day, or a stern exhortation to morality in others. Indeed, that's the addictive moment, served up to the Enemy by an organization of ostensibly "godly men"—who in fact are simply using religion to hide from the shame of their own sin-addiction.

Where shame abides, addictions abound.

And warriors are lost.

In fact, both the liberal-universalist churches and the demonic New Age revival today feed largely on this longing for a spirituality that promises safety from such shame-based "Christianity." They simply discount the Father God as parochial or sexist, eliminate sin and the need for a savior, and voila! A self-affirming spirituality of denial, tailor-made for an addictive society hellbent to hide its brokenness and need.

The conservative churches, meanwhile, are busy exhorting others to morality.

Nobody's simply confessing his need for God.

Consider sexual impotence. Does a man's sexual "performance" improve, is he healed or even motivated to "do better," by his wife's telling him, "You've got to try harder!"?

Rather, the shame he feels for not being able to do what he wants, and should be able to do, is only exacerbated. Such exhortation only drives him further into despair; he fears his sexuality as an occasion for failure, and his impotence becomes more deeply rooted.

Diversion begins to look easier than renewal, and sexually addictive behaviors beckon.

To overcome his impotence, in fact, a man may need Christian counseling to help him identify and be healed of some past trauma that has made him fear and thereby withdraw from even godly sexual encounters with his wife. Often, an unfathered man felt emasculated by his mother as a boy and projects that fear onto his wife. In any case, the impotent man will certainly need a wife with compassion, patience, and even a sense of humor—not a woman who posts a "godly performance" checklist on their bedroom wall.

In fact, the Bible says, "The husband should fulfill his marital duty to his wife" (1 Cor. 7:3, NIV). The man hiding from relationship in religion would therefore conclude, "A true man of God should perform well enough sexually to satisfy his wife. When he doesn't, he just needs to be told to obey the Scriptures."

That's enough to give a husband a headache at bedtime.

No one exposes the limits of exhortation so sharply as an addict.

Certainly, exhortation can be an effective weapon in behalf of men who can, but won't—who lack motivation, not ability. A coach, for example, properly exhorts players who've been pre-selected for their ability to compete succesfully at their league's level.

Again, I regularly jog a three-mile path, and often the urge to quit strikes before the end. Because I know my distance ability, I can exhort myself, *I know this isn't always fun, but you'll feel a lot better when you're done, so let's get on with it!* I wouldn't push myself to run a marathon, on the other hand, unless I'd prepared myself appropriately.

If a man has sought a lifestyle of surrender through prayer, vulnerable fellowship, committed accountability, and possibly counseling, eventually he may reach a point where godly self-ex-amination becomes addictive introspection if he's not exhorted to move outward—even as an army from a beachhead. After an operation, a man must leave the hospital for the barracks and get on with the destiny that the operation presumably facilitated.

The biblical faith sees exhortation not as a coercive technique, but rather, a gift of the Holy Spirit to fulfill the Father's purposes (Rom. 12:8). Its faithful use, therefore, requires proper discern-ment.

In Kingdom warfare, for example, it may be appropriate to exhort the man who truly "can't do it" on his own strength, but only when you sense God has said, "Urge him to step out in this instance, because I will give him what he needs to exceed his natural abilities." In such cases, you need witnesses to confirm that supernatural word of faith (1 Cor. 12:9; 14:29).

The same is true for exhorting yourself.

In a moving example, 1988 Winter Olympic figure skater Brian Boitano recalled stepping onto the ice for what became his gold-medal performance. The American crowd began chanting, "Boitano!" and the Canadians, "Orser!" for their own favorite, Brian Orser.

As a *Newsweek* reporter tells it,

> But somehow with Boitano's first glide the "Battle of the Brians" receded, and the only battle going on was between two voices in his head. One kept saying, "You're going to blow it"; the other retorted, "Shut up! Concentrate!"
>
> When he reached the critical triple-flip/triple-toe-loop combination, Boitano was rewarded with transcendence. "I went to vault off my toes and the ice just exploded under me," he recalls. "It felt like someone was lifting me up under the armpits and then they just set me down light as a feather." From that soaring moment, the rest remains a blur—the triumphant finish, the crowd exploding from its seats, Boitano hiding in a bathroom stall while his rivals skated and, finally, his ascent to the highest podium.

Boitano's experience, in fact, suggests the word of faith: "It was exactly how I had always envisioned it, so I wasn't sure I wasn't dreaming," he says. "It wasn't until they played the national anthem—much faster than I had imagined—that I knew for sure it was all real."[4]

How, then, do you know when the voice urging you to press on is the Lord's promising he'll provide what you need, or the Enemy's suckering you into failure?

The Holy Spirit will prompt you when to exhort a brother—usually after he's been to the cross for healing and needs a boost to more fully experience and integrate his growth. A man who hasn't gone to the cross himself can't discern such a timely need in another, and his exhortations serve only to mask his own fear of surrender. He thereby short-circuits God's healing process.

Of course, sometimes you get no clear "word of faith," and you just have to pray, "Help, Father!" and step out on the ice. In fact, sometimes you fall flat on your butt—literally, like Boitano in the '94 Olympics, even after years of grueling preparation for his comeback. That doesn't necessarily mean you didn't discern correctly; for his own good reasons, God can tell a man to enter a political race, for example, but not intend for him to win.

The Father's purposes—and sense of victory—are not our own (Isaiah 55:8-9). The bottom line is trusting that your Father loves you and will use whatever experience you give him to convince you. Perhaps, like Brian Boitano, a twenty-four-year-old needs most to experience the gold-medal victory as he'd envisioned it, and a thirty-year-old needs later to learn a different kind of strength and victory.

The addict, then, denies the truth and indulges his pride, saying, "I will, because I can." The victim sees only half the truth and says, "I won't, because I can't." The Kingdom warrior surrenders to the Full and Living Truth and says, "God will, because I can't."

It's the difference, as another has said, between telling God, "I can do it with your help," and confessing, "You can do it with my cooperation."

From Addiction to Addiction

Consumed by shame, however, the addict dares not accept his human limitations—the alcoholic fancies he can drink forever; the homosexual or playboy, that he can safely have as many sex partners as he wants; the religious addict, that he's saved by telling others how to be righteous. In fact, his addiction often grows from an effort to quiet the shaming inner voice that says, *You should succeed, but you won't.*

Unwilling to surrender, he can't discern God's call. He either capitulates to the voice of shame by giving in to his addiction, or he battles it in his own strength by overcompensating—then burns out and gives in.

Thus, the man trapped in alcoholism, homosexuality, or false religion fancies, "I'm just fine and don't see why others tell me I need help!" That is, "What's wrong with having a few drinks?" or, "God made me gay and that makes it good!" or, "But I'm just proclaiming the Word of God!"

In fact, every addict has already experienced surrendering to a power greater than himself, namely, the Enemy—that is, the power beckoned by the addictive substance or behavior. Hence the fatal flaw in a secularized twelve-step program: We must surrender not just to "a power greater than ourselves" (Step 3), for which any demon would qualify (James 2:19). Indeed, we must give ourselves up to the one and only Power who has demonstrated he is greater than the Enemy, that we might witness to the ancient proclamation, "The Spirit who is in you is more powerful than the spirit in those who belong to the world" (1 John 4:4).

The battle to overcome addiction, therefore, is appropriately cast in the realm of the spirit, where "higher powers" must compete for our surrender and demonstrate which is indeed the highest.

Likewise, our human sin-addiction manifests as a natural tendency to deny that we are creatures of God and need him to rule our broken lives. That is, we give ourselves up to something other than the God who is truth, because we don't want to face the humbling truth about our sinful human condition and our inability to save ourselves from its effects.

I therefore define addictive behavior as "doing something consistently in order to avoid facing the truth about yourself."

This, at last, allows us to minister without judging each other, saving us from the self-righteous assumption that "As long as I do not drink alcohol or do drugs to excess, I am not subject to addictions." Rather, as human beings trapped in our shameful condition of sin, we will all in some way find ourselves manifesting addictive behaviors until Jesus returns.

Because we humans are both a proud and creative species, we devise a broad range of activities to avoid the humbling truth about ourselves—including not only substance abuse, but also compulsive behaviors in sexuality, relationships, and even religion. In recent years, for example, the twelve-step program has expanded its "Anonymous" groups from AA (Alcoholics) to include OA (Overeaters), SA (Sexaholics), CODA (Codependents) and even FA (Fundamentalists).

The variety of addictions underscores that "Satan cannot drive out Satan" (Matt. 12:26, NIV). That is, you can't overcome one addiction by switching to another one, but only by giving yourself up to Jesus instead—as the apostle Paul exhorted the Ephesians.

Thus, psychologists have identified an "addictive personality" in those who flee the source of their compulsion by leaping from more frowned-upon addictive behaviors to more "acceptable" ones. That way they're less likely to be confronted with the truth by others. They stop drinking and start smoking, break off an abusive relationship and begin overeating, swear off homosexual encounters and embrace shame-based religion.

Significantly, the addictive personality requires a "high" akin to the keyed-up excitement, danger, or adventure of living on the edge. It's like an adrenaline addiction. In addictive relationships, for example, it's the electricity of always being on the verge of splitting up. The one thing an addicted man can't handle is peace and security in a relationship. It's too unfamiliar; he feels more in control running on the coping mechanisms from his out-of-control boyhood family.

Men surrendered to Jesus don't need this conjured, addictive "excitement." In fact, it's the counterfeit vitality of life in the Spirit—that is, living out of control, without surrendering to God's control; never knowing what's going to happen, without trusting God's purposes.

Like shamed children, we imagine that if the Father God really knew the truth about us, he'd reject and abandon us. The Psalmist, however, proclaims a different image of God: "My father and mother may abandon me, but the Lord will take care of me" (Ps. 27:10).

We deny the painful truth of our brokenness, therefore, and eventually discover that our mere willpower can't suppress it. Naively, we give ourselves up to substances or behaviors that promise to do it for us. As adults, we fancy that we can lock past wounds down in the basement and out of sight, and those monsters will no longer affect us because we've forgotten them.

And then, a man wonders why he hears an occasional roar coming up from within his spirit—a terrifying dream, a shocking impulse, an overwhelming sadness at a song or movie. Thus the Father gets your attention and effectively invites you to come to

177

him at last for healing. Jesus is asking, *Will you let me go down in your basement and clean out your house so you can surrender to me, learn to trust me, and thereby not need to hide from the truth behind addictions?*

A man will never know why he's hamstrung by subconscious insecurities until he allows Jesus to walk with him into the depths of his soul, to see what he's held down there because he hasn't trusted God to overcome it. He imagines that with any opening of the basement door, like a crack in the dike, his subconscious will erupt and overwhelm him with a flood of horrible, dammed-up emotions that Jesus can't handle.

Without Jesus, however, that fear is often realized. A popular secular method for surfacing truth, for example, is hypnosis—in which a person is drawn into a wholly passive emotional and spiritual state, open and vulnerable to "outside" suggestion, both human and demonic.

At best, hypnosis is unnecessary for Christians, who have access to all truth through the Holy Spirit (John 16:13; 1 Cor. 12:8)—who respects our will, even to say no.

It's natural to shut down to painful experiences and hide them in the subconscious.

The Enemy, on the other hand, if he can't keep a man in denial avoiding the truth, will invade and shatter his boundaries with the truth, regardless of whether he's ready or not—like the false exhorters. I've ministered to men devastated when earlier hypnosis had surfaced past traumas that they had not yet developed the emotional and spiritual security to face or integrate.

In a further example, the current legal battles over "false memory syndrome" reveal the clear limitations of natural knowledge.

A lying demon can easily speak to a person under stress, whether influenced by a counselor or through hypnosis, whenever he is surrendered to someone other than Jesus.

But the Holy Spirit will reveal only the truth, and then, only when he's prepared you to hear it. That's the truth that sets you free, as opposed to the truth that binds you in shame—that leaves you anguishing, "If it's true, I should be able to deal with this traumatic memory, but I can't!"

Meanwhile, the world remains forever bound in its self-serving myopia: no secular law court will recognize evidence brought by the Holy Spirit and therefore can't discern the difference from that brought by the Enemy.

In any case, if you've ever allowed yourself to be hypnotized—even for "entertainment"—you need to be spiritually cleansed by someone surrendered to Jesus who honors the workings of his Holy Spirit.

The Father God, who has created and stood by us in our worst pain, knows how to approach each man's deepest wounds, and his Holy Spirit will reveal no more than what we can handle at any given time.

If I sense the Father has prepared a man to face some painful memory, I "test" that word of knowledge by urging the man, "Tell God how badly you want to see the truth and break through this memory block to healing!" If his intensity toward the Father matches that needed to face the pain, he's ready for the operation.

If the man is not ready to storm the gates of heaven after the truth, he'll run from the pain it bears. No man will entertain the unmanageable truth about himself until he knows his Father stands by him in it—not to shame him, but to deliver him from its deadly effects.

Addiction, therefore, is the Enemy's blackmail. Only the truth can overcome its shame and break the blackmailer's grip. "Go ahead and tell the world the worst truth about me," the Kingdom warrior can say; "I've already been to Jesus with it all, and I'm OK with him!" As the apostle Paul put it, the "real Jew," that is, the real man of God, "receives his praise from God, not from man" (Rom. 2:29).

This is a major strength of the twelve-step program, in which persons overcome shame by speaking out the truth of their affliction to an audience of others who share it, and receive immediate affirmation.

"I'm Bob and I'm an alcoholic," a man says as he stands to speak at an AA meeting. He's met with a rousing, welcome chorus of "Hi, Bob!"

Translation: "You're safe here. You don't have to be afraid of the truth about yourself. We're with you in it."

The Blackmailer has no takers here.

For Kingdom warriors, the issue is not whether people will find out the truth about me, but whether I will take responsibility for my condition and seek help to overcome its negative effects. The more I focus on the latter, the less I fear the former.

It's a blessed cycle: The more I walk in the truth with Jesus, the less shame I bear, the more I feel like a man, the less I feel compelled to hide, the more I ask Jesus to surface the truth in me, the more he heals me, the more I feel like a man, and so on.

A man learns to honor the truth by submitting to it—and discovering thereby the freedom it bears.

For example, track star Danny Harris was ranked number one in the world in the four-hundred-meter intermediate hurdles in 1990, then in 1992 tested positive for cocaine. During his four-year suspension from competition, he began working a twelve-step program and obtained a reinstatement hearing with USA Track & Field.

As one sportswriter reported,

> When Danny Harris told friends he had agreed to be interviewed by a reporter, they warned him that the article might be negative. He laughed. What could anyone write about him that he hasn't confessed in Alcoholics Anonymous and Cocaine Anonymous meetings?
>
> "If all you do is write, 'Danny Harris is an addict' . . . 100 times and nothing else, I won't complain," he said, "because every word of it would be true. If God doesn't want me to run again, as much as I miss it, I can accept that and go on. But I have a good feeling about the hearing because my life is good. I'm not the same person I was before."[5]

The twelve-step program espouses such "tough love"—that is, love wed to truth—to break the destructive cycle of striving, failing, shaming, falling. Essentially, this is the biblical sword of truth, wielded with love by a fellow sinner.

In twelve-step vocabulary, a man might stand to speak at a church gathering by announcing, "I'm Bill, and I'm a sinner, saved only by grace through faith in Jesus Christ." Whereupon all the others would shout in brotherly support, "Hi, Bill!"

Too often, however, men come to the church seeking a religious mask to hide their sin—like the Pharisees.

Thus, the grace of AA is rarely evidenced in churches. For the average man struggling against addictive impulses, church is the last place he would think to go for help—because too often he sees there the same shame-based fear of truth that fuels his compulsions. Hence, the term, "religious addiction"—that is, using religious practices to hide sin instead of to surface and heal it—like the Pharisees, "who were sure of their own goodness and despised everybody else" (Luke 18:9).

Freedom in the Truth

The truth unburdens you. Lies, however, require ever-increasing energy to sustain. Ask any addict. The shame that could at first be quelled by a beer soon requires a six-pack; the inadequacy that once could be hidden with an occasional visit to a prostitute now requires daily masturbation and pornographic movies.

"How do you know when an addict is lying?" asks a twelve-step joke.

The answer: "When his lips are moving."

As Mark Twain once said, "It's easier to tell the truth; you don't have to remember so much."

What, then, can set an addict free? Nothing but the blood of Jesus—which sets a man free to face the truth, the whole truth, and nothing but the truth.

Granted, not every man is ready to hear the truth Jesus bears.

Someone once told me, "I know God is after me, but I just can't let go of all my desires and plans for myself. I keep running away from him because I'm afraid he'll make me do something I don't want to do. Can you give me some helpful advice?"

I prayed quickly. "Yes," I said. "Run as long as you can."

Translation: When the lie begins to require more than you can give and all your addictive efforts to contain it not only fail but are destroying you, cry out for Jesus. The more determined your cry, the more ready you are for his deliverance.

If the essence of masculinity is walking in the truth, then addictions and the lies that fuel them are the most clear threat to men today. It may be helpful to list here some truths I have seen the Holy Spirit minister to men in various addictive behaviors:

- An overeater came to see that he had been sexually molested as a boy and had experienced some pleasure in that. Disgusted and ashamed, he hated his body and wanted to make it as unattractive as possible to others so none would molest him again or stir the shame-ridden urge of sexual desire in him.
- A man addicted to late-night TV realized he'd been emotionally abused by his father and felt safer alone at night, when everyone else was asleep.
- A man who couldn't get through a weekend without watching several TV football games saw that he was vicariously drawing from those games the vitality he lacked in his own life.
- A man trapped in homosexual activity confessed his longing for a physical embrace and masculine approval from his distant, judgmental father.
- A man who jumped from one woman to another came to see his widowed mother had been seductive towards him. As a result, his natural, God-given love for his mother was adulterated with sexual desires. Therefore, he could only see love for a woman as sexual, and in successive "conquests" he was acting out bonding with and leaving his mother.

If the root of addictions is a lie, then the addict requires others who are equally afraid of the truth to foster the lie by walking with him in it. Hence, the term *codependent*.

The codependent is addicted to the addict; that is, he uses the other's addiction as an excuse to avoid facing the painful truth about himself. "It's her problem," the husband of an alcoholic wife might say. He criticizes her for drinking, seeks sympathy for himself from others, and wonders why she can't be as righteously self-controlled as he.

The codependent never owns up to his own pain, often because his parents were caught up in their own addictive behaviors and never taught him his feelings were important. He therefore can't see the reality of evil, even its efforts to destroy him. He can't stand up for himself—or for others.

Even as the codependent covers up for the alcoholic parent or spouse, so as a Christian he wants to make God look good. If, for example, he prays and the person is not healed, it was his own "lack of faith."

As a boy, he thought, *Dad got drunk because I was a bad boy—if I just try harder to be good, he'll stop drinking.* As an adult Christian, he reacts to misfortune: "God's punishing me. If I can just try harder and do it right next time, he'll bless me."

Whereas the alcoholic says, "I can control my drinking," the codependent says, "I can control my alcoholic."

Ultimately, he excuses or accommodates her outrageous behavior. But he never holds her ultimately accountable for it. He treats her like a child because he fears a mature woman who would hold him accountable for his charade. If she ever did stop drinking, he'd have to face the truth of his own deep insecurities—that is, why he chose such a woman to bond with in the first place. Indeed, if she left him, he'd have to find another addict to preoccupy him.

Such a man must begin taking responsibility for his own life and cease building it around his wife's addiction. He can seek Christian counseling, recovery groups, and prayer partners, ask Jesus how he's praying for his wife, and draw appropriate boundaries.

He can tell her, "I am committed to you to work our problem out together. Whatever you decide, I'm going ahead to get my own healing. You're free to go on drinking. I can't stop you. But if you refuse to recognize your need for help and join me, you must do it alone. I'll grieve, I'll cry. But I won't let you destroy me as well as yourself."

The common question of the flesh, "How long should I hang

183

in there?" is answered simply—but not easily: "As long as it takes"—that is, as long as it takes for the Father to accomplish his purposes in this situation. Jesus essentially asked that question on the cross, and when he yielded wholly to the Father—"Not my will, but Thine be done"—the Father shaped him in the pain for his destiny.

Beg the Father to use the situation for all he can to surface whatever truth you need to face. As long as the surgeon has you cut open for an operation, you might as well have him work on whatever else in there needs healing—unless you want to go through another operation later.

You'll know how long to hang in there. The Father will let you know in his time, and it'll be confirmed by faithful brothers—that is, men who have sought the Father's will for you and not just taken up "your side." In many cases, when the man can at last stand firmly in the truth, the woman leaves him, because he will no longer serve as a foil for her lies.

A spirit of "addiction" may be present and can be cast out when the man has renounced it himself and committed to a discipline of the flesh, such as a Christ-centered twelve-step program. Often deep emotional or spiritual wounds must be healed as well to secure the deliverance.

The fountainhead of addictions, therefore, is the will to avoid suffering. Performance-oriented religion, for example, is addictive inasmuch as it keeps you from suffering the shame of your hopelessly sinful nature. Again, the codependent short-circuits the healing process precisely in trying to save the addict from suffering.

The problem is not that the addict suffers from his addiction, but that he hasn't dared to suffer deeply his real wounds. He doesn't trust any power greater than himself to save him. To avoid suffering, therefore, is to avoid the God of the Cross—and thereby, to avoid the crucible of pain wherein God shapes a man for his destiny as a warrior.

Thus addiction has been called a "spiritual disease," and its most refined—that is, diabolic—forms are not found on skid row, but in religious institutions. It was not alcoholics, after all, who killed Jesus, but indeed religious men—who, by the way, condemned him for befriending drinkers (Matt 11:28-29).

What then constitutes healing of addiction?

When the energy formerly given over to the compulsive behavior is given over instead to Father God (Eph 5:18).

Does that mean, for example, that a man previously surrendered to alcoholic or homosexual behavior will never again think of having a drink or same-sex partner?

Probably not, until Jesus returns.

Surrendering to Jesus instead of your addictive compulsions restores in you the freedom at last to choose, where before you were enslaved. After that, it's between you and Father God.

Certainly, I've seen God work such a complete healing in a few men. But on the average, overcoming addictive behaviors follows the pattern of overcoming our sin-nature. As fallen creatures in a fallen world, however, we'll never be free of sinful impulses, and the most common ones that come to you will likely come out of your old, particular compulsion.

The Father's emotional healing of past wounds, for example, is not a spiritual lobotomy. You'll always remember the painful events, but when you surrender them to Jesus, he takes the sting out of them and they no longer have power to control your will. Indeed, he transforms them into weapons for his victory when we reach out with his healing to others trapped in similar compulsions (2 Cor. 1:3-4).

That's likely why God doesn't remove all memory of our addictive behaviors—so we can help others by testifying to his saving grace in such suffering. A man who hasn't forgotten what addictive impulses feel like has greater credibility among those still trapped by them.

In fact, the Father promises us something better than freedom from all sinful impulses—namely himself, present with us in the battle, drawing us unto himself as his sons, and deploying us as his warriors into a world addicted to sin.

As a sin-addict, with a body that's taking me to death, I'll take it.

Thankfully and joyfully.

TEN

Battling for the Child:
Honoring the Boy in Yourself

At that time the disciples came to Jesus, asking,
"Who is the greatest in the Kingdom of heaven?" So
Jesus called a child, had him stand in front of them, and said,
". . . Unless you change and become like children,
you will never enter the Kingdom of heaven. The greatest in the
Kingdom of heaven is the one who humbles himself and
becomes like this child. And whoever welcomes in my name
one such child as this, welcomes me." Matthew 18:1-5

"You know, we really need to begin thinking about whether or not we're going to start a family," Mary said one morning over breakfast, a few months before our first anniversary.

Suddenly the newspaper I was scanning seemed to grab my attention. "Uh, well, I guess . . . I mean, well, yeah, I think that's probably a good idea," I mumbled, fidgeting with the pages.

"So how do you feel about being a father?" Mary asked.

A woman gets to the bottom line fast on this kind of issue. So fast I almost choked on my raisin toast.

"Being a father? Oh, excited . . . ," I allowed, hesitating.

"Feel" questions are not my favorite; nervously, I turned to the next page and stared vacantly at the tire sale. Sighing at last, I laid down my paper and turned to Mary. "But scared."

It was true. Neither of us had ever had children. Yet at forty-six, I'd thought about it off and on over the years. Mary was over forty herself, and we didn't have a lot of time left.

Still, we had a good life. We loved each other, enjoyed our jobs and the freedom to come and go. We exercised well and slept nights—all the way through.

"Your life will never be the same," everyone with children warned us. But as we talked honestly that morning, we realized that was precisely the point. I didn't want my life to be the same. I'd already traveled the world, pastored churches, written books, been on radio and TV shows.

Exciting as all this had been at the time, the prospect of a repeat cycle by itself now felt flat. "If you never have children," I recalled my father saying years before, "you'll miss out on one of life's greatest adventures."

We tried to imagine what it would be like to have a child and wondered, "How would we fit a child into our schedules?"

Eventually, we looked in the Bible for passages about children—and were humbled and convicted. Children, we saw, are not a burden who obstruct "the good life," but blessings from God who facilitate the best life:

"May the Lord give you children," the psalmist proclaimed, "you and you descendants! May you be blessed by the Lord, who made heaven and earth!" (Ps. 115:14-15). "Children are a gift from the Lord; they are a real blessing" (Ps. 127:3). And again, "Your wife will be like a fruitful vine within your house; your children will be like olive shoots around your table. Lo, thus shall the man be blessed who fears the Lord" (Ps. 128:3-4, RSV). Introducing his family to his brother Esau, Jacob declared, "These, sir, are the children whom God has been good enough to give me" (Gen. 33:5).

These words not only turned us around intellectually, but brought us to our knees together at the foot of our bed. There we confessed and begged God's forgiveness for our compulsive independence and nearsighted view of happiness and freedom.

We surrendered and poured out our hearts, telling God and each other at last how much we longed for a child, and we cried out the pain for years of not having one. We confessed that we had stopped hoping for fear of being disappointed—we had chickened out and hadn't trusted God to stand with us in grief as well as in joy.

We had become so intent on doing our own thing because we had not trusted God to do his thing. To paraphrase Jesus in the opening quote, we had not "welcomed" the child in his name— we had not surrendered to his purposes in us as parents—and had thereby not welcomed Jesus. Because he respects our own will enough to await our invitation, we had been cruising along on our own self-centered terms and missing God's mark.

As we talked and prayed over the next few days, we thought of several other Christian couples who had been trying unsuccessfully to become pregnant—among them, my prayer partner and his wife. We decided to invite them all to our home to pray together.

Ten couples came that Sunday evening, including friends who had recently moved and drove two hours to be there, and a non-Christian couple who were friends of another.

As the oldest couple, Mary and I had naively thought we were the only ones with "extra" problems and had basically started the group to pray for us. As we all began sharing our stories that night, however, years of longing, prayer, persistent efforts, and disappointments poured out from everyone, even the youngest. Tears flowed as couples told of painful miscarriages, operations, medications, special procedures—all for nought.

As we later surrendered to Jesus in prayer together, I felt a deep pain similar to what Mary and I had experienced at the foot of our bed—but now for the others there as well. "Jesus, come and minister to our terrible pain and disappointment!" I prayed. "We love you. We've given our lives to you. We know you love children and we've offered ourselves to be parents according to your will. Surely you want children who will praise you more than you want grieving couples!"

Moments later, I felt a distinct shift in my spirit from grief to

189

anger. I sensed the Enemy was determined to sabotage what was happening that night because it threatened a larger agenda of his that extended far beyond our little group. I sensed a spirit of "infertility" and the group agreed; together we bound and cast it out, asking for God's blessing of fertility for us all.

Later, when we had all shared our stories and prayed for each other, we covenanted to meet one Sunday evening a month thereafter.

The next month, the couple from out of town—who had miscarried earlier that year—announced that they had conceived later at the hotel the night of our first meeting! During prayer later, the husband was stirred to call out the rest of us men. We prayed for wisdom and courage to overcome our fears of being fathers, for hearts to love our wives through these difficult times. And then we husbands circled together arm-in-arm and invited all our wives to join hands together in the middle.

These are my beloved daughters! I sensed the Father's saying as we men embraced the women with our circle and prayed for their protection, comfort, healing, and fulfillment as women. "I don't know how to thank all you men," one woman said, wiping her tears to a chorus of "amen!" from the others.

The Father honors men who step out as his warriors, even unto blessing their families.

As we finished, I could sense the Father's strength flowing through us men as if he had been wanting us to bless his daughters like this for a long time. *These are my sons!* I heard in my spirit and sensed the Father's beaming proudly.

The next month, Mary and I had our own announcement to make. On our first anniversary, we had conceived!

Within the next two years, seven of the ten couples in the group had babies, including three who had miscarriages before finally delivering successfully. The three couples who remained childless included one who later divorced, another who realized they were not emotionally ready yet, and the non-Christians—who nevertheless felt "really touched" by what they had experienced among us.

Looking back, we realized that our battle against infertility had several fronts. Most of the women needed physical healing in order to conceive. All had received medical treatment before coming to the group and continued to see their doctors during the process.

I don't believe that infertility is necessarily caused by a spiritual problem, but I do believe that it may be. In our case, at times we sensed a clear spiritual attack, and often we battled more specific spiritual oppression in individual couples. Even now I can't say to what extent our infertility was caused by a spiritual problem or simply by the fallen nature of this world. The Bible rarely accomodates the spiritual/physical distinctions that our modern scientific minds prefer.

We had no formulas and no easy answers to this terribly painful issue—just a faith that God works in our suffering as he sees fit, as we surrender it to him and keep pushing ahead into the battle.

Certainly we were reminded that the Enemy hates children— especially those with Christian parents who will guide them to focus their energies on serving God. With abortion, he destroys children before they are born. But he knows Christian couples won't abort, so he has to start earlier to keep us from delivering or even conceiving.

In traveling around the country, I have heard similar accounts that confirm a current, widespread attack upon Christian couples trying to have children. All the accounts report great difficulty until the couple enlisted support from other believers. One pastor told me that during his annual denominational confer- ence, a speaker felt led to invite couples needing special help in having children to come to the altar for prayer. To everyone's amazement, more than one hundred couples came forth.

Some, he knew, had conceived other children years earlier, but now could not. We wondered: Had the Enemy stepped up this attack in recent years?

Child Sacrifices

Today, even as in the Bible, the Enemy seeks to destroy God's children of destiny. The pharaoh attempted to kill baby Moses, called to deliver God's people from his slaveholder's grasp (Exod.

1:6-16). King Herod sought to kill the baby Jesus, called to proclaim God's Kingdom (Matt. 2:16ff.).

In each case, the Enemy attacked all Jewish babies in an effort to kill the one sought. Similarly, the Enemy attacks all babies of believing Christians today, whether potential or born, in an effort to sabotage God's purposes in this world—even as in biblical times, to destroy Jesus and keep him from growing and maturing among us.

In fact, the spiritual Enemy of Israel manifests in gods that often require child sacrifice. Thus, when King Josiah sought to restore Israel to right relationship with God, he "desecrated Topheth, the pagan place of worship in Hinnom Valley, so that no one could sacrifice his son or daughter as a burnt offering to the god Molech" (2 Kings 23:10).

Furthermore, child sacrifice is linked with occult spirituality:

> Don't sacrifice your children in the fires on your altars; and don't let your people practice divination or look for omens or use spells or charms, and don't let them consult the spirits of the dead. The Lord your God hates people who do these disgusting things, and that is why he is driving those nations out of the land as you advance. Be completely faithful to the Lord. (Deut. 18:10-13)

New Age spirituality, therefore, often accommodates abortion.

Indeed, the ancient pagan gods are worshiped among us even today at abortion clinics. The gods of the world are distinguished from the God of Israel in that the former exist to serve me—my nation, my race, my clan, my family—whereas God calls us to serve him. As any father with spit-up on his pajamas knows, a baby doesn't serve the parents, but in fact requires adult self-sacrifice. The self-centered pagan gods, on the other hand, ultimately require child sacrifice, from abortion to neglect. "My life is my own and I will do what makes life easiest for me" is their creed.

Ironically, most proabortion rhetoric assures that having un-wanted children fosters child abuse. From a spiritual perspective, however, abortion not only depreciates the value of a child's life, but also beckons infanticide over the land—each of which fosters child abuse.

Our experience with the couples' group, meanwhile, caused me to realize that the Lord had lost no time in drawing Mary and me into his battle for children. In fact, the morning after Mary had moved alone into our newly rented home two weeks before the wedding, she called me, upset. "There's something awfully oppressive and scary here," she said. "I prayed against it all night, but couldn't sense what it is. You've got to come and pray over the house today!"

That evening, as we prayed quietly in the living room, I felt the heaviness myself, but got no words or images. "This is weird," Mary said, "but the word *infanticide* keeps coming to mind. What in the world would killing babies have to do with our house?"

I had no idea. We weren't even married yet, so we hadn't talked seriously about having children ourselves.

Was it a spirit over Los Angeles? We prayed—and sensed rather that the spirit was localized to our property. The landlord, who had lived in our front home previously and now lived in the adjoining cottage out back, was into New Age spirituality—the mail included pieces from Scientology, Rosicrucians, and the like. We cleansed the home from occult spirits—but still felt no release from "infanticide."

Had the owners had an abortion? Unlikely; both were older, and they had only bought the house a few years earlier, long after their childbearing years. Had they engaged in ritual abuse? Unlikely; they both seemed genuinely humane and friendly.

Puzzled, I could only bind the spirit and send it away. When I moved in after the wedding, the attacks ceased—until I left town for conferences, and then Mary would again experience night-mares and oppression.

Meanwhile, over the next year, we received unforwarded mail to a particular doctor, whom I will refer to as Dr. Smith. The landlord told us this doctor had been the previous owner and used the rear cottage as an office.

Months after we began hosting the couples group, Mary and I were praying for a child together one night in the living room. Suddenly, a gruesome image came to my mind of babies being crushed and killed. By that time, we were onto the Enemy's scheme to destroy Christian children, so we assumed the image indicated a spirit aimed at our group. We prayed protection over ourselves and others in the group—but the image persisted.

Suddenly, Mary sat bolt upright. "Remember the 'infanticide' spirit?!" she exclaimed.

I did, indeed—and we prayed against it again. Still, we puzzled over its affinity for our home and, as our pregnancy progressed, became heaven-bent to rid our place of its influence. I fasted. I prayed alone, and with other men. I began each conference asking the men there to pray a covering over my home.

And then, late one evening when I was out of town, Mary called me excitedly at my hotel. "I think I solved the 'infanticide' mystery!" she declared. Our insurance company, she said, had called and asked her to compare our gynecologist's fees with others in the area, giving her a list of five other doctors. "Guess who was on the list?" she asked.

"Who?" I asked, baffled.

"Dr. Smith!" she exclaimed. "It didn't strike me until earlier tonight as I was praying for the baby. Dr. Smith is a gynecologist, and worked out of the rear cottage. I checked it out, and Dr. Smith does abortions. I'll bet some were done, or at least advocated on this property!"

Amazing! I thought. But it made sense. At the next couples' group, we shared our story. Together we set the cross between ourselves and Dr. Smith, renounced any killings on our property, offered up the spirits of the aborted children to Jesus, and prayed vigorously against the spirit of "infanticide" in our home and over the group.

Mary slept fine during my next trip and was never bothered again.

This power encounter cleared the way for a truth encounter.

One day midway in the pregnancy, Mary said she felt I was withdrawing emotionally—and I knew she was right.

"Father, help me!" I wrote in my prayer journal. "I don't want to be closed off to my child!"

That night, as Mary and I prayed on our knees at the foot of our bed, I begged God to bring out the truth, and to set me free.

"Lord, I feel so inadequate to be a father," I confessed at last. I wrote down later what I sensed from the Father God in reply: *You're afraid and withdraw because your father was unable to demonstrate confidence in you. But I have confidence in you, that you will surrender and come to me. It's not that you have what it takes to be a father, but that I have what it takes to make you a father. I trust you, my son, that you will come to me and let me teach you, let me father you—and you will father your child with confidence, knowing I am with you.*

"Thank you for your confidence in me, Father!" I said, hesitating. "I want to surrender to you and trust you.

"Still, you know I've never spent much time around children. At my age, I'm afraid I just won't have the patience for a child's crying and fussing all the time."

You will enjoy him, I heard.

Not only did I feel reassured, but the masculine pronoun seized me. I was going to have a *son!*

Later, Mary and I reflected on our relatively old age for childbearing and decided to review the story of the aging Zechariah and Elizabeth:

> But the angel said to him, "Do not be afraid, Zechariah; your prayer has been heard. Your wife Elizabeth will bear you a son, and you are to give him the name John. He will be a joy and a delight to you." (Luke 1:13-14, NIV).

There it was again: "A joy and a delight"—even as I'd heard while praying earlier.

In Hebrew, "John" is "Johannon," meaning "God is gracious." Given my age, the mistakes I'd managed to pack into those years, and the genuinely new life I now felt beckoning in my son—not to mention that Mary's middle name is Elizabeth!—we decided to name our boy John.

Over the next weeks, Mary and I spent much time at the foot of our bed praying. One night, I asked the Father to prepare me for a son by telling me something of his destiny. *He will be a warrior after my own heart,* I sensed. Thus, to John we added "Miguel," the guardian angel over Israel (Jude 9), in Latino form to reflect his maternal ancestry.

To us, John-Miguel is God's grace and his victory.

Learning to Respect the Child

When I see him as a toddler today, engaging life with such headlong openness and delight, I sometimes catch myself worrying, *Lord, how can this carefree, happy little boy ever be a warrior?*

I recall John-Miguel's first major battle at birth—related in the introduction to *Father & Son*—and I have an idea. Then, even as I write this chapter, he contracts a blistering diaper rash and cries out to me, "Daddy, talk to Jesus!"—and I know.

Indeed, I remember with chagrin that this very misconception of my flesh about warriors has prompted God's calling in my life—and this book itself.

This, indeed, is a warrior after the Lord's own heart, not my heart of flesh. He's a Kingdom warrior, a holy soldier set apart from the world's definition—not cold and violent, but boldly engaged with life and joyfully surrendered to Jesus. In his presence, I'm humbled before God, even as a child. My little son—*mi guerrerito*—has prompted a new prayer within me: "Father, draw me close to John-Miguel, and teach me as he grows what it means to be a warrior after your own heart."

As Mary and I continued asking the Lord to prepare us for parenthood, we examined related Old Testament passages and began to understand the roots of Jesus' regard for children. The God of Israel, we realized, reveals himself primarily not in nature or ideas, but in history—in his acts among men and women. Without history, we have no relationship with the true and living God. And without children there's no history.

You don't need children to witness to a god of nature or a god of philosophical principles. The sun and wise insights are nice, but they are no substitute in God's heart for a child. Religions centered about such gods can only have a lower regard for children than those born out of Judaism—just look at the Canaanite nature-worshipers who practiced child sacrifice, or the New Age earth-worshipers today who entertain abortions.

Children, however, witness to the God of history, his committed presence and ongoing power. "You and your children must obey these rules forever," Moses commanded the people of God at the Passover. "When your children ask you, 'What does this ritual mean?' you will answer, 'It is the sacrifice of Passover to honor the Lord, because he passed over the houses of the Israelites in Egypt. He killed the Egyptians, but spared us'" (Exod. 12:24, 26-27).

"The greatest in the kingdom of heaven," Jesus therefore said, "is the one who humbles himself and becomes like this child." The humble child is the gateway to the Kingdom of heaven, the entrance to the "place" where God rules as King. We're thereby enabled to become the men he created us to be.

In order to convict his self-centered, status-seeking disciples, Jesus could've lifted up an old man, a pregnant woman, king, religious leader, or any other likely object of human esteem. But instead, he chose a child.

This is no maudlin, Pollyanna diversion, but a profound statement about the very nature of God himself. The doorway to the heart of the Father God is a humble child. He is the God who not only honors children, but who became a child in a manger. Indeed, he gives us children as an act of blessing and grace—a real-life, historical, one-more-chance opening to his heart.

"The Holy Spirit is like my children," my seminary pastor, Rev. Herb Davis of the Eliot Church of Newton (MA), used to say. "When we're taking a trip in the car, I set my watch and make sure all the kids go to the bathroom before we leave. When we hit the turnpike a few minutes later, I see that open road, click in my cruise control, lean back at last and feel pretty self-satisfied. And just about then, I hear a small voice from the backseat: 'Daddy, I have to go!'"

Children are fundamentally upsetting to those who cling for security to their own controlled agendas—no matter how "religious." A graphic example of children interrupting a religious agenda with God's agenda is when parents brought their children to Jesus to bless them. The disciples, who had their own plans for Jesus, "saw them and scolded them for doing so."

Jesus, however, has his own plan:

> But Jesus called the children to him and said, "Let the children come to me and do not stop them, because the Kingdom of God belongs to such as these. Remember this! Whoever does not receive the Kingdom of God like a child will never enter it." (Luke 18:16-17)

If indeed the Kingdom of God, which we battle to restore, "belongs to" and is thereby reflected in the child, then drawing close to the child becomes a primary training exercise for God's warrior.

The child reminds us of what we're fighting for, when the powers of the world are literally hell-bent to make us forget. That is, the warrior of the flesh fights for his own selfish desires and scoffs, "Let the women take care of the babies and kids."

The Kingdom warrior, however, fights for God's will, against self-centered desires in both himself and in others. To paraphrase Jesus, he proclaims, "Let me be close to the children, and let neither my macho insecurities or anyone else's get in their way, because my Commander-in-Chief has revealed his victory in them!"

If we allow Jesus to bless the child, if we draw close to and respect the child as a legitimate signal to God's kingdom, we will be reminded of God's purposes and restored to his intent. We who have been deceived unto death will rediscover at last the pathway to the Father God and be restored to victorious life in relationship with the Conqueror.

And now quickly: Be wise as a serpent. Think like the Enemy. Do you see?

Of all creatures on earth, the child is the greatest threat to the

Enemy's purposes, and therefore, the relentless focus of his attack—from violent Saturday morning TV cartoons and sexual molestations to abortion and infertility. The Kingdom warrior's primary battle must therefore be to protect, uphold, and usher the child into saving relationship with the Father God.

A man learns this battle insofar as he brings the little boy in himself to Jesus. If he loses touch with this childlike part of himself, he can't be a warrior for the Kingdom of God. If enough men suppress the little boy within their hearts, and consequently, distance themselves from children, the pathway to the Father is lost, along with the world Jesus died to save.

As any father of a two-year-old knows, becoming "like a child" means not only being humble and open, but also expressing your needs and feelings freely. Many men today, however, were essentially scolded and shamed as children with, "You shouldn't feel that way!" In other words, "Big Bompas don't cry."

When Jesus says, "Unless you change and become like children," he's saying, "Unless you stop condemning and honor the part of yourself that longs to be free of shame."

As one Christian writer declares,

> The defiant-sounding "No!" of the two-year-old is not rebellion, but the beginning of the assertion of selfhood. The parent who whacks a two-year-old across the face in response to such a "No!" is not correcting rebellion, but quenching selfhood. The child is not intending to rebel—he or she doesn't even know what rebellion is. A two-year-old "No!" is an expression that "I am!" Since the child is made in the image of I AM, what more appropriate declaration?[1]

Simply teaching a child to obey external authority doesn't equip him for battling the powers of the world. Rather, he must develop an inner sense of what's truly best for him and strength to maintain boundaries that protect that. Another writer, in fact, has declared that an adolescent can't effectively say no to self-destructive practices, like drugs and premarital sex, if he hasn't been free to say no to his parents as a boy.

Certainly you don't have to give in to the boy's every desire, but you must honor him and not cause him to feel ashamed of his impulses and feelings. That's how a boy learns to honor others—even you. When he says *no* you can ask him how he feels about your directive and explain your reasons. He may protest, but if you respect him like that, you can stand by your limits without fear of destroying your relationship.

At the same time, you don't need to be afraid that reconsidering your decision on the merits of his desires and feelings will make him disrespect you. As long as you're honoring his heart and not fearing his rejection, it can be a true gesture of strength and love: "I can see now how important this is to you, Son, and so I'll set aside my plans this time for you."

Honoring the Child in Yourself

Unless a man goes to Jesus for healing Father-input, however, he "fathers" himself the same way his dad did.

Bill, a thirty-five-year-old sales manager, told me his father had been "hard on discipline," and every time he asked for anything fun as a boy, from an ice cream to a movie, the father would automatically snap, "No!"

"That made me feel ashamed for even wanting an ice cream and really shut me down," he sighed. "Today, my wife says I'm a 'wet blanket' most of the time, and she's right. I feel ashamed sometimes for even wanting to have fun. I hate it—I can't seem to let myself—or anyone else—enjoy life!"

Bill was squelching the little boy in his heart just as his dad had done decades earlier.

Realizing this, Bill could see how his father's harshness had affected his attitude toward his own son. "He asked for an ice cream the other day when we were out at the store and I just automatically snapped, 'No!' He cried and told me how good it would taste. He'd eaten a good lunch and I had the money; there really wasn't any reason in the world to deny him that little pleasure.

"In fact, I knew that was Dad's voice saying, 'No'—but I just couldn't stop it."

Bill shook his head in dismay. "I understand why Dad was so tight, coming through the Depression and World War II. I know he wasn't being malicious or anything; his circumstances just forced him to be that way.

"But still, it did hurt me, and I have to deal with that—or I end up hurting my boy, too."

I hesitated. "So . . . did you get the ice cream?"

Bill laughed nervously. "No. After I snapped at him, I was afraid to be inconsistent and back down on my word."

I assured him that from a little boy's perspective—and very likely, God's—any damage done by inconsistency would weigh less than that done by consistently denying his son the joy of simple pleasures. In fact, I suggested the next time that happened, he kneel down and tell his son, "I'm sorry for snapping at you like that. My own daddy did that to me and it hurt me, too. I want you to enjoy [an ice cream], so let's go ahead and have one together."

"Oh, but he can't talk that good," Bill declared. "He wouldn't understand those words."

"But you do," I said. "And if you say them sincerely, he'll catch the spirit of them. In fact, it'd be good for both of you. Your little boy is a gift to you from your Daddy God, partly to give you another chance at being a boy yourself. Show your appreciation by letting your son teach you how to enjoy life."

I smiled and added, "Your wife will be as thankful as you."

We then prayed against a generational history of deprivation and asked the Holy Spirit to open Bill to receive the fullness of the Father's goodness—from ice cream to salvation in Jesus (John 10:10).

Human nature can't understand that the humble, needy, vulnerable—even unprotected—child beckons the rule of God in a man's life, and on earth itself. Yet, to respond to that child is to know the heart of the Father God for ourselves, even as men.

"But I don't know what my son needs from me," many men have told me.

"That's because your father didn't honor your needs as a boy and made you feel ashamed of them," I reply. "What, in fact, did you need as a boy from your own dad?"

Sadly, this question is often met with a long pause.

Long-suppressed pain and anger scream silently in the man who has never given those feelings a voice.

He's forgotten what he needed from Dad because he didn't get it—and may even have been shamed and/or punished for asking. Indeed, he's believed he can never get it and has built a lifestyle of false satisfactions to cover his shame—all of which would have to crumble and fall if he were to face his true and deep need for Dad.

At times I envy my son. At two, he just says out loud what he needs and how he feels about it. Already, however, shades of shame occasionally dart fearfully across his eyes. I pray the Father will keep healing me so I can help my son stay real; as long as he stays in touch with himself, even if he gets a little loud at times, I can always help him learn later how to express his needs and feelings appropriately. A flame can always be stoked or redirected; but once it's out, it's dead.

I've prayed with enough men to know the Holy Spirit can resurrect it—but it usually takes a long, long time.

That's why we tremble when a woman asks, "How do you feel?" It stirs the terrible pain from when our spirits were quenched as boys, and the shame for not being able to know something that any normal human being should—and that most women do.

If I as his father disregard and don't honor my son's needs and feelings, he'll learn to dishonor them himself. Ashamed, he'll suppress them below consciousness, thereby handing them over to the powers of darkness to generate destructive lusts and fantasies. Thus abandoned to his father's feelings and needs, he must abandon himself as an adult to someone else's—and become the classic codependent, always giving to wife, boss, and others, but resentful that no one ever gives to him.

Compliant children often grow up and marry addicts, to re-create the painful but familiar scenario of living with a demanding parent. Accustomed to being at the mercy of other people's agendas, they lack an inner directedness and seek others to direct them.

Without that centeredness, it's hard for a man to hold others accountable. He withdraws from speaking the truth, because he's afraid the other will lash back and hurt/punish him or will speak with the same condemning spirit that invaded him.

Christian psychologist Jim Wilder makes this point powerfully in his insightful *Life Passages for Men*:

> The sign of a complete boy is that he can ask for and receive what he needs with joy and without guilt or shame. While this will appear selfish to some, it is absolutely essential as a foundation for giving as an adult. The one who cannot receive freely cannot give freely.[2]

Furthermore, a man who has lost touch with his own needs and feelings falls prey to the Law, which, like Dad, dictates what he should need and feel—conveniently but tragically obscuring his true and authentic cry for relationship with the Father. As an adult, he either becomes a rigid, religiously correct Christian or rebels and becomes a rigid, politically correct liberal.

Like the warrior of the world, he may grit his teeth and submit to authority, but can't surrender to his true Commander. Indeed, he remains as insensitive to the needs and feelings of others as to his own and thereby forfeits his license to battle in behalf of others.

As Wilder notes, "The problem for those who try to become men without first becoming boys is that they can only give if they are compelled to do so by shame or guilt or fear."[3]

Indeed, the man who hasn't honored the child within himself can't discern his own best interests and becomes a danger both to himself and others:

> Men who do not know how to be boys will fall asleep at the wheel, because they didn't believe they needed sleep. They will believe the billboard that shows a glass of whiskey and the caption: "What a successful executive earns in a day." It

will be a life of pain, as they fail to ask or ask amiss and so fail to receive. As pretenders to the throne, they demand in fear what they would be freely given in love, while they flee the power wielded by those entitled to possess and give.[4]

That is, the man who doesn't honor the child in himself, ultimately withdraws from, and can't manifest the blessing of, his manhood to others.

Having battled thus to overcome his own shame—to save the boy in himself—the Kingdom warrior is now ready to battle in behalf of his own children.

ELEVEN

Battling for the Child:
Honoring Your Son

If anyone should cause one of these little ones to lose his faith in me,
it would be better for that person to have a large millstone tied
around his neck and be drowned in the deep sea. Matthew 18:6

The coyotes go right for the baby lambs. Virginia sheepherder
George Bird[1]

HERE we see the Kingdom warrior's standard for evaluating adult
attitudes and behaviors toward children: Does it undermine, or
does it foster a child's faith in Jesus?

Indeed, Jesus reserved his most fierce lashing for those who
undermine a child's faith in him: They're not just to be tossed
overboard for a slap on the wrist, but weighted down; not just
with something heavy, but "a large millstone"; not just in the
hands, but "around his neck"; not just in the shallows, but "the
deep sea."

Jesus' fury in defense of children compares only with that
against the Pharisees, for hiding their sin behind religious exhortation (Matt. 23). And indeed, his root concern is the same in
both cases: Those who lack relationship with the Father hide

from the shameful truth about themselves—and ultimately crucify those who enjoy relationship with the Father and walk freely in his truth.

Men trapped in false religion don't value children as Jesus does. Children, like Jesus, do not fear the truth; men who do, like the Pharisees, fear children.

In the old fairy tale, a couple of swindling tailors pump the king's ego by promising to make him a magnificent garment. In reality, however, they make nothing, but "present" it to the king with pomp and regal pantomime. The king is ashamed to face the truth that he's been bilked. Everyone else sees the sham but colludes in silence, afraid to make the king look bad. He parades naked around the kingdom—until at last a child upends the impostors' scheme and restores the kingdom to sanity by shouting the truth: "The king has no clothes on!"

The Enemy may pick off a president or king here, a pastor or TV evangelist there. But his most refined, state-of-the-art efforts to deceive and destroy focus on children. If he can deter, distract, undermine, seduce, or otherwise cut the children off from relationship with the Father God, he will have won the battle against the God of history. For the next generation will forget him. Cut off from the Father, they and their families will be utterly defenseless.

The Enemy attacks most deliberately and forcefully at our weak spots. Clearly, the child is the weakest, most vulnerable and impressionable member of the community.

The coyotes go first for the baby lambs.

The Vulnerability of Children

We didn't take John-Miguel out of the house until he was several weeks old, because he had no immunities, no resistance to powers in the world that would harm him. He will need us, in fact, to feed, clothe, and house him, likely for eighteen years.

Even as a seedling needs more attention than a tree, the child is fundamentally dependent and unable to manage life on its own. Those who value independence and self-reliance will therefore fear, pull away from, and even scorn the child, who bears the truth that mocks our adult pride—namely, that we can't manage our lives alone but need God and each other (Rom. 7:24).

German culture, for example, values order and structure based upon self-reliance and hard work—and apparently doesn't affirm the value of children. A *Newsweek* feature titled "Be Kinder to Your 'Kinder'" declares that "Germans' chilly attitude toward children is such an established fact of life that there's even a word for it: *kinderunfreundlich*, or 'child unfriendly.' You quickly learn to keep your kinder out of the way."[2]

Youth minister Angela Merkel of the German Federation for the Protection of Children estimates that nearly a million German children are "severely abused" each year. "It's a scandal," she says. "We Germans treat house pets better than children."

The double-edged sword of truth, however, bears upon America as well. Early in 1994, a Carnegie Corporation study on the developmental requirements of young children was reported in a news feature titled, "It's Bad News for America's Kids": more than 25 percent of American children today are born out of wedlock, one-quarter of mothers get little or no prenatal care, infants are the fastest-growing category of children entering foster care, and one in three victims of physical abuse is a baby.[3]

Noting that "the earliest years of a child's life are society's most neglected age group," the study warned that "the seeds for many of society's future problems take deep and lasting root when the concerns of this age group are overlooked." Indeed, "the children themselves are not quiet, they are crying out for help. But these sounds rarely become sound bites. Babies seldom make the news. They do not commit crimes, do drugs or drop out of school."

The Enemy is destroying our children and thereby claiming our future.

Where are the Kingdom warriors?

We men have valued independence and self-reliance more than dependence and community (see my chapter "Rational and Independent, Faithless and Alone" in *Healing the Masculine Soul*). We tend to withdraw from, and thereby abandon, our children either physically or emotionally, even as we learned from Dad to abandon the dependent boy within ourselves. Abandonment, after all, is the essence of the father-wound both in and through us.

With worldly eyes, we see no strength or dignity in being dependent. Predicating our manhood on the lie of independence, we can only fabricate a false masculinity out of violence and pride. That is, we haven't dared know the Father, and therefore we can't affirm the strength and sonship he gives to men who confess their dependence upon him.

In fact, the child's vulnerability reminds us of when we were vulnerable as boys and were abandoned. The storehouse of pain from that trauma in every man's masculine soul cripples the warrior because it dams the free flow of care, love, and even godly discipline—the kind that doesn't "provoke anger" (Eph. 6:4, RSV)—from our hearts to our children.

Kevin, a twenty-six-year-old father of a six-month-old boy, sought my help one day for "a lot of crazy feelings" toward his son. The boy had begun to cry one day, and Kevin was startled by an intense anger that suddenly flared within him. Immediately, he turned the baby over to his wife, went into their bedroom, and fell on his knees.

"I begged the Father to help me," Kevin said. "'Why in the world,' I asked him, 'would I feel such anger when my son needs me to hold and comfort him? Heal me, Father, so I can give him what he needs from me!'"

When we prayed later, Kevin remembered his mother's telling him years before that he'd cried incessantly as a colicky baby. His older sister was only two, and their father had left the home. The family lived in substandard housing; diapers for two infants had to be washed by hand in the bathtub, with only a line for drying—indoors during the Midwest winter.

At home, the stress became unbearable. Kevin's mother had told him that one night she put him in a rocker-cradle beside the bed "and vowed to rock me until I stopped crying. It took the entire night, almost eight hours—but I finally gave up and fell quiet."

We prayed further, and eventually Kevin sighed. "I don't judge my mother for what she did. Times were awfully tough, and she did an amazing job by herself. But . . ." His voice trailed off into the silence.

I prayed and waited. "But as a father," I finally said, "you dare not deny its very real effects upon you. In fact, your son won't allow you to; just being in his presence triggers the pain and forces you either to act out or get help."

Kevin nodded. "Pushing all that down was bad enough. But then after that I always heard, 'Big boys don't cry' and 'Stop crying, or I'll give you something to cry about!' I guess I just felt ashamed of my pain."

And so Kevin shut down and ostracized the hurting little boy within him, splitting off from his feelings and true self.

"When did you cry last?" I asked.

Keven hung his head, shaking it slowly. "I really can't remember."

He'd lost the child, and with him the gateway to God's Kingdom and any sense of his own calling in it. He could only try his best to do what someone else said was "right," but had no credible inner-core resonance born out of trusting relationship. Unable to trust God to stand with him in his pain, he became fearful of making a mistake and being abandoned, and thereby became vulnerable to false, performance-oriented religion.

His infant son's crying had tapped this painful memory of his own crying unheeded at the same age, suppressed in his heart unto anger. As we prayed further, Kevin begged Jesus to set him free from its effects so he could stand with his son in his own pain. He asked Jesus to hold him as that crying little boy in the crib—and at long last poured out his anger and pain to him.

He enlisted a prayer partner and others to pray for him.

Eventually, Kevin began to cry for his mother and pray fiercely for her. Having dared at last to feel his own pain, he could at last feel his mother's pain in those trying times years ago—and release her the more cleanly from his own natural anger and judgment.

Kevin told me he doesn't feel anger anymore when his son cries. He doesn't have to because he's given his to Jesus. Instead, he feels the boy's hurt—because he's dared to feel his own. He doesn't run away from his son's pain; it doesn't threaten to surface his own and overwhelm him. Because he let Jesus stand with him in his own pain, he can let him stand with his crying son through him.

"Now, I just pick him up and hold him," Kevin told me, smiling. "I pray out loud and ask Jesus for his love and healing."

When a Child Cries

The Father God can use confusing, painful times to draw a father and son into relationship both with each other and with him.

Recently, John-Miguel awoke from his nap while Mary was out of the house a while and began crying hysterically for "Mommy!" I tried a bottle, fresh diaper, and holding him, but could not get his attention to make him stop. In desperation, I tried reciting his favorite nursery rhyme, and he paused.

"Say 'Jesus'!" he sniffled through his tears—almost as if chiding me, "Why are you wasting time talking about all that other stuff? Take me where I can get what I really need." Amazed—and chagrined—I immediately began singing a prayer to Jesus, and soon he fell asleep.

Drawing close to the child, I glimpsed the Kingdom of God.

Indeed, a child's faith in Jesus blazes the trail to God's Kingdom on earth. As a father-warrior, I don't want to cause my child to lose that faith. If he does, I lose the trail, too.

If the essence of faith is trusting that God is present to honor my authentic needs, I am determined to demonstrate such a presence to my son. Sadly, however, many Christian men think that the only way to instill strength of character in a son is by "teaching him independence"—when often that's just abandoning him, even as Dad did to you.

Some Christians, for example, advocate "training" infants to sleep by leaving the baby to cry out alone in successively longer intervals. Yet we learn faith in knowing, "I cry out in need and someone comes." Faith will not come easily therefore to the child who experiences "I cry out and no one comes."

As the psalmist proclaimed,

In my distress I called upon the Lord; to my God I cried for help. From his temple he heard my voice, and my cry to him reached his ears. . . . He bowed the heavens, and came down; thick darkness was under his feet. He rode on a cherub, and flew; he came swiftly upon the wings of the wind. (Ps. 18:6, 9-10, RSV; see also Ps. 99:6)

"But you can't let your baby manipulate you into doing everything his way," advocates counter.

On the contrary, a child learns to manipulate when his needs are *not* met—forcing him to conclude, "No one will hear my direct and honest cry; therefore, my only hope of getting my needs met is to deceive and manipulate."

Significantly, the let-them-cry-it-out program comes packaged in isolated Scriptures, but never the words or character of Jesus. Would Jesus—also named "Emmanuel," that is, "God with Us"—leave a child to cry alone in the night?

Alan, a forty-two-year-old Christian, told me that when his twenty-year-old daughter was just four months old, "Her sin-nature took over and she got it into her mind to run the family by keeping us up all night." Overruling his wife's tearful objections, he insisted that the little baby be left to cry alone at night—"To teach her as soon as possible God's family order: that she's the child and we're the parents."

As we talked later about events that shaped our lives, Alan shared his deep pain from when his daughter had gone "through a rebellious stage" and tried to commit suicide at fifteen.

"I was at work when they called," he said, shaking his head sadly even then, "and raced to the hospital. When I saw her, I threw my arms around her and begged her, 'Oh, honey, please tell me: What in the world's been upsetting you so much? Why didn't you come and talk to me? When did you ever get the idea I wouldn't be there for you?'"

I believe the answer is partly, "In the crib at four months old."

As Mary puts it, "You either stay up nights with them when they're babies, or you stay up when they're teenagers."

Granted, leaving a baby to cry alone doesn't in itself necessarily lead to suicide later. But I believe it leaves children vulnerable to the Enemy by teaching them, in effect, not to cry out for help when later needs arise—and in fact, may dull their sensitivity to where they can't even recognize their needs.

A man who has not been taught to listen to the pain of his own abandonment can't hear it in his child. This technique attracts people who were never taught while growing up to honor their own authentic needs and feelings and who therefore can't honor their children's. The father who was emotionally discounted, and in that sense, taken advantage of as a child, fears being similarly disparaged as an adult. He sees his own child's actions through the distorted lens of his own wounds.

He hides from his own abandonment wounds—and justifies abandoning his own child in turn—by imagining that his baby cries not out of genuine need but, rather, in order to manipulate him. Blinded by his own shame and fear, he sees not a helpless child who needs his love and protection, but rather, a scheming opponent who threatens his authority.

He projects onto his son his own boyhood urge to overrule Dad's authority. Thus, he can't see the difference between a child's whining for another piece of candy and crying alone in the darkness—or between "spoiling" children and simply meeting their genuine needs.

Meanwhile, we're accountable to Jesus not to give or deny the child everything he or she demands but, rather, to uphold the child's faith. Sadly, the average man today doesn't know how to uphold a child's faith, because his own father didn't uphold his.

Like Alan, he's cut himself off from his true needs and feelings so deeply that he can't trust even his wife's anguish and his child's tears more than his fear of losing power. Longing to feel like a man amid shameful self-doubts, desperate to be accepted in a culture of men who have never known godly father-love, he's easily seduced by the false promises of wielding "manly discipline"—and he'll wound his wife and children to get it.

In fact, virtually every couple who espouses the cry-it-out program has told me in a variety of ways, "It tears my heart out to hear our baby crying like that from the other room."

The worldly man, as a fugitive from the truth, discounts that anguish as sentimental—dare we say *female?*—foolishness. I believe, however, that it's the very anguished heart of Father God himself, which he instills in every father for the child's protection.

What tears my heart out, therefore, is knowing that children cry out fearfully at night while the ones they need and trust most lay unmoving across the hall—because I see parents inflicting on their children the destructive wounds of their own childhood and crippling the faith of a generation to come.

When I talk to these parents, I'm strangely reminded of the women I've counseled after abortions—who've been told that they've done no harm to any child, that in fact, it's ultimately for everybody's own good. These women have been lied to, and their aching mother's heart knows it.

But they haven't been taught to honor their own hearts, and so they capitulate to the Enemy's spirit of shame. "My feelings must be wrong," they imagine, "because all the authorities around me—whether 'pro-choice feminists' or 'Christian family experts'—say something else."

"After all, your child must learn reality," many Christian fathers declare. "You have to teach them that in the real world someone doesn't always come running when you cry!"

I agree that a man must teach his child reality. Indeed, that's precisely why Jesus came: to afford us a *more authentic reality* than the world can know—that is, to bear life as Father God intends it, and in that ultimate sense, more accurate than the world's indifference. After all, what is more real: the world's indifference or the Father's enduring love?

We teach best what we know best. And men today know abandonment all too well. The Christian father's job, however, is not to capitulate to the world and inflict children with its abandonment, but rather to surrender to the Father and provide children with his protective, ever-present love—so they can later maintain their faith in Jesus among powers that are hell-bent to destroy it.

Furthermore, the boy who hears his parents say, "I love you" and then watches them leave him alone in the darkness will associate love with abandonment. He learns not independence, but codependence—a false and addictive "love" for others who similarly discount his needs and abandon him.

"But you are the adults, who have the authority in the home, and you need your sleep," these Christians uniformly protest. "You can't let your child run your life."

Is this not the same rationale for abortion, translated from, "No child will interfere with my right to live as I please"?

Authority in the Kingdom of God is not to arrogate power and privilege over the weaker members, but to serve them (Matt. 20:25-28).

A Call to Arms

Mary and I have not slept a full night since our son was born two and a half years ago. I want to sleep, and I want my family to sleep, as much as anyone. But more than that, I want my son to learn faith in Jesus. I consider that to be my sacred responsibility to him as his father and to the Father God as his warrior.

We've prayed over and again for wisdom when John-Miguel awakes crying at night. In praying as well with numerous others for confirmation, I have no sense that he has sought to manipulate us with his tears, but rather, that he is hurting and afraid.

Immediately after his traumatic birth (see the introduction to *Father & Son*) the doctors suspected he had an infection. In our exhaustion, we unwisely allowed them to take him away from Mary off and on for two days in order to treat him. It turned out he had no infection, and other doctors we consulted later criticized our original doctor's decision. The Lord showed us later John-Miguel's fear of abandonment from that separation experience, and we've prayed nightly for the Father's security and peace to replace that in his heart.

The fact that praying and singing to Jesus has settled him down, since before he could talk or understand what that name meant, suggests that in crying out at night, he is at times responding to an attack from the Enemy—who knows full well the name of Jesus (Mark 1:23-24). Certainly we knew from his conception that as a Christian child he would be a threat to the Enemy, and thereby would be subject to such attacks—especially while sleeping at night, when everyone's defenses are down.

At times he's cried out for his mother at night, and I've decided Mary must have rest. I've gone to him myself, and he has protested and cried. I tell him Mommy needs rest, that Daddy is with him and won't leave him alone. And I hold him as he cries, singing often about Jesus until he eventually nods off.

We keep praying and keep getting up. Most Christian men— like Alan—leap to admonish me that it's my manly responsibility to be decisive, overrule my wife's feelings, and protect her by "being realistic" and letting my son "cry it out."

Meanwhile, we believe our approach is fully in accord with the Scriptures and the character of the Father God who gave them. At times we sadly take refuge among non-Christian friends, who often seem less concerned about being right and more willing to be real about a child's deepest needs.

Mary bears the bulk of this nighttime work. It takes a toll on her and gives us less time together. But we agree that we don't want John-Miguel to cry alone at night. My cooperation and support for her is therefore essential. When I can't take over at night, either because I have professional responsibilities or John-Miguel won't settle down without her, I pray, "Father, how can I support Mary in some other way?"

Sometimes, for example, I get her flowers, take her out to dinner, surprise her with thank-you/love notes, give her time alone or with friends by taking John-Miguel with me Saturdays, Sundays after church, or early mornings. Still, I recognize I could do more—but can never really do enough; there's no way to compensate for such a mother's true labor of love.

Meanwhile, the fruit of our battling—even against our own tired flesh!—is a toddler who not only asks me to pray to Jesus for him, but is beginning to do so himself now as I hold and encourage him. Our willingness to both pray and walk through his nighttime cries seems to have fostered within him a genuine, growing faith in Jesus.

Discipline through Trust

My brothers, we're at war. The battle is intensifying to where the next generation will be attacked with a vengeance and fury beyond anything we or our fathers could've imagined.

I remember as a high school freshman in 1960 seeing a girl's knee—and excitedly telling the other boys about it later in P.E. Today, virtually naked women leer from highway billboards and TV commercials.

We must do everything we can now to prepare our children for the struggle that lies before them.

As Jesus demonstrated on the cross, winning at Kingdom warfare requires great sacrifice. The stakes are high, and the battle for the child is paramount. Like any other war, it can't be won by men who allow the desires of their flesh to rule them— even the desire to sleep.

"Why are you sleeping?" Jesus demanded of his disciples as he sweat blood the night before he was crucificed. "Get up and pray that you will not fall into temptation" (Luke 22:46)—that is, to believe that our adult desires are so much more important than children's needs.

Fathering in this present age is for warriors. It's not for men who would rather sleep through the night, read their newspaper uninterrupted, wear a shirt more than once without getting it cleaned, have a cheerful, attentive, and alluring wife twenty-four hours a day—or otherwise control their own lives and mediate their own pleasures.

Tell me you know it's not the best for your children to let them cry alone at night, but it's just too hard for you to get up again and again, night after night. Believe me, I can sympathize. I'll pray for you and your children. I'll weep with you.

But don't tell me that letting your son cry himself to sleep is the Christian way.

Rather than impose some order out of my own desires—like the disciples who told the children not to bother Jesus—I want to discern and meet my child's genuine needs. I figure that's the price of parenthood. I don't want to control my child so that his mother and I may enjoy order, but rather, to help him develop trust so that later he might have faith in Jesus and thereby enjoy Father God's order.

Dr. William Sears, Christian pediatrician for over twenty years and father of eight children, has written numerous best-selling books, several along with his wife Martha, a pediatric nurse. A bold and noteworthy exception to most Christian child-care writers, Sears declares that godly discipline seeks not simply to change immediate behavior, but to help the child "operate from a set of inner controls rather than external force."

Such lasting, inner transformation requires a "connected" relationship with the parent:

> Discipline is not something you do to a child. It is something you do with a child. . . . The connected child desires to please. Discipline is a relationship between parent and child that can be summed up in one word—trust. The child who trusts his authority figure is easier to discipline.

"Discipline," Sears concludes, "begins as a relationship, not a list of methods."[4]

Indeed, that's how God does it. He begins with relationship by demonstrating his trustworthiness: He loves us and saves us. And then, at last, he says, "Let me show you how I designed you to function" (Exod. 20:1ff.). After the Exodus from Egypt to the Promised Land, therefore, God gave his people the Law. But the mere "external force" of the Law made us forget the trusting relationship that made us want to keep it.

And so the Father made the ultimate sacrifice—and demonstrated conclusively that we can trust him—by sending Jesus as a New Covenant through which to "put my law within them and write it on their hearts" (Jer. 31:31-34).

If the goal is to change the child's immediate behavior, then the punishment of the Old Covenant will work fine. But if it's to draw the child into eternal relationship with the Father, then the self-sacrificing love of the New Covenant must prevail.

Punishment forces the child to do what someone else wants; discipline enables him to do what's best for him—understanding that ultimately he wants to do the right thing, but can't on his own (Rom. 7:18). Punishment requires a big stick; discipline, a big heart. Punishment sets father against son; discipline requires Dad to come alongside the boy with love and encouragement.

The average man today, however, has learned rules and not relationship from his father—even as his father and grandfather before him. He knows what it's like to be set against Dad, but not to have Dad walk alongside him in difficult choices. Like ancient Israel, the Law's fear of making a mistake has overshadowed his needs and precluded relationship with Dad.

Only sacrificial love, from the heart of the Lawmaker, can resurrect that memory in himself and thereby restore the next generation to the relationship that fosters "inner controls." We men today must therefore receive and appropriate Jesus' sacrifice for us and in turn make godly sacrifices for our sons.

For me, that means giving up my ego, confessing my inadequacy, trusting the Father God's grace, and pressing on to let him father me so that I may learn thereby how to father my son.

I'm still learning.

But I've learned enough by now to be troubled by much Christian teaching on "child discipline" today, the bulk of which focuses primarily on obedience—just like most teaching to men. This approach comes from men who never learned to trust their fathers with their brokenness. Unlike that of Dr. Sears, such teaching rarely uses the word *trust*. Rather, like the above-mentioned Alan, it presumes a power struggle, pits parent against child, and relies ultimately upon corporal punishment to enforce the parent's authority.

Under the New Covenant, the locus of authority is in relationship, not law. It's the difference between "I don't want you to do that" and "Don't do that, or else!"

"But," you may protest, "your son has a sin-nature that you as his father must confront."

Absolutely; I see it all too often.

But how does Jesus demonstrate that God overcomes our inborn sin-nature?

The Cross offers a hint: He did not come with a whip.

I don't want my son's sin-nature to rule him—or me. As a Christian, however, I serve a different Kingdom than the world, and therefore I relate to power differently from men surrendered to the world. I don't want to offer my son punishment that scares him into obedience. The Enemy can do that. Rather, I want to give him a relationship with me that builds his faith in Jesus. I haven't got time, therefore, for courses on "biblical parenting" that simply teach "How to Make Your Child Obey You." Give me, rather, a Christian course on "How to Earn Your Child's Trust."

That's what Father God did for me through the Cross.

That's his way to overcome human sin-nature.

If a father's love teaches a boy to want God's best for himself, how then does a father most convincingly demonstrate love for his son?

Father God answered that question on the cross. "But God has shown us how much he loves us," as the apostle Paul put it. "It was while we were still sinners that Christ died for us!" (Rom. 5:8). A father most effectively sacrifices his pride in his son's behalf, therefore, when the boy is "wrong."

In his jolting *Spare the Child: The Religious Roots of Punishment and the Psychological Impact of Physical Abuse*—a book that should be required reading for every Christian father—Philip Greven notes that nineteenth-century evangelist Dwight Moody "had been whipped as a boy," but did not whip his own children. As Moody's son William wrote later, "In his home, grace was the ruling principle and not law, and the sorest punishment of a child was the sense that the father's loving heart had been grieved by waywardness or folly."

As a boy, Moody's son Paul had a friend visiting him one evening. When bedtime approached, Moody told Paul to bid his friend goodnight. Returning moments later, he found the boys still at play and "commanded" the boy to go to bed. As Paul recalled,

> I retreated immediately and in tears, for it was an almost unheard-of thing that he should speak with such directness or give an order unaccompanied by a smile. But I had barely

gotten into my little bed before he was kneeling beside it in tears and seeking my forgiveness for having spoken so harshly.[5]

Paul never forgot. In fact, he came to see how his father's humility and honesty shaped his faith:

Half a century must have passed since then and while it is not the earliest of my recollections, I think it is the most vivid, and I can still see that room in the twilight and that large bearded figure, the great shoulders bowed above me, and hear the broken voice and the tenderness in it.

I like best to think of him that way. Before then and after I saw him holding the attention of thousands of people, but asking the forgiveness of his unconsciously disobedient little boy for having spoken harshly seemed to me then and seems to me now a finer and a greater thing and to it I owe more than I owe to any of his sermons. For to this I am indebted for an understanding of the meaning of the Fatherhood of God, and a belief in the love of God had its beginnings that night in my childish mind.[6]

Unlike Moody, most Christian fathers today seem obsessed with upholding roles and ensuring that the child not "get the upper hand." Could this reflect a boyhood anger at Dad for being passive, as in, "I'm not going to let myself get pushed around like Dad did"? Or indeed, could it reflect an abiding fear—such as Moody resisted—of disobeying Dad by not punishing your own son as he did? That is, "I want to be a man like Dad, so I'd better do what he did. After all, I'm still alive; it didn't hurt me all that much."

I wonder: When Dad sets up relationship with his son from infancy as over-and-against each other, does that not ensure that the boy's natural rebellious urges will become destructive?

Father God declared in closing his Old Covenant that he would "turn the hearts of the fathers to their children, and the hearts of the children to their fathers; or else I will come and strike the land with a curse" (Mal. 4:6, NIV). Whatever its source, this father-vs-child approach to discipline among men today beckons God's curse and not the blessing of his ministry among us in Jesus. Its jockeying for a power advantage beckons punishment as a means of establishing your authority and forcing obedience—as if the child had no desire whatsoever to please the father, or any willingness to trust the father's judgment.

Or indeed, as if—contrary to what Jesus said—the child and the Kingdom of heaven were utterly incompatible.

Again, I hear the common rationalization, "But you've got to teach him the way things are in the real world."

On the contrary, as a Christian father, I do not want to teach my son power plays and fear. The world will teach him that very well all by itself when he's out there beyond my embrace—or indeed, when he becomes man enough to face its brokenness in himself.

Rather, I want to teach him what Father God has taught me—what the world can never teach him, and indeed, what he must learn if he is to defeat the world—enduring faith in Jesus. As John declared, "Every child of God is able to defeat the world. And we win the victory over the world by means of our faith. Who can defeat the world? Only the person who believes that Jesus is the Son of God" (1 John 5:4-5).

I want to to build a relationship with my son that demonstrates that in the company of men surrendered to Jesus he has a safe place, an emotional sanctuary set apart from the ruthless powers of the world. I want to be a place where he's not only accountable for his sins, but loved, afforded mercy and healing, and called as a son to battle alongside Jesus and other men for the Father's Kingdom (John 16:33; 2 Cor. 2:14).

My little boy has a very strong will, which I respect as a gift from God. He's a warrior. The battle in this world against God's Kingdom is fierce, and the Enemy devours weak-willed men. As his father, I don't want to break his will, but rather, to show him the true victory that comes in surrendering it to Jesus. I've only been a father for a few years, but that's long enough to know how hard, if not impossible, that is to do. And so I pray for the Father's wisdom constantly.

But if I break his will by abandoning, shaming, hitting, or otherwise coercing him into "obedience," he cannnot know the fulfillment and joy of truly wanting to follow Jesus out of his own, heartfelt longing.

A faith based on anything less simply won't endure the coming onslaught.

Threats, coercion, and fear mark the Enemy's game. His power to employ such weapons successfully is far greater than mine and will sooner or later overpower and subvert any fear-driven will in my son to obey my commands—or even God's. My unique authority in John-Miguel's life as his father is to mediate the Father God's love to him—something the Enemy can never do.

I've heard men say, "The Bible says to use the rod." Indeed, as others have noted, the shepherd doesn't use his rod punitively, to beat the sheep, but lovingly, to draw them out of danger and back into the safety of the fold. The warrior-king David did not sing, "Thy rod and thy staff terrify me into obedience," but rather, "Even if I go through the deepest darkness, I will not be afraid, Lord, for you are with me. Your shepherd's rod and staff protect me" (Ps. 23:4).

Thus, John declared, "There is no fear in love; perfect love drives out all fear. So then, love has not been made perfect in any one who is afraid, because fear has to do with punishment" (1 John 4:18).

Again, this by no means relieves me of the responsibility to teach my son boundaries that ensure his own safety and respect the dignity of others.

Suppose your little boy were to pick up a baseball bat for the first time and hit a ball far across the yard through a window. You wouldn't punish him; he's just naively trying out his stength. You wouldn't tell him, "You're no good at hitting," and never give him a baseball again. Sure, you'd make sure he fixed the window—but then you'd take him out to a field and help him develop his skill properly by showing him how to do it even better.

Every little boy I've seen who has been taught to honor his

feelings seems naturally to have a bold curiosity, a readiness to reach out and test his limits—to shout in the kitchen at the top of his lungs just to see what it sounds like, to throw himself laughing against someone five times his weight and yell, "Daddy, wrestle!"—or even, "No!"

These are the precious stirrings of masculinity, the stuff of which warriors are made and for which this broken world cries out to be refined and matured. It begs for a father to notice, encourage, and focus properly. It's appropriate to tell your boy, "You've got a strong voice. But it hurts other people in the house, so let's do it only outside"—instead of, "Stop yelling so loud!"

You don't have to abandon your son who says, "No!" and punish him for insubordination. You just have to engage him in relationship. Then you can stand with him in his upset and say, "You don't want to do what Daddy says, do you?" You can allow him to respond, and then either adjust your plan accordingly or explain to him why it's important to do as you've told him, and stick by it.

When a father kills such impulses by punishing the boy to break his will—spanking him or shaming him with "You're a bad boy!"—God grieves, because he's losing a warrior. Only the Father God can heal such a wound in a boy and resurrect such masculine strengths in the man—and it takes a long, long time.

I don't want my son to spend those years in Father God's hospital, but rather, in his barracks.

If I were in any way to break my son's will in order to gain the short-term goal of obedience or "respect"—to accommodate my will or even God's—I would answer to God for crippling his warrior and thereby serving the Enemy. The battle we face today requires warriors who have surrendered their will to God for their own good; boys who have been shamed or otherwise coerced into "doing God's will" most often rebel and join the Enemy when they leave the church or home where God's will is valued.

I am therefore determined to do what I can to make my son even more strong-willed in the future. If the price for that now is some upset to my ordered ego, more time and energy required to reconcile our differences, may God help me to pay it.

His battle ahead requires it.

Certainly, at times he wants to do things that are either not good for him or the rest of the family, and I draw limits on his behavior. I tell him he can't do it and explain why not. In response, he may reject my explanation, cry, and run around demanding his way. I don't begrudge him his feelings. He's free to get angry and disagree.

Sure, it tires me out sometimes. But it doesn't diminish my authority.

I tell him I understand he's angry we can't do it his way. But we're still going to have to do it Daddy's way this time, and he'll have to trust me on this for now. I promise him that, as soon as we can, we'll find a way to do something that he'd like to do.

Again, as with those who let their infants cry alone, I hear as a means of justifying spankings and whippings almost exclusive reference to Old Testament texts—often by the same men who are otherwise quick to point out how the New Testament supercedes the Old, and indeed, differs precisely in promoting the love rather than the fear of God.

Listen to the story:

> Some people brought children to Jesus for him to place his hands on them, but the disciples scolded the people. When Jesus noticed this, he was angry and said to his disciples, "Let the children come to me, and do not stop them, because the Kingdom of God belongs to such as these. I assure you that whoever does not receive the Kingdom of God like a child will never enter it." Then he took the children in his arms, placed his hands on each of them, and blessed them. (Mark 10:13-16)

I'll stack that text up against anything the Old Covenant can offer.

Law and Grace in Parenting

In *Spare the Child,* Philip Greven suggests that our readiness as fathers to strike our sons explains why we men grow up so ready not only to tolerate but to perpetrate violence in our culture.[7]

A boy picks up his moral cues from Dad: "Dad hits me when he doesn't like what I've done. Therefore, men resolve differences by violence. If Dad did it, it's OK. I can hit people myself, especially when I think they've done wrong and therefore deserve it."

Often, a boy who's been spanked won't respond later to love, but only to more spanking. The Law, that is, has supplanted the Spirit within him. God's story of Israel says clearly that a son lost in the Law can be restored to appreciate and respond to relationship with the Father only through crucifixion.

In this case, that might mean the father's dying to his pride and asking the child's forgiveness, then begging Jesus to show him whatever brokenness in himself has led him to resort to the Law, and how to become hospitable again to his Spirit's rule.

Don, a senior executive in his late fifties with two grown sons, balked as I shared these views—until I asked him if he'd hit his sons when they were younger.

"Actually," he said, "I did once in a while . . . in the beginning." Smiling thinly, he paused and looked away, knitting his brow, then added, "Until I stopped."

I waited a moment. "What happened?" I asked finally.

With a deep breath, he turned back to me. "This sounds so foolishly simple, but one day when Barry was about ten and Cal was twelve, I heard them yelling at each other out back. I got there in time to see Cal haul off and punch Barry.

"When I saw Barry lying there on the ground, I was so mad at Cal, I grabbed him by the shoulder and hit him really hard, a couple of times, on his shoulder, knocking him down. I stopped, and suddenly I saw both of my boys lying there hurting—kind of like one of those frozen frames in the movies. Somehow, it struck me then: How could I tell a boy it's wrong to hit someone, and then do exactly the same thing myself?"

Don lowered his eyes.

"I felt confused, and . . . really didn't know what to do. All I knew was I had to show my boys some other way to handle their differences, or they'd grow up getting into stuff like that with other guys, and probably even their own sons.

"I fumbled around and told both boys I was sorry I'd set the wrong example for them, that I didn't want them to hit each other, that it just makes things worse in the long run."

Shrugging his shoulders, Don looked up and sighed. "I never hit either of them again. Sure, we had our natural share of run-ins after that, and I stuck by certain limits on their behavior. I can't say that we worked everything out just fine all the time—but I just did my best to talk it out with them."

I had to ask. "Do your sons spank their kids today?"

Don smiled broadly, with a hint of pride. "No," he said, "they don't."

My brother-reader: If this chapter is half as hard for you to accept as it's been for me to write, then I know you're struggling with it—or even against it.

I invite you: Keep struggling.

With me.

With all of us who, like our fathers in their time, long to give our sons what we never received ourselves.

With all of us who don't know how to do it, but are beginning to know who does it.

One thing is sure: The brokenness among us men today is deeper and the battle we face is more demanding than ever before. If it's tough for us now, it's going to be even tougher for our sons.

As Kingdom warriors, we must begin to pioneer new frontiers of faith—honoring our fathers for what God gave us through them, and pushing on to deeper healing in our own time. Like our biblical forebears who boldly set out into the wilderness toward the Promised Land, we must trust anew the God who promises sustenance "which neither you nor your fathers had known" (Deut. 8:3, NIV).

We're all learning.

I certainly hope that I can look back a year from now and see things I'd do differently. That's called "growth." Only mercy and grace makes it possible; without it, I'd either shut down in remorse, or stonewall my mistakes behind elaborate rationalizations—and shut down my son.

I could never have written this chapter before my own son was born. Years ago, even as I taught around the country on the father-wound, friends told me, "You'll never really understand God's love for you until you become a father yourself."

They were right. If the Father God loves me only as much as I love my son, I'm home free. And yet, I know he loves my son even more than I do.

Finding Manhood in Fathering

Even in closing this chapter shortly after my son's second birthday, I find myself angry. As a man, I feel as if I've been lied to, even cheated out of a supreme pleasure virtually my entire adult life.

My previous experience, from Peace Corps to pastoring, had prepared me for the hard work of fathering—the dirty diapers, sleepless nights, pruned social life, Di-Gel dinners, and sex fasts.

But I was not prepared for the joy. I suspect that's why God had to tip me off to it, as he did for Zechariah.

When your little son, sitting in your lap at breakfast as you squint at a newspaper spotted with oatmeal, turns suddenly and announces, "I like my daddy!" you know "the Lord's unfailing love and mercy still continue, fresh as the morning, as sure as the sunrise" (Lam. 3:22-23).

You know you've been redeemed. And when he bumps his head and cries, "Daddy, talk to Jesus!" you know why.

Why was I not told about such joy in being a father?

The answer, clearly, is that we men have not learned to value the child.

True, my dad told me I'd miss out on one of life's greatest adventures if I never became a father myself. I can now say he was right. I'm grateful for that fatherly word.

But never in all my adult travels did any other older man tell me even that much about being a father—neither while studying at the very finest universities, attending churches of virtually every denomination, listening to politicians of every stripe, or reading the most esteemed authors.

From cereal boxes to sermons, various men told me that

nothing in this world is more satisfying than winning a ball game, having sex with a woman, making money, succeeding profession- ally, serving the poor, praying in tongues, reading the Bible.

Each of those activities can be very good. But never in my fifty years did an older man tell me the truth: No life experience makes you feel more like a man, more in touch with God's very heart, more determined to battle for his Kingdom, and thereby, more genuinely alive than being a father.

I've been ripped off. It's only been a few years since my son was born, but that's long enough to catch on.

I rage, I rage—until at last, I weep.

Because in my heart, I know the tragic truth: My older broth- ers have not lied to me. They've only told me what they genu- inely believed to be true, out of their own brokenness.

At a 1994 conference on healing at the Anaheim (CA) Vine- yard Christian Fellowship, author Francis MacNutt taught on reconciliation between Christians. He closed by bringing to the altar representatives from various churches—from a Catholic priest to an African American woman pastor—to sit barefoot before basins of water.

He then invited anyone who had judged and thus hindered God's workings in and through any of these groups to come forward, wash the representative's feet, and ask forgiveness.

The congregation waited as MacNutt introduced each repre- sentative standing in a line across the altar and then turned to give them instructions. A friend of mine who was there described for me the remarkable scene which then unfolded.

Suddenly, quietly, a boy of perhaps ten walked up onto the altar and stood at the far end of the line. When the adult representatives had been introduced and received their instruc- tions, MacNutt began to call the congregation forth.

"Who's the boy?" someone interrupted, shouting from the congregation.

Puzzled, the line turned to see, along with the thousands of others. A separate children's program was in progress elsewhere, and presumably only adults were present in the sanctuary. The adult in line nearest the boy leaned down and asked him what he was doing there. The boy whispered a reply and, telephone-game style, the representatives relayed the message back to MacNutt, who repeated it in the microphone: "The Lord told me to come up."

No more was said, and soon lines formed in front of the adult representatives. For some time, the boy simply sat there alone.

Eventually, several present began to understand.

And then, one man went forward. He knelt before the boy to wash his feet and ask his forgiveness for having discounted children and thereby their witness to God's kingdom.

Lord Jesus, bring us the truth that sets us free! Teach us to know the Father, so we can honor the child, even the child within us all.

We have honored ourselves like men and welcomed the Enemy.

Lord Jesus, teach us to humble ourselves like a child, so we can welcome you.

Amen! Come, little boy!

Amen! Come, Lord Jesus!

TWELVE

Weeping Warrior

*I am worn out with grief; every night my bed is damp from
my weeping; my pillow is soaked with tears. I can hardly see;
my eyes are so swollen from the weeping caused by my enemies.
Keep away from me, you evil men! The Lord hears my weeping;
he listens to my cry for help and will answer my prayer. My enemies
will know the bitter shame of defeat; in sudden confusion they
will be driven away. Psalms 6:6-10*

Jesus wept. John 11:35

HUMAN nature doesn't associate crying with warriors, whom we
imagine instead as stoic and unfeeling, focused only on getting
the job done. But if Jesus' job—and therefore, his warriors'
battle—is to reestablish God's kingdom authority in the world,
then we must begin to allow weapons our human authority can't
affirm.[1]

The notion of crying as a weapon must therefore be redeemed
from the notion of "manipulation." The issue becomes confusing
for Christians when a televangelist like Jimmy Swaggart is

caught with a prostitute, weeps penitently on TV, and is caught with yet another prostitute soon thereafter.

By definition, spiritual weapons are designed to achieve God's purposes and not our own. As the apostle Paul declared,

> It is true that we live in the world, but we do not fight from wordly motives. The weapons we use in our fight are not the world's weapons but God's powerful weapons, which we use to destroy strongholds. We destroy false arguments; we pull down every proud obstacle that is raised against the knowledge of God; we take every thought captive and make it obey Christ. (2 Cor. 10:3-5)

We manipulate when we fear losing control over another and being hurt. In that sense, Swaggart manipulated. He used crying to mask the truth of his sexual addiction—to control people's judgment and protect himself from being shamed. As Christians, however, our task is to lay at the Cross our own human impulse to control others in order to save ourselves, and let Jesus—"God Saves" in Hebrew—control the situation.

But for most men, the problem is not using tears to manipulate others, but rather withholding tears to control ourselves.

Tears, in fact, are occasioned by lack of control: If you could control others, they wouldn't be able to hurt you in the first place. Thus, human nature says, "Fortify your defenses; don't dare open up and cry!"

No human response causes us to let go of our defenses more completely than heartfelt crying. Therefore no response so hospitably invites the power of God, and thereby threatens the Enemy.

The question "When did you cry last?" can indicate how much you've sold out to the world and its compulsion to seize control apart from God. When I was nearly thirty, someone asked me this, and I couldn't recall. Today, I'd respond, "Do you mean, 'When did I cry this morning?' 'When this afternoon?' or 'When this evening?'"

Holding on to my pain takes more energy than I've got to spare in my fifties.

A man who's dared face his own wounds won't withdraw from others who are wounded—not even from Jesus, wounded on the cross and grieving even today for this broken world (Heb. 7:25; 9:24).

Because God hurts for his children (Jer. 8:21), the closer you draw to God, the more you can feel his hurt for others. Whatever situation in the world prompts you to cry can indicate the Father's call to ministry in you.

When we left our church in Los Angeles, for example, the senior pastor prayed for our family at the altar on Sunday, "We release Gordon and Mary now to new occasions for you to break their hearts for your kingdom." On the way home that afternoon, Mary remarked, "You know, it's true. When I started my ministry here as a counselor years ago, I always used to cry for my clients. But that's stopped. Now when I cry, it's usually for John-Miguel's hurts and needs, or just for what a blessing he is."

That realization confirmed Mary's sense that indeed God had called her to a new ministry, from counseling adults to mothering and ministering to children. After Mary's experience, I prayed "Father, give me a piece of your broken heart for this world, and show me whose pain you're leading me to minister to."

I realized myself later that I had wept for the church and parishioners while pastoring there, but that had stopped. My tears now were for John-Miguel and the wounded men at my conferences—often prompted as I wrote my books. Thus, God confirmed that he had called me from pastoring to fathering, conference ministry, and writing.

To a young man anxious to be regarded as "manly" by virtue of his own strength, tears bring shame. To a maturing man, determined to know the truth his pride has hidden, tears free him from shame at last.

Stuffed Pain, Pent-up Tears

Still, it's not easy to undo a lifelong pattern of repressing your tears, and most of us as we age struggle with mixed feelings about crying. Studying Spanish years ago in my twenties, I memorized part of a poem titled, "Juventud" ("Youth"):

> *Juventud, divino tesoro*
> *Ya te vas para no volver;*
> *Quando quiero llorar, no lloro,*
> *Y a veces, lloro sin querer.*
> (Youth, divine treasure
> So quickly you go, never to return;
> When I want to cry, I don't,
> And at times, I cry without wanting to)

One grace of aging is that you no longer have the energy to stuff your pain down. Mature men, virtually by definition, are determined to use their energy more constructively than in suppressing reality.

At the same time, your own will can't easily dismantle defenses that it constructed years ago. Because we learn well to fortify our defenses in proportion to the threat, often the dam within us is broken not by frontal assault of great tragedy or confrontation—which may only prompt stronger defenses—but rather, by disarming acts of kindness and love.

Thirty-two-year-old Gregory Withrow, for example, testified recently before a California Senate Judiciary Committee hearing about his former life as a "skinhead" organizer of the racist Aryan Youth Movement. "The only emotions I knew before were hate and fear," he said.

Neither exhortations to righteousness nor stiff legal injunctions persuaded Withrow to renounce his violent bigotry. He simply met his fiancée. "This woman showed me love," he said, "and that is why I decided to drop out."[2]

Withrow's former fellow skinheads very likely learned as boys themselves the rejection that they wield against others. Never taught to value themselves, they must devalue others in order to fabricate a self-worth by comparison. All that adds up to deep pain in a man, the kind that only affirming love can reach.

I suspect that most of us men learn to cry from a woman rather than a man—even as boys many heard Dad say, "Stop crying or I'll give you something to cry about!" Such threats teach a boy not to trust the man with his pain, but to go instead to Mom, the woman for safety and comfort.

Dad's job, however, is to reveal the Father God's heart to his son—that is, to give him something to rejoice about in a world that already offers far more to cry about than any one man can bear.

Too many men have learned from Dad to suppress their pain and tears—and not simply by example.

Jay, at thirty-six, had achieved many awards for hard work on the job but had no close male friends and only broken relationships with women. "Dad used to whip me hard as a boy," he told me. "I cried at first, but after a while I decided I wasn't about to give him the satisfaction of seeing he could hurt me like that. So I just stopped crying, no matter how hard he hit me.

"Once, I remember he took out his belt and hit me so hard I had bruises for weeks after. It was all I could do to grit my teeth and hold back the tears. But I guess my pride and hatred of him was stronger than my pain, because I didn't let out a drop. He finally threw his belt down in disgust and stomped out."

"And so," I offered poignantly, "you won."

Indeed, Jay had won at his dad's game but lost his masculine soul. Filled with hatred and all alone, he dropped his eyes as his boyhood tears shoved against the prison bars of his heart.

Believing that "real men don't cry" has cost us men dearly. It's cut us off from our own selves, from others, and from God. For God's warriors, the consequences are especially grave.

The weeping willow bends and survives the storm intact; the hard oak cracks and falls.

When you hold back genuine tears, you refuse to trust Jesus and give him your pain. Human nature is simply too self-centered to facilitate godly resolution, and in repressing your pain into the darkness you offer it to the Enemy to use against you. Often a man thinks he's nobly mastering his pain by shoving it down, but in fact, he's just treating himself the way he was treated as a boy.

It's a vicious cycle that only Jesus can break.

A friend with a three-year-old son told me that they'd recently invited for dinner another family with a ten-year-old named Judy. His son quickly began tagging after Judy, who showed a genuine, friendly interest in her toddler protégé. During dessert, my friend told his son that Judy would have to go home after dinner.

Minutes later, the boy began pounding on his plate with a spoon and shouting meaningless phrases. After all polite requests to stop proved fruitless, the wife ordered the boy off to his bedroom alone, and he ran off defiantly, slamming the door.

"I could hear him pounding on something," my friend said, "and after a while, I got so frustrated I decided to go in and show him who's boss. Before I opened his door, I managed to get ahold of myself enough to ask Jesus for help. When I went in and saw him, kind of huddled against the wall, somehow I just knew I was missing the mark.

"I sat down beside him and prayed some more. 'You're pretty angry, aren't you?' I said. He just sat there, kind of stone-faced.

"And then it struck me. 'Are you sad that Judy's going home?' He looked at me and snapped *no* so angrily, I knew I was on to something. I began saying over and over to him, 'Are you sad that Judy's going home?' He kept saying no, and I thought maybe I'd made a mistake. But finally, he broke down and just bawled. 'I don't want her to go!' he said, crying and crying.

"The upshot is, a few minutes later, we were all back at the table having a great time chatting. When Judy finally left with her family, he said good-bye with a big smile—and went on with his business."

I remember once when I said something that hurt John-Miguel's feelings, and he cried. I knelt down, held him, and said I was sorry. Before long, we were laughing and playing together again. "I'm worried," I said to Mary that night. "Do you think he'll carry that wound around?"

"As long as he can cry, he'll be OK," she said. "It's when he doesn't cry that we need to worry."

Heartfelt tears can melt walls of defense and allow the Father to enter a man's heart.

I remember the first time I cried with Mary.

Our courtship was as terrifying for me as it was glorious. I knew she loved me and that I loved her. Many others had prayed and confirmed my sense that the Father had brought her to me as an immeasurable gift of grace.

Even before we met, others had said what a powerful ministry team we'd make. Predictably, as soon as I asked her to marry me, the Enemy attacked with a vengeance, focusing on my deeply rooted defenses from past wounds.

The more I allowed myself to want Mary's love, the more frightened I became that I wouldn't get it, which made me feel ashamed and afraid to talk. This fear urged me instead either to run or to control her—but I was determined to stay, and I treasured her love precisely because it came unsolicited from her heart.

Over and again I prayed, begging Jesus to open me up to receive the gift he was giving me. Yet, even as the wedding approached, I was losing weight and racked with tension and back pain in an effort to bear my feelings.

The morning I picked Mary up to get the wedding rings, I knew I no longer had the emotional or physical energy to hold my feelings down. When she met me at her apartment door with purse in hand, I asked if we could talk first before going. We sat down on her couch, and I took a deep breath.

"Jesus, take me through this!" I prayed quietly and leaned into my fear. "I need to tell you I'm afraid," I said.

Mary looked at me a moment, and said, "I know. It's a big move for both of us. I'm afraid, too."

No condemnation. No shame. No argument. Just the two of us together on the threshold of an awesome commitment, afraid and yet determined to stay open to what God was doing between us. I was overwhelmed. Before I knew it, I was crying, sobbing uncontrollably as we held each other.

We were late at the jeweler's—but emotionally right on time for the wedding! After several other times of just releasing my fears and crying, the Enemy gave up. My back began to loosen up; I discovered Mary was a great cook, and I was back to normal weight before you could say, "I do."

Why are we afraid to cry? Usually, because when you're crying, your defenses are never more fully down and you're wide open to getting hurt worse. Crying disarms you. Indeed, that's why the purest tears are spiritual weapons and most definitely not "the world's mighty weapons."

For the wounded, fearful man who has become so well defended that he can't access his own inner feelings, tears are a blessing that flush out his clogged spirit. Often trapped in loneliness, he wants to be disarmed, because he knows he can't either love or be loved when his energies are consumed in defending himself.

A man who can't cry is a dangerous man. He's lost touch with reality. He doesn't know his own pain and therefore is incapable of acknowledging anyone else's. He hurts others and remains unaffected himself.

Holocaust survivor Elie Wiesel tells of a man who worried after seeing the death-camp horror, "Will I ever cry again?" Translation: Has living amid the inhumanity of Evil caused me to build such formidable defenses that I've become desensitized, and thereby dehumanized?[3]

Significantly, the man did not worry, "Will I ever laugh again?" Laughter is simply not the more reliable indicator of reality. If you can't cry, you've lost touch with your own heart and can't laugh genuinely. Satan laughs; he can deceive and manipulate, but can't cry heartfelt tears. I can't imagine Hitler's crying, yet I've seen photos of him laughing with Nazi henchmen.

When his friend Lazarus died, Jesus wept. Occasionally I read Christian commentators who wish the Scriptures said somewhere that Jesus laughed. I don't worry about that. I know he laughed heartily, because I know he cried deeply.

As the psalmist declared, "Those who sow in tears shall reap with songs of joy" (Ps. 126:5, NEB).

Surrendering to Tears

If, indeed, the father-wound among men today is a wound of absence, then its healing requires grieving the loss of Dad's presence and love. Thus Robert Bly, grandfather of the secular men's movement, discussed men's "remoteness from their fathers" in his first men's conferences in the early eighties and was surprised at the response:

> Often the younger males would begin to talk and within five minutes they would be weeping. The amount of grief and anguish in the younger males was astounding! The river was deep.[4]

Letting go of past wounds takes a lot of tears. As others have said, the only way out is through. Until a man learns to face and grieve his genuine losses, his energies are consumed in defenses. He can't be free to trust his destiny in the Lord, open to receive direction, or real enough to walk it out.

After a divorce, for example, the world tells him, "Go out and enjoy yourself with a lot of new women. That'll make you forget the past and feel better!" Years later, he's only learned how to hide his true feelings with quick sex, which only makes it harder for him to enjoy a fulfilling relationship with a woman. The Father, however, says, "Come to me, Son, and let me hold you. Pour out your pain to me. I'll use it as an occasion to strengthen our relationship, draw you closer to my purposes, and prepare you for a suitable companion to walk with you in them."

Crying in Father God's arms melts your pride and brings you close to his heart.

In fact, God can use your tears to disarm another, even as your own self. Because no gesture so radically drops our defenses as authentic tears, never are we so safe as with someone who's crying.

At thirty-five, Jerry and his wife had threatened divorce and often withdrew emotionally from each other.

One day, he called me excitedly to report "an amazing breakthrough" in his marriage. "I was literally on my way out the door to sign the divorce papers," he exclaimed. "I'd tried everything that day—threats, pulling away, kindness. I prayed and prayed, but nothing ever seemed to change."

He paused and sighed, a mixture of joy and awe.

"As we stood there in the doorway arguing, somehow I just stopped. A helpless sort of feeling came over me, and it struck me that all my arguing was part of a vicious cycle, a Ping-Pong volley of defenses, that I had no idea how to stop. And then, before I knew it, I was crying. Right there in front of my wife. It was like a dam broke, and it all came out. As I cried, I just told her how much what she'd done had hurt me, and how much I wanted us to be together.

"Suddenly, I realized she was touching me, and soon we were sitting down together on the couch, holding each other and talking about how we could each make things different."

He paused, as if reflecting. "It was like a whole new world from where we'd been just minutes before."

Certainly, Jerry and his wife had much further work to do; his crying was no miracle cure for years of destructive patterns.

Neither Jerry nor his wife had grown up in a home that provided emotional safety. Jerry had seen his father and mother angry often but had never seen either drop their defenses and cry. He was so well defended emotionally that he never would have allowed himself to cry even alone, much less as a way of manipulating his wife.

In crying before his wife, Jerry had never dropped his guard so completely as an adult. The Father honored his courage and used his tears to open his heart, see the truth, and speak it with love—which set him and his wife free to a new level of acceptance and cooperation.

I believe God answered his prayers with those tears—dispelling his fear and gaining new access to his marriage, which had formerly been in the Destroyer's grip. Daring to walk in his own powerlessness, Jerry at last experienced the Lord's power.

I do not offer Jerry's story as a model technique for restoring a marriage, but as an example of how a man's surrender to tears allowed God greater freedom to work in his life. With his tears and the truth they bore, Jerry severed the Enemy's grip on his marriage through him and released it to God. Shifting his focus from trying to change his wife, Jerry did what he as a man could do at that time and surrendered to God. After Jerry had thereby allowed God to restore relationship with himself, any restoration of relationship with his wife was an issue between God and her.

Jerry sought help from a Christian counselor and began meeting with other men for prayer, encouragement, and accountability. "The more responsibility I took for putting myself where God could change me, the less I worried about changing her," he told me. "It was terrifying to let go like that—but the more I cried and spoke honestly instead of lashing back, the more secure I felt."

In surrendering to Jesus, Jerry was not practicing a technique with guaranteed specific results, but inviting a relationship with assured Presence. In fact, as Jerry committed himself to face and take his own pains to Jesus regardless of his wife's response, she could no longer justify her hurtful behavior as a reaction to him. Sadly, she herself refused to surrender to Jesus, and eventually she divorced him.

Jerry was crushed—but not destroyed. "I've never been hurt so badly in all my life," he said, "but over time, the more I learned to hold on to Jesus, the more I could let go of her. There were plenty more tears to cry and some hard truth to speak and to hear. But I decided that, as long as I had to deal with this awful situation, I'd better use it to get as much healing as possible, so it wouldn't happen again."

He sighed. "I didn't always do it right, but I really did hang in there with Jesus. For the first time in my life, I could look myself in the mirror and see a man—even a son of my Father God!"

That spiritual/emotional grounding not only sustained Jerry through the divorce but allowed his grieving to deepen his relationship with the Father—thus preserving and preparing him for a healthier marriage in the future. The Enemy's hold on his destiny was broken. Jerry was freed to refocus his energy later from battling one-on-one at home to battling side-by-side with a genuine helpmate in his vocation.

Even as over the months I praised God with Jerry for this healing in his masculine soul, a battle rose within me. As a boy, I had learned that crying is a sign of weakness, which simply exposes you to destruction. From Popeye and Superman to John Wayne and Luke Skywalker, the message from the world was clear: To save yourself, wield physical force faster and more destructively than the other.

Yet, in crying before his wife, Jerry did not set out to save himself; that would have been manipulation. Rather, he sacrificed his pride and lost himself, like Jesus. As a result, he was saved for God's purposes and not consumed by resentment.

Clearly, heartfelt tears can release a situation to the purposes of God when grinding anger only binds the situation more tightly to the self-centered purposes of human beings. As James noted, "Man's anger does not achieve God's righteous purpose" (James 1:20).

Several days after Jerry first called me, in fact, I was praying with a group of fellow pastors for spiritual renewal. As many visions of sin and rejection of God came to our minds to pray against, we were at once convicted of our own sin and led first into prayers of repentance for ourselves. As our own confessions poured forth, soon God's grieving for the sin of our society was revealed to us, and one pastor prayed aloud, "Lord, teach us to be weeping prophets!"

Almost matter-of-factly, I said, "Amen." But then tears filled my eyes and I knew that, even as God hated our sin, nevertheless he wants us as sinners to know his deep pain at our turning away from him. I knew that in some mysterious way understood only by God, my tears and those of the other pastors there were releasing us to the healing power of God—far more effectively than any angry sermon denouncing sin.

I once asked a grandmother and longtime member of a church I pastored, "Why did you first come to this church years ago?"

"When my son was just a little boy about four, we had been going to another church for some time," she replied. "And then one Sunday as we were leaving, I was holding his hand walking to the car and he stopped and looked up at me. 'Mommy,' he said, looking troubled, 'Why is that man talking up in front always so angry?'"

She sighed and smiled thinly. "We never went back."

"Children and dogs know," as the saying goes. The man who is quicker to be angry at than to weep for sinners is properly suspect. Likely, he hasn't let God show him his own sin, even God's own grief for our sin, and the Enemy will work through just such a blind spot. Indeed, like King David, the warrior of God knows his own natural perceptions are adulterated with pride—that he can't see himself honestly, and therefore must beg God to show him his own sin so he can be redeemed and his blind spots covered (Ps. 139:23-24).

It's amazing, but true: We're loved regardless of our wrongdoing—so deeply, in fact, that God weeps for us in our brokenness and gave up his Son to make us worthy of his love.

Kingdom warriors have struggled with the truth—so hard for the flesh to grasp—that "mercy triumphs over judgment" (James 2:13). Men who have experienced that truth will recognize God's word of mercy as it comes to them for others, because they've experienced their own need for it.

When Jesus wept before raising Lazarus, everyone there saw his tears as a sign not of his weakness but, rather, of his love: "See how he loved him!" If indeed God is love, then such tears herald the saving presence of God.

Lazarus' sister Mary was angry at Jesus for delaying his arrival and blamed him for her brother's death. But she didn't stop at her anger and judge Jesus.

Rather, she wept at the greater loss—which prompted the Lord's compassion and released the situation to God's greater purposes of mercy:

> When Mary reached the place where Jesus was and saw him, she fell at his feet and said, "Lord, if you had been here, my brother would not have died."
> When Jesus saw her weeping, and the Jews who had come along with her also weeping, he was deeply moved in spirit and troubled. (John 11:32-33, NIV)

We have every reason to believe that Jesus is still moved to saving action by our tears and, indeed, still weeps himself with and for God's people—as even now he "is at the right hand of God and is also interceding for us" (Rom. 8:34, NIV).

Indeed, insofar as Jesus bore our sins to the cross, God proclaimed in him that our hurts are his hurts (Jer. 8:21, RSV). Jerry's weeping before his wife, for example, certainly reflected his own pain over the rift between them.

But if it had reflected nothing but his own pain, it could not have borne saving power—such as that of a child playing with a knife, who cries when the parent takes it away. Rather, Jerry's tears reflected as well the pain of Jesus at seeing division and destruction ravage a man and woman called by God to live united in love. In thus giving Jesus a chance to express his pain through him, Jerry offered himself up as a vehicle for God's saving power.

Founding pastor John Wimber of the Vineyard Ministries in Anaheim, California, tells a poignant story. Early in his ministry, a woman came to him at a particularly busy moment and said matter-of-factly, "I have a word for you from the Lord."

With strained courtesy, he noted that he was in a hurry and urged her to proceed quickly—whereupon the woman burst forth crying. For several minutes she spoke not a word as tears flowed down her cheeks.

Puzzled, Wimber waited respectfully, until his patience reached its limit. "Could you please just give me the word, so I can get on with my schedule?" he asked.

The woman sobbed deeply and then, gathering her breath, said simply, "That's it."

The tears were God's message to Wimber, as if God was saying to Wimber, *I love you so much it hurts me to see you wasting all the talent and energy I've given you chasing after the wind.*

"It was like a gigantic blow to my solar plexus," he declared:

> I had figured if God was going to speak to me, he could have spoken about a hundred sins. I had a long list (and rationale for each of them). But what God did bypassed all my barriers. I wandered out of that [encounter] shaken. I knew that I had somehow wounded the Lord. In my relationship with God, I had hurt him.[5]

The woman who approached Wimber was bold. This weeping warrior was thereby used by God to run an end around on his well-fortified ego to reach his heart. There followed in Wimber's life a painfully upsetting but deeply renewing period of humility and healing. "In that season," he said, "the Lord told me, 'John, I've seen your ministry. And now I'm going to show you mine.'"

In secular language, tears can be God's judo maneuver that uses the other person's ego-weight against them.

African American Ben Kinchlow, former cohost of *The 700 Club*, wrote in his autobiography of his early adult rage at the racism he experienced. One evening, a friendly white minister, John Corcoran, invited him and his wife to dinner, and during their conversation Kinchlow began talking about those experiences. Soon his anger burst forth in fury:

> I clenched my fists in a final spasm of anger and, breathing heavily, stared hard across the table into the face of Corcoran, this nondescript, sandy-haired young preacher with the long nose. He looked into my eyes. I wanted him to feel my hatred, my contempt, my anger, my pain. . . . Several seconds went by, and I found my rage subsiding, like a storm that had blown itself out. . . . Suddenly it dawned on me. John was crying.

Later, Kinchlow reflected on that surprising experience:

> He was crying—not because he was embarrassed or angry with me, but because he cared. He cared for me, the angry, overwhelmed, black young American. In that instant I knew somewhere inside that he loved me with a love that exceeded anything I had ever felt for anyone or anything. That man loved me.

Corcoran wept not fearfully, as a child, because Kinchlow's rage had frighened or hurt him, but faithfully, as a mature Christian. That is, he saw with the compassionate eyes of Jesus the terrible pain in his guest that had prompted that rage.

Clearly, this momentous opportunity to witness the transforming, victorious love of Jesus would've been utterly lost had Corcoran chosen instead to suppress his tears as "unmanly"—and defend white people, quote Scriptures on controlling anger, or jump on the bandwagon by denigrating other whites.

Kinchlow later talks about that experience as "the night John Corcoran saw the real Ben Kinchlow and cried":

> I encountered at that dinner the sort of concern and compassion Jesus spoke so much about and that his followers later wrote about in the New Testament. I know now that John was living out Paul the apostle's appeal to the Christians that they "bear one another's burdens, and so fulfill the law of Christ" (Gal. 6:2, RSV). Although I was not yet a Christian, he actually had taken upon himself my suffering and frustration, thoroughly identifying with me.[6]

This Christian warrior's weeping portrays graphically the difference between God's power and the white "wannabee," who cops a variety of hip African American styles and lingo in an effort to demonstrate he's not racist. The latter—popular among white activists—lacks any transforming power precisely because it's rooted in maintaining emotional barriers and avoiding the truth.

The Kingdom warrior knows that he must identify with others' suffering at some level in order to endure in the battle to alleviate it. Compassion is the hallmark of his calling, his very license for fighting in the other's behalf.

A word of wisdom, if not caution, is appropriate here. Clearly, you can bring God's Word to another only insofar as you have laid down your own word at the Cross. If you haven't yielded your own personal wounds to Jesus for his healing, another's pain will simply trigger your own instead of the Lord's.

When ministering to others, you will follow your own cue instead of the Lord's. You're likely to begin crying before Jesus begins and to continue crying after he may have stopped and would proceed to speak more directly. As a result, the other person simply feels guilty that his suffering has made you cry.

The Weeping Warrior versus the Avenging Warrior

If one task of God's warrior is to clear the pathway to Jesus, then God is calling warriors to demonstrate his compassion to others as a major way of turning their hearts to him. Certainly, it is always easier to bring a word of judgment than to weep for another. The former makes us appear strong and righteous, while the latter makes us appear weak and foolish.

The weeping warrior has given up his own strength and righteousness to take on the weakness and the foolishness of the Cross instead: "For the foolishness of God is wiser than man's wisdom, and the weakness of God is stronger than man's strength" (1 Cor. 1:25, NIV).

The story is told of St. Francis of Sales:

> One day when he was hearing confessions, a man came to his confessional and accused himself of many grievous sins without showing any signs of sorrow. The Saint began to weep and continued shedding abundant tears till the man finished his confession. When it was done, he asked the Saint why he wept so much.
>
> "My child," he said, "I weep because you do not weep. You have by our great sins crucified the Son of God, and you seem to have no sorrow for what you have done."
>
> These few words touched the sinner's heart, and he also began to weep. God showed him at that moment the greatness of his sins, and he became penitent.[7]

Because the role of the weeping warrior so radically challenges the role of the judging, avenging warrior—which our flesh welcomes—responding to such a call can at first be confusing and upsetting. You may not even recognize it.

I once mentioned this issue of the weeping warrior to a friend and fellow pastor, and he told me of an incident that had taken place ten years earlier during a business meeting at his old-line denomination's regional headquarters. Seated around a large conference table with perhaps a dozen officials and other committee representatives, he became increasingly disturbed as discussions of church growth, public policy, and other important concerns included no attempt or apparent desire to seek God's word.

"We had some pretty heavy decisions to make and just weren't getting anywhere," he said. "Finally, I just couldn't stand it any longer, and I spoke up. I told them that since we were Christians, why not offer up our concerns and issues to Jesus first and trust that he would lead us from there?

"Before I knew it, I was pleading with them to pray together and allow Jesus to come and help us. I recall noticing that they all had blank looks on their faces, as if they didn't understand a word I was saying. And then, without thinking, I suddenly just broke into tears—right there in front of all those other ministers and denominational executives!"

He shook his head in wonder and dismay. "When I finally pulled myself together and stopped crying, the room was absolutely silent, and everyone sat there around the table with the same blank, puzzled looks on their faces—only now embarrassed as well. I just wanted to shrivel up and crawl into a hole somewhere!

"Finally, the chairman kind of shuffled his papers and everyone turned back to the discussion. I never said another word at that meeting, and all the ride home on the freeway alone in my car, I kept asking myself, *Why in the world did I do such a crazy thing? I mean, am I really that emotionally unstable?*"

My friend confessed that the memory of that event was so embarrassing that he had simply put it out of his mind until he and I began talking. At once I praised God for the insights he had given me by then, and I explained to my friend that very likely, he had neither been crazy nor emotionally unstable, but rather, had simply heeded God's call to be a weeping warrior. He had boldly presented the tears of Jesus, wounded by his pastors' rejection.

He sighed deeply and then smiled brightly. "Of course!" He

exclaimed, amazed and relieved. "I can't believe I never realized that over all these years!"

Jesus wants the pathway to himself clear and open. His true warriors, therefore, are determined to "tear down every proud obstacle that is raised against the knowledge of God."

To the flesh, crying is a weakness unto death.

Indeed.

To the warrior of the crucified and risen Christ, it's a death unto victory.

THIRTEEN

"Male Headship" and Battling for the Woman

Submit yourselves to one another because of your reverence for Christ. Wives, submit yourselves to your husbands as to the Lord. For a husband has authority over his wife just as Christ has authority over the church; and Christ is himself the Savior of the church, his body. And so wives must submit themselves completely to their husbands just as the church submits itself to Christ. Husbands, love your wives just as Christ loved the church and gave his life for it. Ephesians 5:21-25

THE PASTOR opened his three-page letter by thanking me for writing my book and then came right to the point. "Do you believe in 'male headship'?" he asked—and followed with a long and detailed argument just in case I didn't know it's "biblical."

I hear this question regularly, from radio shows to conferences. Sadly, it often comes from men who are not really seeking the truth, but, rather, a way to hide from the truth women bear us. That is, they're convinced "The Bible teaches male headship" and seize upon that as a license to silence and dominate women.

It makes you wonder: What are we so afraid women will say?

Nobody knows your wounds better than the one who suffers

their effects, and no other adult suffers a man's wounds more than his wife. Women are therefore in a unique position to bear us profound truth about our brokenness. The man who flees that truth will find the woman pressing him for it.

The warrior of God, however, doesn't want chinks in his armor; he understands that the truth will set him free from his shame, and so he presses the Father for it: "Show me myself the way you see me."

Often the Father answers that prayer through the woman.

A simple question will gauge how much of your marriage you've surrendered to the Father for his purposes: When was the last time you asked your wife, "Honey, where do you think I need healing in my life?" It's simple—but not easy. If you and your wife haven't spent time at the Cross together, you've probably never asked her that question. Instead, you've likely hurt each other so much that you don't trust her to speak the truth with love, and she doesn't trust you to listen even if she did.

The great concern for "male headship" today doesn't, therefore, surprise me. I know how badly we men are wounded, how deliberately we've been taught to be ashamed of our wounds and, thus, how sorely we're tempted to hide them. In the armies of the world, emotional intimacy among the ranks inhibits the task; in the army of God, it *is* the task, for broken relationships and isolation beckon the Enemy.

Women and Healing the Masculine Soul

We men suffer the loss of valuable discernment when women are silenced. We've only recently begun to realize this. I'm amazed that my own grandmother, for example, was not allowed to vote as a young woman. I can only pray that my son will be healed enough as a man to be similarly amazed when years from now he learns about the sexism his own grandmother—and even his mother—had to endure.

In the mid-sixties, a male friend told me he'd been nailed during his law school interview by this riddle-question: A father and his son are in a serious car accident. The father dies, and the boy is taken to a hospital emergency room. The chief surgeon at the hospital is assigned the operation, but declares that someone else must do it: "I can't operate on that child; he's my son."

How is that possible?[1] Hint: Neither the dead man nor the chief surgeon is the boy's stepfather (see footnote for the answer).

At twenty-five, I was stumped too. Chagrined, I had to chuckle later at a woman's bumper sticker, "Adam Was a First Draft."

More recently, at fifty, that same old chagrin winked at me in the split-second it took me to "get" the following joke, told by an African American newspaperwoman in a column titled "Pseudo-Equality":

> David N. Dinkins, then the mayor of New York, was riding through the city in his limousine with his wife, Joyce. Looking out the window, they recognized a man doing manual labor on the roadside as "John," a former suitor of Mrs. Dinkins'. Seeing him, the mayor smiled a bit smugly at his wife.
>
> "You must be so glad," he said, "to be married to the powerful mayor in the limo rather than to poor John shoveling alongside the road."
>
> His wife smiled. "If I'd married John, he'd be with me in the mayor's limo."[2]

As women began asserting their needs and revealing men's prejudice, they essentially took over the masculine mantle of truth-teller, which we men had dropped in fear. God's warriors today, therefore, battle to relieve women of their truth-telling burden for us men, to take back that mantle—and its responsibility—for ourselves.

As Jesus demonstrated on the cross, however, truth-tellers don't die of old age. Men seeking to deny their brokenness no more welcome that ministry from other men than from women; non-Christians discount you as "too religious," while Christians discredit you as not religious enough, that is, "worldly." It was the most religious men, after all, who killed Jesus for speaking the truth about them—not the atheists.

Granted, I'm not perfect—just ask Mary—but I try to stay open to constructive criticism and honor the truth. Frankly, I want my wife to be that way, and I can't very well ask her for something I'm not willing to give myself. I'm suspicious, therefore, of men who defame as "unbiblical" or "too masculine" a woman who brings just criticism against us men, no matter how harshly.

If she's pointing out some way we men commonly hurt others, the question for us isn't "Why can't that woman be more biblically submissive?" but rather "Why have we men strayed so far from the Cross and each other that a woman has to tell us the truth?" Indeed, how can we get healed and be a blessing to others instead of hurting them?

I often hear men complain that women have taken over the church. But any pastor knows the truth: Ask for volunteers to work with the children, organize a prayer-ministry team, or teach the high schoolers, and more women than men respond.

The late Kathryn Kuhlman was once challenged by a delegation of male pastors for her public healing ministry. "Don't you believe a man should be doing this instead of you?" they demanded.

"Indeed I do," she replied. "In fact, I believe God sought out many men to do it, but they all refused, and so he had to ask me. And I said yes."

One pastor even told me he asked for volunteers to help design a men's ministry and was shocked when several women stepped forth!

Women have a high stake in our healing. It's as if they've come across the desert and gathered at the banks of the river—but they know they can't enter the Promised Land without men alongside.

In fact, I believe that a new women's movement is coming. The old, secular one begun in the sixties cut itself off from men in order to lift the standard of truth where we'd dropped it. This allowed women to move into positions formerly restricted to men—such as company executives, vice presidents, firefighters. The new women's movement will proceed as men seize and lift high the standard of truth in the name of Jesus. Covered by such authentic masculinity, women will experience at last the freedom to pursue authentic femininity.

What that will look like has to be worked out between women and the Father. Our business as men is to be sure we're walking in his truth—holding ourselves accountable even as we hold women accountable. As we do our part, we then can only trust the Father to bring us together with women appropriately to serve his Kingdom.

A man surrendered to the Father doesn't have to fear the woman's strength. Indeed, he can celebrate it as a complement to his own, necessary to fulfill their common destiny.

Taking Responsibility

I appreciate women's desire for our healing. But the severity today of our brokenness and the Enemy we face requires that we take responsibility for seeking it ourselves. We need to walk into the Promised Land, not be carried there by women. Indeed, we must lead the way as warrior/scouts, facing and battling the giants stirred there against godly men. Only then are we ready to walk with the woman and face the giants that are stirred there against a godly marriage.

When planning my men's conferences, therefore, I tell the host pastor to avoid getting women to do any preparation work. Those who treat adult males like irresponsible boys don't help us become men. Doing the work ourselves is part of our healing, which the Father will build on during the conference itself.

A faithful farmer takes time to till the soil and await the harvest. Pastors who want men healed must take the time to invest in relationships with the brothers at church and wait until they're ready to orchestrate the conference themselves. Being respected like that teaches men self-respect and motivates us to take responsibility for our own healing.

It also avoids predictably hurt feelings among women "helpers." For example, one host pastor where I taught believed strongly in "male headship." At the same time, he had a woman do all the planning legwork for their men's conference—a considerable task. Another male staff member scoffed that they just didn't think they could get any men to do the job. Friday evening, they assigned their hardworking woman to sit out front and handle the registration table.

She was altogether friendly and had left before I spoke. But as the first person incoming participants met, the woman's presence confused and unnerved a number of men. Predictably, she overheard a comment or two, went home hurt, and called the pastor's wife.

To my dismay, the pastor stood up before I spoke the next morning and chastised the men for their "insensitivity to the woman." In fact, he said, we men need to be healed of our "fear of being around women"—whereupon he produced an "I'm Sorry" card for her and urged every man to sign it.

Later, I told the staff member that I could understand the woman feeling hurt, but I felt it was insensitive to the men to have her present.

"But you don't understand how hard she worked for this conference!" he retorted.

On the contrary, I did—and that was precisely the problem, because it reflected the staff's disrespect of the men.

"Male headship" can't mean "getting women to do the work for us."

We need sisters praying for us, not mothers doing for us.

In fact, that conference was one of my least attended, and I can't help wondering: Does the Father bless with fruitfulness only where men take responsibility for themselves? Not just at men's conferences, but even in churches themselves?

Healed Men Don't Wound Others

Women are sinners, too. Indeed, I've met women who have clearly capitulated to the Enemy in his efforts to destroy men. But my license to criticize such women comes only out of my readiness to own up to our own brokenness. When we face the Lord on Judgment Day and he asks us, "Why didn't you men own up to your sin so I could heal you and send you out victoriously into battle?" it won't cut it to reply, "Well, gee, Father, you just don't know how bitter and nasty those feminists were!"

Jesus knows all too well how bitter and nasty we human beings can be. He's got the nail scars to prove it—and they didn't come from women. What he doesn't know is how faithful we can be. That's the Big Unknown he's banking on at the cross, namely, that we won't yield to the Enemy and stonewall unto death against the truth, but instead, will yield to his mercy and let him restore us unto new life.

Women have been badly wounded by men brandishing "male headship" as a machete. I'm not surprised, therefore, when angry women demand, "How dare you talk about 'men's wounds'! What about about all the wounds men have caused us women?"

"I want to get men healed," I simply say. "Don't you?"

End of conversation.

Those confrontations push my "shame buttons" and set off alarms in my gut. But I've learned that the other person's anger usually hides a deep hurt; defending myself only exacerbates the other's hurt and distances me from the truth.

I ask my confronters to treat me with the same respect I afford them. But whether or not they do, I dare not run from the truth they bear.

I call on Jesus as my Defender and ask him to show me any truth I need to hear amid the chaff of vengeance. Above all, I try to remember: the one who can stay surrendered to Jesus is the leader.

We men need to confess that often we've sacrificed women's souls to our pride—indeed, that we've dumped our wounds onto women instead of onto Jesus.

Healed men don't wound others.

In fact, I was humbled into this new perspectve by a group of women while at Stanford graduate school in the late sixties. The feminist movement had just begun gathering momentum on campus and was not without its angry voices. One day the student paper reported a terrible rape/murder the night before in the university chapel. That afternoon I was on campus talking with a woman about something else when another woman, a mutual friend, came up.

257

"Did you hear about the awful murder?" she asked after a moment.

I nodded—and I dropped my eyes before the women as a hint of shame struck me.

Frowning, the first woman shook her head in dismay. "Yeah—I sure hope they get that guy."

I swallowed nervously, steeling myself for a vengeful feminist outburst.

"Me, too," the other said. "He sure needs help."

Stunned by such radical compassion, I sat speechless.

I minister to men, therefore, not because we've hurt women, but because we've withdrawn from the Father's healing. We've given the powers of sin and death rein, both in and through us.

For the Kingdom warrior, therefore, the question is not, "Should there be ultimate authority in this world?" nor even, "Should it be Jesus?" That's already been settled for us: God sent Jesus to establish his throne (Phil. 2:9-11). We thank him for doing so, because, left to our own lordship, we strut right into the hands of the Enemy.

If, as the apostle Paul declares in the opening Scripture, a husband's authority is derived from Jesus', the true question for God's warrior becomes, "How does Jesus establish and exercise his Kingdom authority among us?"

The warrior of the flesh values obedience over trust and therefore strives to determine who obeys whom (Luke 9:46-47). Whether father or company boss, he believes that authority is established not by character but by position—not by power to inspire trust, but rather, to coerce obedience.

"Religious" men use shame instead of guns: "If you don't agree with me, you're not a true Christian." Like the armies of the world, the warriors of religion believe people function properly only when everyone wears their rank insignia clearly on their sleeve, and those who violate that order are "dishonorably" discharged—that is, shamed and excommunicated.

Among Kingdom warriors, however, the mantle of leadership isn't something that ambitious men seize, but rather, that faithful men receive. The man shouting, "I'm the leader!" most often isn't.

Even as the Spirit fulfills the Law, the commander who inspires trust among his troops precludes this hierarchy. As with King David's followers, the men would seek his authority over them even if the Law had not ordered it (2 Sam. 5:1-3).

Without such trust, the effort to establish authority becomes an effort to determine, "Who tells the other what to do?" This readily translates: "Who gets to do what he wants without being hindered by the feelings and needs of others?" Who can't be told the truth, and therefore gets to hide his sin and the pain of its effects?

Hence, the obsession of the flesh with "male headship"—yet another religious principle behind which to hide our shame and consequent fear of genuine intimacy with a woman.

Jesus, meanwhile, has stated clearly the requirement for leadership in his Kingdom. When the disciples argued over "who was the greatest," he said to them, "Whoever wants to be first must place himself last of all and be the servant of all" (Mark 9:35).

Similarly, when the wife of Zebedee asked Jesus, "Promise me that these two sons of mine will sit at your right and your left when you are King," he replied to the young men, "You don't know what you are asking for. . . . Can you drink the cup of suffering that I am about to drink?" (Matt. 20:21-22).

Like the sons of Zebedee, the men most focused on their transcendent headship can't see their present responsibility. Like children, they want the goodies but don't want to pay the price.

They like to hear the Bible say, "a husband has authority over his wife," but not "husbands, love your wives just as Christ loved the church and gave his life for it." It's like singing the hosannas of Palm Sunday and the alleluias of Easter without singing the Good Friday chorus of Psalm 22, "My God, my God, why have you abandoned me?"

The flesh fancies that you don't have to give up your life—or your pride—for your wife unless she first acknowledges you as her head. The Kingdom warrior, however, knows that as the leader, he initiates. He may hope the woman follows and grieve if she doesn't. But God has risked granting her free will even as he granted it to men; whether she responds or not is a matter between her and God, and not within the man's power to control.

Jesus didn't wait for our righteousness before going to the cross on our behalf (1 John 4:10). If he did, he'd still be waiting, because we have no righteousness without him. Jesus did not go to the cross because we are righteous, but rather, because he is righteous—that is, faithful to the Father's call.

Because women are sinners, too, part of the Kingdom warrior's job description is to bear God's truth to the woman with the Father's heart of love. Instead of complaining, "But she won't acknowledge me as head of this family!" he must dare to ask himself the warrior's question: "Have I acted like the head of the family?" That is, as Jesus modeled headship, "Have I laid down my life for my wife"—for example, by sacrificing pride and agendas, and sincerely trying to listen to her?

Indeed, have your told your wife Who's the leader of your family (hint: It's not you) by demonstrating your own surrender to him?

As any man who's tried it knows, that's no formula for making a woman submissive. The Kingdom warrior, however, seeks primarily not to make the woman submit to him, but to submit to Jesus himself.

That's spiritual leadership in the home.

The woman is free to kick you in the face when you surrender to the Father—even as we nailed Jesus. But every man must decide: Do you want to be a tyrant in the kingdom of the flesh, or a leader in the Kingdom of God? A tyrant makes others go where he wants, for his "good"; the Kingdom warrior goes first where the Father wants others to go, for their own good.

I suspect, in fact, that the woman requires a man to initiate sacrificial love in order for her femininity to blossom. While pastoring a church with 80 percent adult singles, for example, I was dismayed at how often men balked at committing to an appropriately eligible woman because she appeared "not feminine enough."

Certainly, like men, women today need gender and sexual

healing. But these men were simply not themselves masculine enough—as indicated in their waiting for the woman to initiate and become feminine before they would become masculine and commit to her. Instead of leading by taking their brokenness to Jesus, they dishonestly dumped it on the women—wounding their feminine souls much as little boys damage little girls' hearts by wielding "cooties."

It's a particularly cruel sham, because any single woman who would provide for herself in today's hard world must exercise a host of masculine character traits—which she can yield only insofar as she has a man committed to walking with her.

It's not that she lacks true femininity, but rather, a true man to draw it out of her.

As I told those single men, if she doesn't respond to your godly masculine initiative and can't appreciate your surrender to Jesus, she's not the woman for you. Letting go may hurt for a little while—but you've saved yourself far greater pain by smoking her out early in the game.

To demand women acknowledge "the man as leader" therefore begs the underlying question, What special powers or prerogatives, in fact, does being a "leader" confer upon a Christian?

Jesus responds directly to this question when he scolds the Pharisees:

> Nor should you be called "Leader," because your one and only leader is the Messiah. The greatest one among you must be your servant. Whoever makes himself great will be humbled, and whoever humbles himself will be made great. (Matt. 23:10-12)

As he demonstrated later on the cross, Jesus says here that the leader in his kingdom is the one who dies first on behalf of the other. The only godly competition between husband and wife, therefore, is in racing to the Cross. In order to be the leader at home, a man must go to the Cross before his wife does, and thereby become more determined to face his sin than she to face hers, more dedicated to serving her than she to serving him.

Power to Defend the Woman

The warrior of the world seeks power over others; the warrior of God seeks power *for* others. "To protect and to serve," as proclaimed on my son's toy policeman's motorcycle, carries the idea.

It's only natural to want power. Here we must understand: God doesn't want to destroy your natural desires; after all, he created them. Rather, he wants to sanctify them—that is, to set them apart for his purposes. God's way of purifying your urge to power, however, is the same as for any desire of the flesh—namely, crucifixion.

He thereby banks on our freewill choice to go to the Cross—even as he did with Jesus.

It's also natural, for example, to want sexual gratification. Sexual desire is good; God created it in us. But he wants to sanctify it, to set it apart for his purposes. Men who have grown to realize that's best for them, that apart from the Father's purposes their energies ultimately serve the Enemy, want their sexual desire to be sanctified.

So they bring it to the Cross. They kneel and confess, "Father, apart from you my sexual desire is out of control and destructive. I want you to bring it under your authority. I give it up to you."

A fair warning: God answers prayer. If you lay your sexual desire at the Cross to be sanctified, it must die until the Father resurrects it in his image.

That means you won't be turned on any longer by every knee or drawn to every skirt. You might not be turned on at all for a while. To whatever extent you saw yourself as "masculine" because of your powerful sex drive and self-sufficiency, you won't feel like a "man" anymore.

That's because the Father is making you into his man.

It'll scare you. But then, the Cross is no tea party. It's not where men fabricate images, but where the Father makes warriors.

You have a right to ask, "For how long?"

You have a right to know: "As long as it takes."

Still, it's up to you as much as to God. Although the Father does the work, you have to cooperate. If the patient fights the surgeon and tries to get off the table too soon, the operation takes longer.

A final note: This process of letting the Father sanctify your sexual desire is entirely appropriate for married men. In fact, the apostle Paul assumes such a period of abstinence at times:

> Do not deny yourselves to each other, unless you first agree to do so for a while in order to spend your time in prayer; but then resume normal marital relations. (1 Cor. 7:5)

In order therefore to fight *for* the woman and not *against* her, a man must humbly surrender his desires and pride at the Cross.

Even in the woman's presence.

I emphasize: It's not enough to do it alone in your prayer closet.

The joke is told, for example, of the pastor who prayed alone on his knees in his home study, "O God, have mercy on me, miserable worm that I am!" His wife happened to be passing by his door and heard him. Later, during an argument, the pastor insisted he was blameless and his wife at fault.

"You're a miserable worm, and I hope God can forgive you for it!" his wife shot back.

"How dare you talk to me like that!" he raged.

"Well," she said matter-of-factly, "you said it yourself first."

The Kingdom leader prays not the prayer of the flesh, "Expose and punish *her* sin, Lord!" but rather, that of the warrior David: "Examine *me*, O God, and know *my* mind; test *me*, and discover *my* thoughts. Find out if there is any evil in *me* and guide *me* in the everlasting way" (Ps. 139:23-24, italics mine).

The only prerogative such a leader can ultimately count on is his Father's approval.

But for a real man, that's enough.

"Who is a real Jew?" as the apostle Paul asked—and here we may substitute *man of God* for *Jew*. "The real [man of God] is the man who is a [man of God] on the inside, that is, whose heart has been circumcised, and this is *the work of God's Spirit, not of the written Law.* [This man] *receives his praise from God, not from man*" (Rom. 2:28-29, italics mine).

Indeed, a real woman—one who honors her own femininity as a daughter of the Father—will rejoice on hearing her husband pray like David, and be thankful for the privilege of walking with such an authentic man.

I learned this lesson one evening when Mary and I could not settle a disagreement. "That's enough!" I finally huffed; "I'm fed up with this arguing!" In the scenario-of-the-flesh, at this point the man disappears behind his newspaper or ball game, or walks out. For the warrior of God, however, the opposite of retreat isn't "Charge!" but rather, "Surrender to the Father."

When you do, you discover he's fed up with your arguing, too. He loves you both. He doesn't like to see his son and daughter surrendered to the Enemy and destroying each other.

Don't get me wrong. Talk to your wife when you need to. Tell her how her actions affect you. But when the talking begins to escalate the hurt with accusing and judging, I know only one way out that leads to deeper love.

I've tried it all: I've retreated, popped Di-Gels, and lain awake on the pillow; I've charged ahead to make my point loudly, and made a worse mess. It just doesn't work.

And so that evening, I reached out my hand to Mary. "Let's go to the Father," I sighed, and led us to our knees. "Father," I prayed, "I give up to you. We can't get through to each other, and all this arguing is just driving us further apart. Is there something I'm not doing or seeing as a man that's getting in your way here? Speak to us, Father, and show us how you see all this."

Hearing my surrender, Mary felt safe and followed suit, asking the Father to show her anything she might need to see about herself as a woman.

Before long, I heard in my mind the words, *This is my daughter.*

"Oh yes, Father," I responded. "Mary's your daughter, and I'm your son. That's why I'm asking you to give us a word to settle this argument!"

I waited, and again I heard, *This is my daughter.*

"Absolutely, Father!" I said. "We're both your children, and surrendered here to you. Now please, Father, help us get on with loving each other!"

I waited . . . and suddenly, a scene from high school days popped into my mind: walking up the driveway to my date's house early Saturday night and ringing the bell. The door opened, and there stood her father, drilling me with his eyes.

"Where are you going with my daughter?" he demanded.

"Well, I mean . . . uh, . . . to the dance at school," I stammered.

"When are you bringing her back here?"

"Uh, well, it's over at ten, so I thought maybe . . ."

"Ten-fifteen!" the father boomed.

That young lady danced with a very respectful—if hurried— young man that night. My feet moved about a beat faster than the music and were headed for the door before the last "lamma-ramma-ding-dong." After finessing a few stop signs, I had her back in the driveway at ten-twelve. Those were the days before bucket seats, but I didn't linger. At ten-thirteen, she was in the door.

The memory clip ended, and I understood. The Father was showing me his heart for Mary, telling me how much he cares for her and that I answer to him for how I treat her.

In that moment, I still felt in the dark as to how to settle our argument. But I knew the light was at hand. "Is there something I'm doing that's making it hard for you to talk honestly with me?" I asked Mary.

There was, and she told me. I did my best to listen and said I'd work on it with my prayer partner. Disarmed, she asked me the same question, and I was able to answer her with the same honesty.

I learned that night to honor the woman even as myself.

And more: Look upon a woman the way you want men to look upon your daughter.

Significantly, long before ever meeting Mary, I'd already learned to surrender to the Father God as a lifestyle. Whatever obstacle I faced, I'd learned first to go to the Cross and ask the Father to show me how I might be frustrating his purposes. Sure, in the beginning I balked at dropping my guard in front of Mary, but I soon realized that if I couldn't trust her like that, we'd be building our marriage on sand.

Even as a man's destiny hinges upon knowing Whose he is, so the sanctity of your marriage—that is, its usefulness to God—hinges upon knowing Whose your wife is. If you don't know she belongs to the Father, you can't recognize and thereby respect her as the "suitable companion to help" fulfill your destiny in him (Gen. 2:18). Indeed, the wounds of the flesh—especially in the heat of an argument—can easily portray her as an enemy instead.

When a couple are hurting each other, and thereby opening a gate for the Enemy into their marriage, the leader's job is to draw both to the Cross so the Father can lead them together into his victory. The man who would lead his family, therefore, does his homework: HE knows the way to the Cross because he's worn a path there himself.

"When a man and a woman get into an argument," my seminary pastor, Rev. Herb Davis used to say, "They always think the big question is, 'Who's right?' But that's the easiest question of all. Each one can answer it in a second: 'I'm right, or I wouldn't be fighting like this!' The real question is, 'What's God trying to teach us?'"

That's the warrior's question, the one that requires greater courage to raise. Indeed, you can't walk in the Father's victory until you surrender your own. You have to give up your right to "win"—even your right to be right.

Seeking your own righteousness is a snipe hunt.

The warrior of the flesh judges the woman in order to establish his righteousness; the Kingdom warrior wants Jesus to save the woman and himself from judgment in order to establish God's righteousness in their marriage.

When the bullets are flying, it's time to bivouac at the Cross. It's one thing to tell your wife, "You're a thoughtless, selfish woman and your behavior is unbiblical!" It's quite another to say, "I'm trying to be accountable to God and other men, doing everything I know to take responsibility for my part in our problem and get healed. I want us to become all that God had in mind when he brought us together. I need you to walk with me in that."

That's fighting for the woman, not against her.

Any woman who rejects you after that—who can't affirm a man's fighting for her—doesn't honor her womanhood as much as you do. She's been terribly wounded in her femininity. You'll need to ask Jesus how he's praying for her healing and what part he wants you to play in that.

Not every woman, of course, will come when the man bids her follow him to the Cross. In fact, that's a good way for a single man to evaluate wife candidates. The Bible cautions against marrying a woman who is "unequally yoked" and not surrendered to the Father—not because she is somehow immoral or unworthy, but because the Enemy attacks godly unions viciously, and only those in which both partners are yoked/submitted to his Overcomer can survive and grow through those attacks.

God's Truth: In the Bible and in Life

The Word of God is not just theology but real life.

Even a man who doesn't accept the Bible as authoritative can experience truth. Like a wayward relative, the truth may not be welcomed, but it can be recognized. That is, truth revealed in the Bible should be evident elsewhere, apart from the Bible—even in our experience.

The light goes on when a man connects his experience of truth with the true Word of God. Instead of striving after a "biblical" standard, he then can rest assured that the Father is leading him into that standard as their relationship grows.

Here again we must remember: While the Bible reveals God's loving will, and thus, where it's best for us to go, it is the Father God—revealed in the living Christ and present among us today in the Holy Spirit—who gets us there. The character traits affirmed in the Bible are a supernatural consequence of ongoing surrender to the Author—not something coerced or achieved by human effort.

Christian character is a fruit of the Father's Spirit, not a reward for performing correctly (Gal. 5:22-25).

When the Bible tells a woman to submit to her husband as to Jesus and the man to love her as Jesus loves his church, that's how

267

we are designed to function best. That truth will bear witness to the degree that both husband and wife are submitted to Jesus. As they allow his Spirit to abide in and among them, each will find themselves supernaturally gravitating toward those positions—not because "the Bible commands it," but because it's genuinely fulfilling.

Similarly, if God intends men to be leaders, we don't have to assert or command it, but only give God a chance to demonstrate it.

Granted, in this "meanwhile" season until Jesus returns, that's not going to happen perfectly in any marriage, even though we can anticipate its perfection in the Spirit. Hence, the temptation to bail out on the Spirit and make it happen ourselves with a little holy arm-twisting: "That's what the Bible says, so you'd better do it!"

Translation: "I'm terrified of genuine intimacy with you—and don't trust Jesus to meet me in my fear—so I need you to become an accomplice in my deception by propping up a mask of righteousness for our marriage." Sadly, many women today have been wounded badly enough themselves to fear intimacy, and they comply.

Clearly, the flesh bears temptations far more serious than sex—such as turning God's Word of love into a weapon of shame.

The Father has something so much better for you.

Granted, it takes time.

Methodist evangelist Tommy Tyson tells how, as a boy on the farm, his first job was to collect the fertile eggs for the hatchery. He noticed that the little chicks had to work hard to peck their way out of the shell, and he decided he could save them some energy and himself some time by cracking the egg open himself with his penknife.

They all flopped out prematurely and died, lacking muscle control otherwise gained through pecking out by themselves.

Stay at the Cross.

Give Jesus a chance. A big chance. Every chance.

Give God a chance to show you that his Word is true. Surrender to Jesus as a lifestyle, a holy habit. Ask him to change your heart so you can love your wife as he does. Let him deal with you.

And let him deal with your wife.

This essential distinction between Law and Spirit was clarified for me soon after Mary and I were married. We had a two-bedroom house—small, but big enough to get dirty. Anxious to head off any labor disputes, I suggested right away that we draw up a list of weekly chores and divvy them up—fair and square. I have dibs on the bathroom and the lawn; Mary gets the kitchen and carpets, etc.

But Mary had another idea.

"I appreciate your not wanting us to fight over keeping the place clean," she said—with a pause that seemed to add, "Especially since you can live with a lot more disorder than I can."

She hesitated, as if counting the cost, and then said, "But what if we just trust each other to see what needs to be done, and do it?"

"Huh?" I blurted out.

Even then, Mary knew that only the living God could expand my vision of housecleaning.

I'd never thought of such a thing. As I did, I knew this was going to be harder than any fifty-fifty work detail—but far more rewarding for our marriage if we could pull it off.

Today, years later, it seems to be working. Maybe it's because Mary's been interceding for me to notice my dirty socks on the floor. More likely, she just has the grace to overlook it when I don't.

But I do try. Not because I have to, but because I want to. In fact, I think at times I do even more than I would've under my housecleaning contract—though I confess I haven't asked Mary about that.

I just thank God I'm a man.

So does Mary.

In fact, she thanks God she's a woman.

So do I.

I frankly don't know whether she sees me as her "head" or not, and, in fact, it's probably better I don't.

I only know that she's my Father's beloved daughter, and I'm his beloved son—and I'm too busy enjoying our marriage to ask.

FOURTEEN

The Woman as Ally

*But remember that in God's plan men and women need
each other. For although the first woman came out of man, all men
have been born from women ever since, and both men
and women come from God their Creator.*
1 Corinthians 11:11-12, TLB

MY WIFE Mary gave me the title for this book.

She also suggested that it would follow up on my previous books for men, and during the writing she's given me invaluable input and feedback.

In fact, at one point it occurred to me—not without a hint of shame—that maybe I'd wimped out. I greatly respect Mary's intelligence and professional expertise. Still, I thought, shouldn't a warrior book for men be wholly orchestrated by the man?

Shame made me bury the issue each time it surfaced, until one day it just wouldn't leave. Frustrated, I prayed and asked the Father to take it away so I could get on with the more important business of writing the book.

But as usual, he had a different perspective.

As I prayed, it struck me: Both the title and focus Mary offered seemed altogether right, and the latter came to her during prayer and worship. I've prayed regularly with several men, often about the book; if necessary, the Father could've spoken through any one of these men instead. Could it be, I wondered, that he specifically chose a woman and not a man to mediate such pivotal input?

Intrigued, I took a deep breath and pushed on: "OK, Father, I give up. Did you deliberately choose a woman to show me these important aspects of the book? And if so, why?"

Waiting, I felt a reassuring, good-natured laugh at my conjured fear.

The shame evaporated.

Humility before the Father delivers you from humiliation before the Enemy.

Indeed, in Mary's foundational contribution to the book, the Father seemed to be saying that the woman is essential to the victory God seeks in and through men today. Thus, to the extent that the Kingdom warrior reflects a man's root identity and destiny, a men's book on Kingdom warfare can't be written without feminine input—any more than a man can be born without a mother.

Together as men we must face and seek healing for our father-wound, surrendered to the Father God and without women present. The woman can acknowlege, even rejoice in the manhood that results, but she can't engender or confirm it.

The image of God, however, is reflected in a unity of both male and female (Gen. 1:27). In order, therefore, to bring the fullness of his Kingdom on earth—to be Kingdom warriors—we must allow our healing among fellow men to lead us into affirming and incorporating the woman's input.

The secular men's movement has taught us to break unhealthy bonds with the mother, grieve our father-wound, and bond with other men in order to become secure in our masculinity. But it can't take us the next step, namely, to bond anew with the woman—not as mother, but at last as a "suitable companion" (Gen. 2:18) to fulfill your God-given destiny. To do that, you

must recognize the woman as your Father's daughter, and thereby, a trustworthy partner—even a holy sister.

So, to be a Kingdom warrior a man must grow beyond pursuing his individual desires to pursuing the Father's created purpose in him—which requires the woman as "a suitable companion" (Gen. 2:18). To become the men God has called us to be, we must reintegrate in and among ourselves what Adam lost with his rib—that is, something essential to the woman's nature. It is a piece of the man's life-puzzle without which the overall picture remains uncertain and incomplete.

As Eve was to Adam, the woman is the part of yourself that the Father has rendered outside and beyond you, in order to teach you relationship. You're thereby drawn to reunite with her physically, emotionally, and spiritually, in order to fulfill your relationship with him. A man must allow the woman to awaken within him a primal longing for an altogether essential and authentic part of himself that no other man can draw forth.

New Job Descriptions

Recently, I attended a bachelor party for a young man in our church. To avoid un-Christian bawdiness, the invitation tactfully suggested "tasteful gifts." The party soon revealed our lack of flavorful Christian alternatives, however, as some twenty of us men sat around simply drinking punch and chatting tentatively. Eventually, I suggested to the host that the married men present might each bless our brother husband-to-be by sharing some helpful lesson from our own marriages.

Agreeing readily, he whistled for attention from the others and presented the proposal. The men shifted as a quiet fell over the room. And then, one brother leapt in boldly with a moving story about how his wife had overlooked shortcomings for which he'd condemned himself.

"If you let her," he declared, "your wife can teach you to be easier on yourself. Somehow, it seems like a woman can be a lot more accepting of you just the way you are, where a man would probably judge you. I guess you'd call it grace. I don't know. I only know that since I've been married it's been like new life for me."

A chorus of amens burst the dam, and a flood of stories then poured out from others whose wives' love had released them from shame-based striving and performing.

Certainly, women can be judgmental and perfectionistic, too. But that doesn't characterize genuine femininity. Indeed, it marks false masculinity, a distortion of godly truth and accountability—precisely, in fact, because it lacks the balancing mercy and grace of true femininity.

As Dr. John Gray, author of the best-selling *Men Are from Mars, Women Are from Venus*, declared in a public address,

> Men are drawn to love. Men need love more than women. That's been what you've given us for centuries. We were drawn to women for love. Women went to men for power and protection, for the provider.
>
> Women today, because they're out in the powerful world, out in their masculine side, they come home and they're feeling, "I need love, too." So we men have to learn the new job description to give women this particular kind of love they need to come back to their feminine, and then the woman can fill us up with love too.[1]

We men, Gray is saying, need today to prime the woman's pump with caring, accepting love. That makes sense—but he doesn't tell us where to get even the prime-cupful of love to start. Only the man who knows Jesus, and thereby knows the Father who is love (1 John 4:16-17), can tell us that.

The flipside of this truth has largely fueled the men's movement. To paraphrase Gray, men today are trying to succeed in relationships at home—that is, in the traditional feminine arena. When we go out into the world, we think, *I need to be more centered in my masculine side with direction and power for my life.*

Often, in order to give the woman that security, we may need her to speak a word of truth when we're hiding from the responsibility it requires. That's the woman's "new job description" among fatherless men who have overbonded to their mothers. She might say, for example, "I love you, and I need you to start facing your wounds and focus your life." A woman whose identity is centered in Father God can prime our masculine pump with such accountability; the woman whose identity is centered in the man dares not.

Of all the traumas that could shock a man into remedial action, my own informal poll suggests that loss of the woman's love is most common. Regardless of who's "at fault," divorce often wakes a man up to face his deepest wounds and seek healing. A men's accountability/support group often provides the man with the security needed to fulfill his "new job description" and respond faithfully to hers.

I'm not saying here that the whole problem among us is our fault as men, that women don't need to be healed and change. Indeed, the excesses of the secular women's movement, from goddess worship to lesbianism, might lead a man to say that women have not pursued a high standard of self-honesty.

I believe we men need to show them how. That's leadership— at least, in the Kingdom of God. Such self-honesty among men will release a new women's movement, which I believe is coming not because men demand it, but because the Father wants it—to cleanse, heal, and restore his daughters, even as he is doing with his sons.

In their first movement, women sought to gain self-esteem that men in our brokenness had denied them. The next movement will proceed on receiving the Father's heart, even as men extend it to them.

My concern here, meanwhile, is not to judge the woman, but to heal the man—even as the Kingdom warrior seeks not to exact vengeance from the woman who has harmed him, but rather, to fulfill his destiny alongside the woman who willingly and faithfully complements it.

While most men need a woman as a suitable companion to fulfill their destiny, some men may not. Scripture indicates the spiritual gift of celibacy (1 Cor. 7:1-7) for a chosen few men, such as the apostle Paul—who thereby do not need the woman to fulfill their calling. As a lifelong ministry gift, however, I believe that anointing is rare, apart from those widowed, and some men may claim it simply to hide from their sexuality.

Men and Mothers

This powerful mystery has become far more real to me since becoming a father. Once, for example, a strange question popped into my mind as I was praising and thanking God for making me a father: *What's the difference between you and your son?*

That's easy, I thought. *Obviously, he's younger and doesn't look exactly like me.* I paused, wondering why such a simple question had come to mind.

And then it struck me: *The son is not the father's clone.*

The difference between a man and his son is the mother. Apart from God's sovereign input, her female chromosome comprises fully half the boy's genetic makeup.

Even as he coupled with the mother physically in conception, the father must dare enter and engage the woman's emotional and spiritual world in order to relate authentically to his son. To know and love his son fully, a father must know and love the boy's mother, and thereby integrate the emotional and spiritual differences that the boy himself embodies.

The son is the sacramental product of both Dad and Mom, the outward and visible sign of the inward and spiritual grace that is their love. When Dad is emotionally and spiritually split from Mom, therefore, a boy remains split in his own spirit, confused and unfocused, unable to integrate his various personality traits and pursue his destiny. As a man, he therefore can't discern a "suitable companion," both because his ambivalence toward Mom makes him insecure around women and because he doesn't know the calling in which his wife would accompany him.

For your son's sake, you must let God give you a respect for his mother, whether you're living with her or not.

Every boy naturally judges himself by his father's standards, and therefore longs for his daddy's acceptance and approval. But a boy who must reject Mom in order to be accepted by Dad can't find self-acceptance.

In any case, a society rife with divorce, unwed mothers, and emotionally absent fathers insures aimlessness, shame, and anxiety among its young men. Ultimately, self-destruction and violence give voice to their inner frustration, "I'm called to be more than I am, but can't make it happen."

John Steinbeck's classic novel *East of Eden* portrays this truth poignantly in two sons who grow up without a mother in a farm home dominated by a rigid and severely religious father. He has told the boys their mother is dead, but nothing more.

The father has renounced and cut himself off from his wife, and thereby, from his sons. Without feminine input, he retreats behind the judgment and perfectionism of false masculinity—and false religion. Having closed his eyes to their mother, he can't see his sons as they truly are and relates to them wholly through their performance—both on the job at his farm and in their Christian moral character. Indeed, he condemns the younger son for manifesting personality traits similar to the mother's.

The older son models desperately after the father with bite-the-bullet, ruthless morality; the younger boy, however, seethes with a creative and unruly restlessness—the classic James Dean character in the 1957 movie version.

As a teenager, the younger son judges and punishes himself even as his father does, until he discovers that his mother is not only alive, but in fact, madam of a whorehouse in a nearby town. Fearful but determined, he visits her and discovers the wellspring of his yearning for freedom and authenticity. While he can't accommodate her lifestyle, he learns to honor his mother and thereby, integrate without shame the part of her that is himself.

His older brother, on the other hand, has so invested in the father's shame and denial—and in a false, unbalanced masculinity—that he can't accommodate the truth of his mother's state.

Trapped in legalism, he can't obey God's Law; he doesn't honor his mother by facing and accepting her.

In order to suppress his natural longing for his mother, he must discount whatever stirs it—namely, all feminine objects of desire and affection. He therefore can't bond emotionally with his girlfriend, whose unrequited affections shift to his more engaging younger brother. Disintegrated, he leaves town in a drunken stupor to enlist in the army for World War I to continue, like his father, to hide behind militant legalism from the mother/woman.

When the older son leaves, the father has a stroke. The woman—who loves the younger son and knows his deep father-wound and the destruction it bodes for their future relationship—approaches the old man's bedside and begs him to grant his healing blessing to his son. Afterwards, she urges the young man to visit his father. Wisely knowing her limits (having primed the pump?) she then leaves.

In a poignant final scene, the younger son enters the bedroom where the old man lies terminally bedridden—impotent by all worldly standards, yet retaining in his fragile breath the awesome power to withhold or grant manhood.

Reconnecting to the mother, however, has recentered the younger son from the fear of his heritage to the hope of his destiny. Thus integrated, he can at last stand—and even bow—in manly integrity. Freed from shame, he approaches his father not with his grievances, but rather, his grief—that is, not with the head-on power play of false masculinity, but with the disarming, honest tears of his father-longing.

The son steps out boldly in his powerlessness and models a compelling surrender. In the face of his own powerlessness and his son's authenticity, the father follows suit and at last releases his own shame. Reaching out a faltering hand, he whispers, "Don't leave me. Stay with me, Son."

Now, he can. And graciously, even gratefully, he does.

Ironically, the younger son has fulfilled the Law more authentically than his legalistic father. The fading camera pans to include a smiling, tearful young woman, and we are assured that his life will unfold in accord with God's promise, "Honor your father and your mother, so that you may live long in the land the Lord your God is giving you" (Exod. 20:12, NIV).

Steinbeck's two fictional sons suggest two types of warriors.

The older battles to avoid the fearful truth about himself; thus disintegrated, he eventually retreats to the ultimate hiding place—rigid, self-righteous legalism. The other son battles boldly to face that truth head-on and integrate it unto self-discovery and fulfillment.

The truth is that we men have mothers. We originate in the woman.

The uncentered boy-of-the-flesh scoffs at Mom's embrace because her very presence announces that he's made of something other than pure masculinity. As a man, he graduates from catching cooties to wife abuse and sexual harassment. His dishonoring the feminine dimension of life is reflected inwardly in a false masculinity, as he also shuns close relationships with other men as homosexual, scoffs at holding babies as inconsequential, and stuffs his emotions, regarding them as petty.

It's false because it denies the truth: that brotherly care and support is essential to manhood, the man who holds his baby shapes that child for life, and the very Creator God of the Universe cares about how you feel (Ps. 8).

As a man secures his identity in the Father, however, he can honor his mother and bond with his wife as a "suitable companion" to carry out their created purposes. Indeed, he can enter the woman's world to court and affirm her. He draws her appropriately away from her father to fullfill her femininity, by giving her something Dad can't and must not—namely, his need for her as a woman to fulfill his destiny.

Sadly, insecure men who fear adult women may try to fulfill themselves through their daughters, seeking her as a partner instead of the mother. Such physical and/or emotional incest destroys a girl's ability later to embrace her own destiny with her husband.

Honoring, and not worshiping his mother, therefore, allows a man to balance his worldview with feminine input. As a Kingdom warrior, he sees warfare itself differently from the world's largely male-directed armies.

The Secular Men's Movement

As a sixth grader, terrified of my emerging sexuality and the girls who beckoned it, I remember preparing a report on the army of ancient Sparta. In those days, I preferred the unbalanced view. Indeed, the severe Spartan military discipline, which included being separated entirely from women, seized my imagination—not as a temporary concession to the world's brokenness, but as a noble lifestyle.

When I became a Christian in my thirties, I learned at last to gather with other men, not to fulfill our manhood apart from the woman, but rather, to be healed and join her in a common destiny.

Robert Bly, poet and godfather of the secular men's movement, declared in a 1983 interview,

> The fifties male was . . . supposed to like football games, be aggressive, stick up for the United States, never cry, and always provide. But this image of the male lacked feminine space. It lacked some sense of flow. It lacked compassion, in a way that led directly to the unbalanced pursuit of the Vietnam war.[2]

Bly affirmed as a male's proper first developmental stage "the journey into the feminine"—that is, bonding to the mother as an infant/boy and internalizing her "soft" traits. To become a man, however, a boy must thereafter embark on the second journey "into the masculine"—namely, bonding to the father as an adolescent and thereby learning to exercise "not macho, brute strength," but rather, "forceful action undertaken, not without compassion, but with resolve."[3]

The boy who lacks a father or older man to call him into that journey, Bly said, remains in the womb, forever dependent upon the mother and unable to move out into his destiny as a man. He thereby grows up living or dying by the woman's agenda, unable to trust masculinity in either himself or other men.

Certainly, Scripture doesn't allow a separate masculine and feminine self within us. We are not spiritual hermaphrodites, somehow equally male-and-female, complete unto ourselves. Rather, God created us as separated parts of a whole, longing to be reunited and refocused as interdependent partners in our common destiny.

Yet I knew Bly was beckoning a deeper truth, for his portrait of men overbonded to Mom and longing to bond with Dad, nailed my generation.

I felt both terrified and excited, as if being wheeled into the operating room. The time of stumbling in the darkness after a diagnosis was over. It was time to push through the father-wound toward healing.

A Christian Approach

As a Christian, however, I knew that all truth about our human nature and destiny can be found in the Bible; that like a tree cut off from its roots, such truth cut off from its source in the living God ultimately can't bear its intended fruit. And so, in dismay, I wondered: *Why have I never heard such powerful truth about men spoken in churches? Where are the Christian men to lead us into an authentic "masculine journey" for God's validation?* For several years I prayed that God would raise up a Christian writer to restore Bly's essential truth to its biblical root.

The true Savior does for us what we can't do for ourselves, but trusts us to do what we can. After several years' waiting in vain, I therefore offered myself to the Lord—and in 1987 wrote *Healing the Masculine Soul*. In it, I portrayed Bly's model of successive feminine and masculine "journeys" as helpful for understanding our predicament as men—but inadequate, because it ignores biblical-spiritual reality.

Today, I believe that model actually to be dangerous inasmuch as it pivots on breaking from the mother, and thereby beckons woman hating when divorced from the larger commandment to honor your mother. The lessons of the boy's "feminine journey," secured in the mother bond from infancy and boyhood, are integrated later as a man only as he fulfills that commandment.

In their anxiety to sever from the mother, however, some Christian men have ignored biblical truth and employed violent symbolic rites aimed against mothers. I was told of a Christian forest retreat, for example, in which men made wooden mother-figures and took turns throwing them off a high cliff into a waterfall, as the other men gathered below cheered.

The mother is a part of the boy; male rites of passage that dishonor the mother only dis-integrate him.

I seek here not to defend motherhood, but to foster manhood. A man who doesn't honor his mother, whether symbolically or in fact, can't honor the feminine dimension of life—even the part of himself that is genetically in Mom and spiritually in his wife (Gen. 2:21-23). He can't fulfill his destiny as a Kingdom warrior; indeed, the Enemy will derail him easily, likely through compulsive sexual behavior or otherwise sabotaging his marriage.

Put it another way: The mother naturally stands between the father and his son. If the son doesn't fulfill his bond to the mother, he will move toward Dad looking over his shoulder and wishing he had bonded with her, not yet equipped to bond freely with a man. Even as we must prepare to receive and affirm our sons as men, therefore, we fathers must beware weaning them too early.

The father's presence, in fact, allows the distinction between honoring the mother and worshiping her. Spiritually, individuating from the mother is the primary renouncing of idols—turning from anything to which you attribute saving power besides the living God revealed in Jesus. Even in the most healthy family, a man has no greater temptation to idolatry than his mother, to whom he was literally connected with an oxygen-and-food lifeline for nine months.

This doesn't mean the boy must renounce his mother—which would violate the commandment—but only his dependence upon her. That is, he must shift his dependency from Mom to the Father God, even as he honors her. Negotiating that delicate but essential transition into manhood requires an interim dependency upon Dad, whose affirmation allows him to distinguish between mom as a person and his dependence upon her. Because he no longer needs Mom in order to survive, he can see her as a person instead of the all-powerful life giver.

The unfathered boy, however, can only reject Mom along with his dependence. He violates God's commandment and suffers the consequences: as a man, he forfeits the "long, good life in the land the Lord your God will give you" (Exod. 20:12, TLB), for dishonoring mom short-circuits a man's intimacy with his wife and, thereby, his/their divine destiny.

Indeed, if Dad hasn't taken his own father-wound to Jesus, he will reject or idolize Mom himself—either deprecating her to mask his wound, or looking to her for his life-energy and direction. Thus, he can't facilitate his son's passage into authentic faith.

The godly father presides over the boy's passage from renouncing the mom-idol to embracing the Father God instead. The father-bond, in fact, becomes the lifeline that enables a boy in that passage to affirm both the mother-given part of himself and femininity in girls without fear of losing his masculinity.

An unfathered man can't affirm femininity without becoming it. Indeed, because he's male, he can only become a false femininity—as, for example, the passive, "soft males" Bly portrayed.

At the same time, because he's born of a woman, and separated from her as Adam from Eve, a man is naturally drawn to reaffirm and bond with the feminine dimension of life. That's why boy meets girl.

If the unfathered man doesn't surrender to Jesus and let the Father God secure him in masculinity, he will seek another power to secure him against femininity—often promised in the tough loner, as the cowboy or Rambo. He will think that a man who exhibits any traditional "feminine" traits, such as hugging another man, enjoying a baby, or crying, is homosexual.

On the contrary, homosexuality generally proceeds from a profound insecurity with masculinity, causing the man either to retreat from it into femininity, or try to seize it wholly apart from the feminine. The homosexual impulse seeks masculinity from other men like a woman, as if it were out there in other men rather than in him awaiting confirmation.

In fact, the man anxious to mask rather than integrate the feminine dimension of his root in Mom will eventually hate that part of himself—and find the Enemy ready to oblige him with a "woman-hating" spirit.

This spirit lurks about male rites of passage that discount the mother. It manifests graphically, for example, in the violently anti-woman lyrics of "gangsta rap" music, sung largely by unfathered men in a sadly perverse attempt to break the mother-bond by themselves.

Men who throw mother-images off cliffs or hip-hop curses on women need to face the truth: It's not the woman you're angry at, but the man. Your deepest wound is not from what Mom has done, but from what Dad hasn't done. Grow up and deal with your father-wound. Stop making women pay for your cowardice.

Women justly fear the men's movement insofar as it fails to honor femininity. *Women Respond to the Men's Movement,* a 1992 collection of critical essays by secular feminists, makes the point ruthlessly.[4] Divorced from biblical reality, however, the secular women's movement can't cast stones, for it has itself failed to honor the mother, and has even fostered woman-hating by repudiating motherhood. Hence the 1994 best-seller *Motherhood Deferred,*[5] in which *New York Times* columnist Anne Taylor Fleming laments being middle-aged and childless, after religiously following the antimom feminist ideology as a young woman.

Such pain and anger draws the Father's heart and is therefore fertile breeding ground for the new women's movement.

In any case, I trust that, as with my previous books, women have nothing to fear from this one—at least, no more than men, since for all of us "it is a fearful thing to fall into the hands of the living God" (Heb. 10:31, RSV). The Kingdom warrior I portray herein seeks to foster the Father God's purpose in women, precisely because we men are life partners in it.

I told Mary before our wedding that when we lived together, I of course wanted and needed to continue praying with her—but I would also continue to pray daily on the phone at 6:30 A.M. with my prayer partner. Uncomfortable at first, she nevertheless withheld judgment and asked me to help her understand. "I can't be the husband you need if I don't have other men to pray for me," I said.

That was enough for her.

Breaking Away from Mom and Dad

The political candidate who knows only what issues he's against can't fulfill the duties of office. Similarly, you don't become a man by default. Simply rejecting and distancing yourself from women only cuts you off from that part of yourself which Eve was of Adam—and short-circuits your destiny together.

The greater a man's bond to Father God, the less his compulsion to denigrate women in order to affirm his manhood. Indeed, he can derive a manly strength from affirming what his mother has borne him and its fulfilled expression in women.

In fact, knowing yourself as the Father's son ensures your respect for women. The unfathered man lacks anchoring in his masculinity and fears that affirming anything feminine will suck him back into the mother's womb.

Christian psychologist Jim Wilder has therefore suggested that only poorly fathered men need the rite-of-passage break from Mom:

> I believe that a boy who had his father's involvement at weaning will not have an identity dominated by his mother. Therefore, there should be no further need for the son to separate from the mother. In his great leap to become someone more glorious than a boy, he will naturally want the support of both parents and the wider community. It seems to me that a boy who was raised by his father to express what is inside himself and seek satisfaction in his efforts will not be in for such a great struggle.[6]

Indeed, in cultures that promote a ritual breaking from the mother as a prerequisite to manhood, fathers often are not engaged in rearing the boy until that time.

In *Healing the Masculine Soul,* I portrayed such a rite among the Ibo people of Nigeria from an earlier, polygamous era—when the boy lived apart from his father in his mother's house, until his initiation. Many American men have told me that account of the father's calling out the boy to himself and the older men made them cry. But—like most men today—these did not have fathers who were emotionally present to them as boys.

The Jewish bar mitzvah, on the other hand, seems not to require the boy's breaking from the mother in order to connect him to his spiritual heritage and the present-day company of men.

To belong securely among men becomes an issue only among those who do not—as the multitude of unfathered men today and their sons. For these, a godly occasion of "calling out" may yet remain relevant. Men who become healed enough for the next generation, however, will bond with sons even before they are born, by praying for the boy even before conception and in the womb. Later, such a boy may well not relate to a rite of passage— at least, not one that focuses primarily on breaking from the mother.

Precisely insofar as we men and our sons are healed, another break will be necessary, one for which the secular men's movement has no vocabulary—namely, the break from the father. For every boy must eventually differentiate from his dad in order to pursue his unique destiny in Father God.

A clinging father is just as burdensome to a boy as a clinging mother; each fears the Father God is unwilling or unable to usher them into their own destiny, and abdicates to the boy. The child becomes the father's destiny, rather than facilitating his recognizing it. The demanding, ambitious father who shoves his son into business or sports is the classic example.

If a man breaks from his mother by leaping into the arms of his father, into whose arms does he leap after breaking from Dad? The secular men's movement has stalled because it's inherently unable to answer this essential question. "The company of men" or "society" are insufficient answers, because even men of the world know that true manhood requires being centered in something more lasting and authentic than popular mores.

Bonding with the Father God

We must pass, then, from Mom to Dad, and from Dad to Father God.

"A person is born physically of human parents, but his is born spiritually of the Spirit," Jesus told Nicodemus. "Do not be surprised because I tell you that you must all be born again" (John 3:6-7).

Bly's feminine and masculine journeys, therefore, may be helpful metaphors to describe our wounds and needs, but fall short at prescribing our destiny as men. The essential journey into relationship with Father God—whose image is a union of both male and female—can't be fulfilled either individually or among men alone. It's short-circuited by lust and catalyzed by marriage.

Men who don't trust Father God to walk with them through their boyhood wounds will attempt to deny their need to bond with Mom and Dad, and will therefore project onto God a false, unbalanced character.

This fragmented faith is evidenced today in the church at large. Conservatives, it would seem, flee Mom and worship a false maculinity, infinitely judgmental and vengeful; liberals flee Dad and worship a false femininity, infinitely tolerant and accepting.

Ideally, then, you first bond to Mother—in the womb, at the breast, and in the home. From her you learn, "I am loved because I am." Later, with your wife, you are reinforced with this unconditional security—epitomized in the marriage vows, "For better or worse, for richer or poorer, in sickness or in health, as long as we both shall live."

In order to confirm that your intrinsic value secured with the woman bears extrinsic value beyond your home and among others in the world, you must move from Mom to Dad.

In the father's presence, then, you learn to enjoy your manhood, humbly celebrate your abilities and face your shortcomings, seek and honor the truth, act within boundaries that promote your own safety and the well-being of others. With Dad, you learn the second essential lesson—a consequence, in fact, of the first: Because I am loved, I can make a difference. Later, in the company of men, you're reinforced in your destiny—clarified and facilitated by a smaller, accountability/support group.

Meanwhile, of course, in this broken world none of us "learn" the respective journey lessons fully, because Dad and Mom are imperfect human beings.

Most of us begin to realize our parents' shortcomings at adolescence. If we haven't been taught about the Father God's love and power—which even Dad and Mom require—we resent our parents for not being all-powerful gods and, thereby, failing to give us what we need.

Hence, "adolescent rebellion."

Addictive behaviors—such as smoking, drinking, and promiscuous sex—often are sparked and fueled by such rebellion. Leaping from Dad into the arms of the world, therefore, is no rite of passage; it's a fall into destruction. Indeed, the powers of the world clearly reveal their insidious intent in offering self-destructive behaviors as rites of passage themselves: At the magic age, a young man can at last legally buy cigarettes and alcohol and attend pornographic movies, just like older men.

These behaviors secure you in the world—not as a man among men, but as a sucker among other addicts.

Compulsive-addictive behaviors attempt to fill the gap where the first and second lessons have fallen short—that is, to make a man forget his painful longing to know "I'm loved because I am" and to focus his abilities productively. When a man honestly faces the destruction these behaviors cause himself, he's ready at last to hear the authentic cry in his masculine soul for a third journey—namely, "Who will rescue me from this body that is taking me to death?" (Rom. 7:24).

Adolescent rebellion tapers off as a man begins to realize it's ultimately self-destructive. Indeed, avenging Dad diverts energy needed otherwise to fulfill your destiny. As a man surrenders to Father God, he sees his own brokenness as well as his dad's. Insofar as he asks God for forgiveness, he receives it—and can give it to his dad. Doing so frees his energies at last to bond with the woman and pursue his manly calling as a son of Father God.

Thus surrendered to Jesus, a man learns the essential third lesson—in fact, the authentic fulfillment of the first two: Because my Father God loves me, he has called and prepared me to make a difference in the world. He does this in and through me insofar as I am surrendered to Jesus, committed to my fellow warriors in the Body of Christ, and bonded with the woman in our common destiny.

Amen.

FIFTEEN

From Jackass to Warhorse

For the message about Christ's death on the cross is nonsense to those who are being lost; but for us who are being saved it is God's power. . . . As for us, we proclaim the crucified Christ, a message that is offensive to the Jews and nonsense to the Gentiles; but for those whom God has called, both Jews and Gentiles, this message is Christ, who is the power of God and the wisdom of God. For what seems to be God's foolishness is wiser than human wisdom, and what seems to be God's weakness is stronger than human strength.
1 Corinthians 1:18, 23-25

WHILE planning a sermon, shortly after beginning work on this book, I prayed as usual and asked the Father what he wanted me to say. Waiting for impressions, images, Scriptures, or ideas, I was puzzled to sense just one word: *Prepare.*

"OK, Father," I said, puzzled. "Prepare for what?"

Prepare, I heard again—and nothing more.

"That's a sermon, Father? Just 'Prepare'?"

Silence.

"But if you won't tell me what to prepare for," I protested, "I can't tell people how!"

Silence.

I sighed, exasperated. If indeed the Lord had spoken, the ball was in my court.

I balked. "Prepare" just sounded dull, even passive. I was about to say, "Lord, how about something more bold and proactive?"—but my curiosity overruled.

Intrigued, I pushed on. "OK, Father," I said. "I let go of my desire for an immediate focus. What are you after here?" Suddenly, it occurred to me that the Father God is the Initiator. Thus, "Prepare" might mean, "I'm about to do something significant; get the people ready to recognize and participate in it."

Now *that* was exciting!

I remembered the above Scripture, "What seems to be God's weakness is stronger than human strength," and my mind leapt ahead: If the Father's not telling me what to prepare for, then he must want me to preach some essential aspect of getting ready for a move of God. Immediately I knew I'd have to sideline my curiosity, surrender control of the larger picture, and focus instead on letting the Father hone the church as a tool fit for his hand—like soldiers at attention, awaiting orders.

The Call to Prepare

Preparing for a move of God, I realized, is an authentic theater of action for Kingdom warriors. Indeed, just seeking to trust the Father God when you've been abandoned as a boy, prompts the very onslaught of hell.

No matter what God was planning that would require our readiness, I knew I could preach no more authentic preparation than his biblical blueprint for the coming of Jesus. And so I turned to the story of the forerunner John the Baptist, appointed by God to proclaim healing for the father-wound (Mal. 4:5-6) as preparation for God's most important move in history:

> "He will go ahead of the Lord, strong and mighty like the prophet Elijah. He will bring fathers and children together again; he will turn disobedient people back to the way of

thinking of the righteous; he will get the Lord's people ready for him" (Luke 1:17).

Indeed, when John is born, his father Zechariah prophesies about his destiny, proclaiming God's trustworthiness by recalling his ancient promises now fulfilled (Luke 1:67-79). In Hebrew, his name itself—Jonathan—means "God is gracious." As a man, John trusts God's plan for him, and faithfully prepares himself by living in the desert—thus identifying with his Hebrew forebears in the Exodus and learning there to depend wholly on the Father and not human strength (Deut. 8:2ff.).

When he appears at last to the world (Luke 3:2-6), John therefore echoes the ancient prophet Isaiah,

> "Comfort my people," says our God. "Comfort them! Encourage the people of Jerusalem. Tell them they have suffered long enough and their sins are now forgiven. I have punished them in full for all their sins."
>
> A voice cries out, "Prepare in the wilderness a road for the Lord! Clear the way in the desert for our God! Fill every valley; level every mountain. The hills will become a plain, and the rough country will be made smooth. Then the glory of the Lord will be revealed, and all mankind will see it. The Lord himself has promised this" (Isa. 40:1-5).

Thus the call to prepare comes from a trustworthy God, who not only keeps his promise, but meets his people in their brokenness with power to fulfill their part in it. It's not designed to warn and punish rebels but, rather, to mobilize and empower sons. As a promise to comfort and renew those who have "suffered long enough" for their sins, it therefore requires you first to receive the Father's healing comfort and forgiveness.

For men crippled by shame, that's a battle.

The call to prepare is not aimed at worldly men, who are too busy building defenses and preparing for their own success to make ways for God to enter their lives. Rather, it's aimed at faithful sons, willing to endure the desert season of discipline and learn from his boot camp.

Like John the Baptist, the Kingdom warrior is therefore called to prepare both himself and his people for God to act in and through them.

And that—as any man who's tried it knows—is no license for passivity. It's a major battle to let go of your own control to the Father and get out of the way for him to act. Similarly, even though a farmer depends on God to make the crop grow, he works hard to prepare the soil by cultivating, planting, and watering (1 Cor. 3:6-9).

Indeed, a Kingdom warrior's faith statement might declare, "As I do what I can, God will do what I can't." Thus, God not only comforted the Israelites on their return from exile, but promised when they set out to rebuild the temple among hostile pagans, "You will succeed, not by military might or by your own strength, but by my spirit" (Zech. 4:6).

Like John and the early Israelites in the desert, the Kingdom warrior prepares himself to hear the Commander's call and receive his strength. He "fills up the valleys" in his life by surrendering to Jesus his doubts and weakness. He "levels off the mountains" by confessing to Jesus his pride and begging him to crucify it. He "smooths the rough places" by asking Jesus to polish and refine his humanly flawed efforts to cooperate with the Father.

Thus, he prepares to receive, proclaim, and walk out the Good News: We who had lost our way to the hospital have been found, even by the Chief Surgeon. We who had deserted the barracks have been recruited, even by the General of the armies.

Entering the hospital for his healing prepares a man to enter the barracks for his destiny. In the hospital, in fact, he learns the authentic relationship with the Father that prepares him for the barracks: born in humility and trust, matured in courage and faithfulness.

Thus, a man leaves the hospital for the barracks—and arrives to discover at last that they are one and the same: the Commander-in-Chief is none other than the Great Physician.

The One who heals is the one who deploys.

Indeed, it's our healing and redemption as men to become Kingdom warriors; it's our battle and destiny to know and proclaim the Father's restoration.

In fact, as the apostle Paul declared, your healing often shapes your battle:

> Let us give thanks to the God and Father of our Lord Jesus Christ, the merciful Father, the God from whom all help comes! He helps us in all our troubles, so that we are able to help others who have all kinds of troubles, using the same help that we ourselves have received from God. (2 Cor. 1:3-4)

You can't give people what you haven't got. And you get it from the Father.

Nevertheless, even as I underscore surrender as the essence of the Kingdom warrior's preparation, I have to restrain an impatient voice within me, *But what about* action? *Once a man has surrendered, surely there's something for him to do as a warrior?*

Indeed, the goal of surrendering is to allow Jesus to shape you as his weapon, so he can deploy you to the action he's designed you for—in fact, the battle he's prepared you to win. As the apostle Paul declared,

> For it is by God's grace that you have been saved through faith. It is not the result of your own efforts, but God's gift, so that no one can boast about it. God has made us what we are, and in our union with Christ Jesus he has created us for a life of good deeds, which he has already prepared for us to do. (Eph. 2:8-10)

Don't worry. The Father has prepared not only your destiny, but the "good deeds" which fulfill it. Insofar as you're surrendered to, and thereby are "in union with" Jesus, he'll show you what they are.

Your Destiny in Christ

The Commander-in-Chief is well able to train and to deploy his men when and where he needs them. He will open your eyes to recognize the battle he's prepared you for, and in his time you will get your draft notice calling you to duty—often through everyday circumstances.

Jesus was flesh as well as spirit. You don't always need supernatural words of knowledge to discern the Father's call. You just need humility. The Father is not banking on "your own efforts" to get the job done, but only your willingness to receive his resources. "God doesn't want our ability," as another has said, "but only our availability."

The Father God doesn't play hide-and-seek with men. He wants you to know your destiny—your role in restoring his Kingdom—even more than you do. Your destiny, however, is shaped in relationship with him. Thus, he may withhold an immediate, clear revelation of it so you will seek and engage him more deeply—even as Jesus at times spoke in parables instead of direct statements (Matt. 13:10-17).

In the Bible, two bodies of water portray two successive passages into a man's destiny, each defining a specific stage of relationship with the Father and his expectation of your own participation.

God created the Israelites to "bring light to the nations," (Isa. 42:6) and thus, portray the way to his heart. When they were slaves in Egypt for hundreds of years, they were not free to serve him and to be who they were created to be. Their first step toward fulfilling their destiny in the Promised Land of freedom was to cry out to God in their bondage and trust him to respond (Deut. 26:7-8).

In response, God brings plagues upon Egypt, forcing the pharaoh to let the Israelites go. Soon after leaving, however, they find themselves pursued from behind by the Egyptian army and blocked ahead by the Red Sea. Helpless, and angry at Moses for leading them into such an apparent dead end, "They were terrified and cried out to the Lord for help" (Exod. 14:10).

At first, Moses simply exhorts the people to trust God, misunderstanding their role in his saving work:

> Don't be afraid! Stand your ground, and you will see what the Lord will do to save you today; you will never see these Egyptians again. The Lord will fight for you, and all you have to do is keep still. (Exod. 14:13-14)

But while God is indeed prepared to fight for his people, he expects more of them than simply to "keep still":

> The Lord said to Moses, "Why are you crying out for help? Tell the people to move forward. Lift up your walking stick and hold it out over the sea. The water will divide, and the Israelites will be able to walk through the sea on dry ground." (Exod. 14:15-16)

God requires his army to put one foot in front of the other and "move forward"; his leader Moses must lift his arm. That's it. No more, and no less. He doesn't require natural human beings to do anything supernatural.[1]

God does the job, but through his people. He won't do for us what we can do, but neither will he require of us what we can't.

The Israelites can't know where to go ahead. But they can turn their backs to the untenable position behind, trust God, and start walking. "You don't have to know where to go," God tells the troops. "You just have to move—and I'll direct you."

It's easier to turn the steering wheel on a car once it's moving.

Similarly, Moses can't make the sea part, but he can lift up his stick. "Just show yourself willing to lead," God tells his commander, "and I'll clear the way."

Most Christians know this classic story of God's saving power at the beginning of the Exodus, but few realize that a similar scenario is played out at the end, when a flooding Jordan River blocks the way into the Promised Land. This time, however, the people's own responsibility assumes a new level of cooperation, appropriate to their new maturity and relationship with the Father from their desert discipline:

> It was harvest time, and the river was in flood.
>
> When the people left the camp to cross the Jordan, the priests went ahead of them, carrying the Covenant Box. *As soon as the priests stepped into the river,* the water stopped flowing and piled up, far upstream. . . . The flow downstream to the Dead Sea was completely cut off, and the people were able to cross over near Jericho. (Josh. 3:14-16, italics mine)

Back at the Red Sea forty years earlier, when God's people were ragged, desperate, helpless, and able only to cry out in faith, he parted the water for them. No risk, no worry; just walk, even on dry land.

But when the people had later come to know God as their saving Father, literally an additional step of faith was required. The river is flooding dangerously, and the leaders must put their feet in it first, before God gives them any further confirmation of his saving presence.

God still parts the water. But greater faith is expected of those who have been through the desert boot camp because they have gained a deeper relationship with the Father. The need for greater faith, in fact, confirms a Kingdom warrior's "promotion": the most seasoned soldier is sent to the most critical battles.

The greater the faith required, the more significant the victory. Jesus' surrender on the cross made him eligible to lead the Father's greatest victory in the Resurrection (Phil. 2:8-11).

You can't part an ocean or river. But when God says he'll do it, you can trust him and put your foot in the water. Similarly, you can't stop yourself from sinning. But when God says he's sent his Son to bear your sin, you can step out into life, trusting him to make a way for you into his promised victory.

Like our ancient Hebrew forebears in faith, you can cry out to the Father God from your bondage, and beg him to open the way out. You don't have to know where to go; you just have to want to get out, and trust your Father to lead you.

Most new Christians recall an overwhelming sense of freedom when they first surrendered to Jesus. But often this initial boost is God giving you strength to persevere in his refining ahead, even as a honeymoon roots a couple in joy for the later ups and downs of marriage.

You have to be strong enough to undergo the operation before the surgeon will schedule you; a man must be healthy enough to know he's sick before God will lead him into the desert ordeal.

You don't get airlifted from slavery to the Promised Land. Rather, you enter the desert, the place of complete and utter neediness, to learn relationship with the Father.

The flesh naturally balks at the humbling desert ordeal, and a proud man can be seduced into believing his emotional and spiritual wounds need not be attended once he's become a Christian. "When you're born again, everything's taken care of," he says. "I don't need any further healing."

But consider the sick man treated by various doctors with no relief. Finally, he finds the truly best specialist in the field, who diagnoses him correctly. He doesn't then say, "Now I don't need the operation." Rather, he says, "At last! Now I'm confident I'll be healed—take me to the operating room!"

As you let the Father draw you to himself through his healing, he leads you to the border of the Promised Land, to reveal the "good deeds" he's prepared you to do for his Kingdom. By then, you know his power and love, and you can step out confidently into the flood of sin that separates you from your destiny.

True Religion

Too often we think that becoming like Jesus means "attaining his moral standard of perfection"—which we can't do—instead of surrendering to the Father, which we can do. I've ministered to men who told me, "I'm so bound up inside, I can't even say, 'Father, I want to do it your way.'" I invite them to pray simply, "Father, I want to want to do it your way. Please change my will."

The issue for Christian men, after all, is not whether or not we'll sin, but rather, whether we have relationship with the one who can save us from its effects. Until Jesus returns, we will sin, and that relationship is both the beginning and the goal of sanctification. It begins with your surrender to Jesus and proceeds in his victory as you receive new life in his Spirit, who motivates you with his desires.

The powers of the world do not list *prepare* and *surrender* under the heading of "action." Readers will find many other books that outline, detail, and exhort men to specific action—much of which may well portray God's goal for us. This book, however, focuses upon God's action and not our own—that is, not on how to act, but rather, how to prepare for and cooperate with God's acting, both in and through you.

Indeed, the original sin, which infects us all and which Jesus died to overcome, is the fantasy "I can do it." Thus, the Snake exhorted Adam and Eve: "Go ahead! You can do it on your own. You don't need God. He doesn't want you to know that, because he's proud and jealous" (Gen. 3:1-5).

The Snake is the classic deceiver: it's not God, but we ourselves who are proud and jealous. The Enemy wants most to keep us from knowing God and from recognizing and responding to his action. And so the Snake's lie focuses on distorting the Father God's character, even projecting our brokenness onto him. Jesus, on the other hand, has come to instill his Spirit of righteousness in us.

Hence, false religion: impelled by pride and designed to hide shame—and to avoid facing authentic needs. It tells a man, "You need to be good," or "You need to do it right"—and thereby produces false warriors, who trust in their own strength and battle with huge chinks in their armor.

True religion, on the other hand, is impelled by humility and designed to reveal grace—and to surface and meet authentic needs. It says, "You need your Father"—and produces true warriors, who face the truth of their brokenness, surrender to the Father God, and battle unto victory in his strength.

False religion, therefore, doesn't require surrender, but rather, sacrifice. As men, we often like to pay for what we get, because doing so reminds us that we're in charge. Pay-as-you-go means "I earned it." Certainly, we can and must make amends for what we do, for our sinful acts against others. But no man can make restitution for who he is—that is, for his sinful human nature.

Men raised by unforgiving fathers, however, will try—and either abandon their destiny when they discover they can't make it happen, or lower the "cost" to a manageable "amount" by discounting their sin-nature: "My condition isn't really that bad. I can try harder, sacrifice a little more, and that should even things up."

Such false religion hides a man's deepest and most authentic need, even as for food and water, to bond with and worship his Father God (Deut. 8:3; Ps. 42:1-2; John 14:8).

A man needs Father God because only he can save us from our rebellious human nature, which draws us away from his created intention for us. True religion therefore turns a man's focus from his apparent desires as a proud rebel to his authentic needs as a beloved son. Because those desires appear in this world as compelling as life itself, true religion proclaims the Cross—it reminds us that as we surrender to Father God and sacrifice our very bodies to him, he overcomes the powers of the world in and about us (Rom. 12:1-2).

Yet the powers of the world do not give up easily, and if they can't compel us to reject Jesus altogether, they will seek to distort his character—especially by playing on our worldly desires and fears.

Imagine, for example, a first-century video ad to promote Christianity. The action leaps out with crowds shouting, "Hosanna!" and waving palm branches outside Jerusalem. The camera then pans to a waist-up shot of Jesus—to cut out the lowly donkey—waving triumphantly. Quick images of people being healed, delivered of demons, leaving prostitution, and bending over bulging fishnets are blended with a rising chorus of "Alleluia!" and focus at last on the 120 worshiping joyously at 9 A.M. on Pentecost day.

"Those who are being lost"—in the apostle Paul's terms from the chapter-opening verses—from New Age spiritualists to everyday hedonists—would see everything they want in such a religion.

But they would not see what they need because they would not see the Cross. Unlike those who "proclaim the crucified Christ," they would not see a warrior faith. In fact, they would be lured into a fantasy that ultimately delivers them into the Enemy's hands.

The Cross is the touchstone, the sine qua non of authentic religion—unlike belief systems that discount others' needs and shun discomfort. The man who wants to fulfill his destiny in life knows he needs to crucify his rebellious nature, to surrender it to the Father to die and be resurrected in his image.

False religion is therefore portrayed clearly in those at Calvary who mocked Jesus, "Save yourself if you are God's Son! Come on down from the cross!" (Matt. 27:40).

The false warrior seeks a savior who can deliver him out of discomfort—from nighttime baby feedings to facing his own sin-nature. If he ever battles the true Enemy of God, it is only to "get him off my turf so I can be happier." The warrior of God, however, knows that he must meet the Enemy on the Enemy's own turf, even in others' lives, in order to claim victory—an enterprise which the Cross proclaims is uncomfortable unto death.

As God's authentic Warrior, on the cross Jesus overrules his natural impulse and chooses not to save himself, but rather, to surrender to God and trust his purposes—thereby allowing God to shape him as a vehicle for saving others.

As the apostle Paul declared,

302

> [Jesus] always had the nature of God, but he did not think that by force he should try to become equal with God. Instead of this, of his own free will he gave up all he had, and took the nature of a servant. He became like man and appeared in human likeness. He was humble and walked the path of obedience all the way to death—his death on the cross. For this reason God raised him to the highest place

above and gave him the name that is greater than any other name. (Phil. 2:6-9)

Like the scoffers at Calvary, false religion disqualifies Jesus as Savior because he doesn't do it all by himself, and come down from the cross to save himself. True religion, on the other hand, proclaims Jesus as the Messiah *precisely because he doesn't cop out and save himself.* Rather, he pushes through the pain of his calling unto victory by surrendering to the Father and trusting his purpose and presence in it.

A man attempts to get down off the cross and save himself when he abandons relationship with Father God and turns instead to performance-oriented, false religion. He proudly offers to God his fatted rams, principles of manhood achieved, moral standards adhered to, resolutions made and promises kept—everything but what the Father must have in order to transform him—namely, a humble, on-your-face confession of utter brokenness and need:

> You do not delight in sacrifice, or I would bring it; you do not take pleasure in burnt offerings. The sacrifices [you want are] a broken spirit; a broken and contrite heart, O God, you will not despise. (Ps. 51:16-17, NIV)

False religion therefore recruits from the vast and tragic pool of men today whose fathers did not affirm their genuine needs. Rather, they learned as boys, "If I can just do it right, my father will love me!" Terrified of the negative corollary—"If I do it wrong, Dad will reject me"—such a man dares not know his own utter inadequacy and, therefore, never knows the Father's utter mercy and love.

Indeed, he projects these boyhood fears of Dad onto other men, convinced that his self-doubts and failures have made him unacceptable among men, and he must therefore hide them. It's tragic, like dying of starvation at a banquet. God does not love us because we do it right; rather, only because God loves us can we do it right (1 John 4:10, 19).

The Kingdom warrior, therefore, is motivated by relationship with the Father, not by blind obedience to the Law. He does God's will not because it's right, but because it's life. It's not a matter of what he should do as a Christian but, rather, of who he is, as a son.

Even as God loves us not because we are obedient, but because he is a Lover, so the true warrior does the Father's will not because being a Christian demands it, but because that's what a son does.

When my son had grown enough teeth as a toddler, I decided one evening it was time they were brushed—assuming my job was essentially to force him to submit as I did it for him. I was gentle as I knelt beside him and told him to open his mouth, but as I tried to stick the brush in, a toddler-scream erupted—loosely translated as "No way, Dad!" I tried a firmer voice, to no avail. I gripped his shoulder, and ordered him to open his mouth—but he drew up rigidly and refused.

Exasperated, I gave up. As he stood there close-mouthed beside me in the bathroom, I set his brush down on the utility table. "All right, forget it!" I sighed, stood, and turned to brush my own teeth. As a rabid foam filled my mouth, I was startled when, out of the corner of my eye, I saw my little son pick up his brush, look intently at me, and then try to do himself what he saw me doing. He was brushing his ears as much as his teeth, but I was stunned—and humbled.

Slowly, I set my brush down, turned and knelt again beside my son. "That's . . . that's good," I encouraged him. "I'm sorry Daddy tried to force you. Yes, just brush it on your teeth like that!" Before long, he was motioning me to show him how to do it better.

That night on my knees in the bathroom, I learned a lesson that has changed my life—and my son's. Just by being his father I have a tremendous and precious authority to model behavior in my son's life. My true and lasting authority in my son's life is based upon our relationship, not my physical power to coerce him. Indeed—contrary to the world's view—I lose my God-given authority as a father precisely when I resort to coercion.

The Father God did not restore his children to righteousness with the coercive punishment of the Law, but rather, the Cross.

And that, my Christian brothers, is the difference between Spirit and Law. Moving in the Father's Holy Spirit requires accepting relationship with him, that is, recognizing you are his son, and surrendering to his renewing victory; to focus exclusively on the Law is to deny relationship, see yourself as an abandoned individual, and surrender to a lonely self-defeat.

Denying the father-wound causes us to forget that a portion of the earthly father's spirit is in his son, animating the boy—for better or worse—to be like Dad. We have forgotten the truth, reflected thus imperfectly in the earthly father-son relationship, that the man who becomes born again as a son of the Father God receives the Holy Spirit in himself (John 3:5-8), which animates him to be like the Father God.

Knowing you are the Father's son thereby frees you from the Law, because the Spirit that prompted the Law is in you, fulfilling his intent (Jer. 31:31ff.). Indeed, as my son wanted to brush his teeth like me, so you'll want to do what your Father God is doing. You'll long to be a part of his work in this world and won't be satisfied until you're doing your part.

Thus a man becomes a Kingdom warrior, trusting God's purposes—no matter how much pain that costs him. He knows that ultimately the Father will honor him, even as the resurrected Jesus—that, indeed, the joy of being honored by the Father not only supercedes, but overcomes the fear of being wounded by the world. The man who has faced his own father-wound knows this insofar as he has dared confess—and grieve—his longing for Dad to honor him.

The apostle Paul therefore declared that the Cross is "nonsense" for those seeking to avoid pain and save themselves. But for those in the process of letting God save them—of surrendering, trusting God's mercy, facing the awful power of sin and death both within and without, confessing, "I can't do what you want me to, Father"—the Cross is the crucible in which the power of God is revealed (Rom. 7:25).

Riding into Battle

As a young man in my early thirties, I learned to play a soft nylon-string guitar and eventually decided to get a steel-string guitar. Friends directed me to a burly, gray-haired owner of a slot-in-the-wall guitar shop several blocks from the beach. When I told him what I wanted, he handed me a steel-string demo. Excitedly, I plucked out a song I'd enjoyed on my old guitar—and winced from the pain in my fingers.

"Can't you make it easier to push the steel strings down?" I begged.

"Sure," he said. "I can lower 'em closer to the neck—but they'll buzz against the neck when you pluck 'em."

Massaging my burning fingertips, I persisted. "But can't you lower the strings and fix it somehow so they don't buzz?"

"Son," the old man said, smiling thinly and scratching his white beard, "you wanna go t' heaven without dyin'!"

Even as the warrior requires basic training, there's no heaven without dying, no resurrection without the Cross, no Promised Land without the desert, no revelation of God's purpose and power without despairing of your own, no knowing Jesus fully as Friend without facing the Enemy.

Through the cross, the Father God has said, "I don't bail out on my sons, even when they are in death's grip. In fact, that's precisely where I shape them into warriors for my Kingdom." That's good news for men in this broken world. It's the wellspring of true religion, and the bedrock faith of Kingdom warriors.

The Sunday-morning Christian "civilian" bases his faith on the good things God has given him—his wife, job, children, car. But the Kingdom warrior knows that such a shallow faith won't endure in this broken world where the Enemy yet lurks. What happens, for example, when the wife leaves him, he gets laid off from work, his children get into drugs, his car breaks down? That's essentially what the Enemy did to Job, and God allowed it as a test of his faith.

We thank God, of course, for his many undeserved blessings.

But we believe he's ultimately real when we meet him in our helplessness before the powers of the world (Ps. 56).

Significantly, therefore, when Jesus at last turns from the Galilean countryside back to Jerusalem to be crucified, he enters the city riding on a lowly donkey—even a foal, the lowest of donkeys.

Certainly, God wants us to be courageous in the face of the Enemy. But the security that fosters such courage deepens only insofar as a man surrenders to his covering. The more humble a man is before the Father God, the more bold he can be before the world—because humble openness to God allows a man to receive his Spirit, the power to overcome all other power, both natural and supernatural (1 John 4:4).

Jesus' character and ministry are portrayed in the Bible with two paradoxical images—which appear as nonsense to men trying to sidestep the Cross—that is, to save themselves from being refined and shaped for the Father's purposes.

On the one hand, we see Jesus' riding the humble donkey, the vehicle of humiliation. Indeed, the man who rides the donkey before God no longer needs most to save face, but to face his Savior. As he becomes secure in the power he mediates from the Father, his manly energies are freed from preserving his own dignity to serving others.

He thereby becomes a leader in the Kingdom of God. "You know that the rulers of the heathen have power over them," as Jesus admonished his disciples,

> And the leaders have complete authority. This, however, is not the way it shall be among you. If one of you wants to be great, he must be the servant of the rest; and if one of you wants to be first, he must be your slave—like the Son of Man, who did not come to be served, but to serve and to give his life to redeem many people. (Matt. 20:25-28)

The donkey is a beast of burden, appropriate for bearing Jesus into the Old Jerusalem, the kingdom of the flesh where reign the powers of the world that despise him—Pilate, Herod, high priest and teachers of the Law. The humble steed bears a man unto death of his own agendas, cleansing him of all pride.

Even as Satan can't cast out Satan, neither can the power of the flesh defeat flesh—which yet rules among us only because the ruler of this present world, even God's spiritual Enemy, has intimidated the men of God into shame and isolation. Humanly devised weapons, from swords to H-bombs, can't defeat this Enemy, but only a power grounded outside the world, even in its Creator.

A radically different power must therefore be demonstrated, one that blazes a path for the men of God to the Father's own heart. Thus, the apostle Paul declared that "the weapons we use in our fight are not the world's weapons but God's powerful weapons" (2 Cor. 10:4).

As another has noted, God's problem with swords and H-bombs is simply that they are not powerful enough to accomplish the job he wants done among men. You can't bomb men into the Father's heart just as you can't pull down proud obstacles riding a stallion. You need a counterpoint to the world's pride in order to transform a man's stubborn heart of flesh into the surrendered heart of a warrior (Ezek. 36:26).

You need a jackass.

But as the jackass does its job and those proud obstacles fall, a new vehicle is required to move a man from his brokenness to his calling, from his healing to its purpose in God's larger plan. You can't ride a jackass from desert to Promised Land, from Cross to Resurrection, from hospital to barracks. As you allow God to gain the victory over your pride, you need a vehicle to carry you into his victory over the world.

You need a warhorse.

And so, after Jesus has gone humbly and faithfully to the cross and allowed God therein to shape him for his destiny, then and only then (Phil. 2:6-11), the resurrected Lord emerges honored by the Father, bold and decisive before the Enemy:

> Then I saw heaven open, and there was a white horse. Its rider is called Faithful and True; it is with justice that he

judges and fights his battles. His eyes were like a flame of fire, and he wore many crowns on his head. He had a name written on him, but no one except himself knows what it is. The robe he wore was covered with blood. His name is "The Word of God." The armies of heaven followed him, riding on white horses and dressed in clean white linen. Out of his mouth came a sharp sword, with which he will defeat the nations. He will rule over them with a rod of iron, and he will trample out the wine in the wine press of the furious anger of the Almighty God. On his robe and on his thigh was written the name: "King of kings and Lord of lords." (Rev. 19:11-16)

Our Commander has called us to a glorious victory. But the story is clear: You can't ride the warhorse into the New Jerusalem until you've ridden the jackass into the Old Jerusalem.

The warhorse is not for men who get down off the cross to play religion: who strive after "biblical principles of manhood," who are so busy following the rules that they have forgotten the Ruler, so anxious to be right that they have forgotten how to be real, so ashamed of their brokenness that they don't trust the Father's grace.

The warhorse is not for those who enjoy the hosannas of Palm Sunday, the alleluias of Easter, and the amens of "biblical morality," but have never dared listen to the Good Friday cry of every honest man's spirit, "My God, my God, why have you abandoned me?" (Ps. 22:1; Matt. 27:46).

The warhorse is not for the men who struggle the hardest to be good, but those who most genuinely confess that they can't be good.

The warhorse is for the born-again, resurrected man, who allows God—even begs him—to kill his fleeting fantasy of worldly manhood in order to gain the eternal dignity of godly sonship. The Enemy exhausts his wordly defenses, brings him naked before the powers of death and sneers, "What do you have to say for yourself now?"

"Nothing," he says, "but 'Jesus'."

And that's enough.

Indeed, in this as-yet-unredeemed world we must become used to both steeds. Battle wounds will force us to ride the donkey into a new death, facing yet deeper needs and fears, being broken and cleansed more deeply, and readied for a new battle. We then ride the warhorse as long as the Lord appoints, until battle wounds reveal the need for yet deeper healing.

And then we get back on the jackass once again—until the Old Jerusalem of the flesh passes away at last to the New Jerusalem of the Father God.

The jackass prepares you for the warhorse.

And the warhorse allows you to welcome the jackass.

Today, as I travel around the U.S. and Canada, I see hundreds of brushfires where individuals and small groups of men have gone to the Cross, surrendered their lives to Jesus, and are now ignited with his Spirit.

Like stars in the dark sky, they are many—yet separate.

The day is coming, however, when the multitude of small fires will connect at last and ignite across the land, even as when the Lord returns victorious his glory will light the heavens as sun, moon, and stars fall together (Rev. 22:5).

A Vision for the Coming Battle

Lately, as I pray at men's conferences, a compelling vision, which I once had several years ago, now comes back often. Before "seeing" anything, I hear in my mind a loud chorus of men shouting boldly—a battle cry of both compassion and determination, as if punctuated with tears and raised fists: "Jesus! Jesus! Jesus!"

I then see a long line of saddled horses in the foreground of a plain facing a dark horizon tumbling with storm clouds. Wind whips the horses' tails and manes as they stand behind Jesus, mounted out front with eyes aflame, pointing ahead as his horse snorts and rears expectantly.

And then, individual men stand beside the horses—broken men, some stooped over, others limping with canes, bandages and splints—and Jesus is helping each mount up.

Suddenly, one man with no apparent affliction leaps up on a horse by himself. Deliberately, compassionately, Jesus goes to him and says, "Get down. You're not ready." Crestfallen, the man dismounts, and Jesus returns to boosting the others onto their horses.

At one conference, I "saw" behind the line of horses a woman kneeling quietly, praying. Later, several men told me their wives and other women at the church had wanted to come to the men's conference, and when it was announced for men only, they covenanted to pray for the men.

Worshiping at another conference, I "saw" in my vision an older, white-haired man standing off in the background. A younger man who had been lifted to his saddle by Jesus dismounted, went over and took the older man's hand. I sensed clearly that this was a son and his father. Together, they walked to another horse. Jesus came beside the two and laid a hand on each. With great compassion and mercy—overriding all past wounding—the son boosted his father up.

"Hallelujah!" rose a shout in my spirit.

More recently, I "saw" a young boy watching as Jesus helped a man mount up; as the man sat upright in the saddle, the boy smiled and proclaimed, "That's my daddy!"

As he demonstrated in sending Jesus, and later, his Holy Spirit, the Father has the battle plan and he's taken the initiative to fulfill it among us. Like it or not—ready or not—he's calling men today to be warriors for his kingdom.

In response, the ageless Enemy is rising to attack and defeat us at our every weak spot. The man surrendered to his flesh will be destroyed; the man surrendered to Jesus will recognize his brokenness at last and bring it to the Father, who will shape it into a weapon for his victory.

The Father knows all too well the limits of our sinful human nature. He doesn't hold us accountable for being unable to strive and accomplish, but only for being unwilling to surrender and trust. A man can't save himself, but he can say yes to the Savior.

As men, the ball's in our court.

We can choose to say no to the Father's call, abandon the

world Jesus died to save, go AWOL, and score one for the Enemy. We can shout, "I can do it!," leap quickly onto a horse by ourselves—and be eliminated as quickly either by the Enemy or by Jesus, who loves us so much he will never send us into battle unprepared. Or, we can choose at last to say yes, fall trembling at Jesus' feet, and trust his victory in and through us.

As boys after WWII in the early 1950s, we often tested each other by asking, "What did your dad do during the war?"

Every son, in every generation, must answer that question if he is to know his heritage as a man. For whatever battles a man runs from, he consigns to his son.

Years from today, when my toddler son approaches manhood, I want to be able to look him in the eye and say, "Son, I've fought the battle of my time to prepare you for yours."

But I can't get there alone.

And so I thank God for what he's given me through my forefathers and look forward to what he will give me through you, my brother, as together we fight onward.

For, even now, through the thunder, the sound of sword sharpening can be heard at brotherly fellowships, of armor mending at the altar.

Like Jesus, your battle is coming.

Like Jesus, your battle is here.

And, like Jesus, your horse is waiting.

NOTES

Introduction

1. Joe Kita, "Our Fathers," *Men's Health*, June 1995, 86.
2. Harry Stein, "The Post-Sensitive Man Is Coming!" *Esquire*, May 1994, 5–6.
3. Ibid., 63.
4. "APA Revises Criteria on Key Sexual Issues," reprinted from *Regeneration News*, Dec. 1994, in *The Standard* (Exodus International), 1st quarter 1995: 10. Specifically, the *Diagnostic and Statistical Manual*, paragraph B, section 302.20, was changed from diagnosing pedophilia as a disorder if "The person has acted out on these urges, or is markedly distressed by them" [1973 *DSM-III*: 285], to "The fantasies, sexual urges, or behaviors cause clinically significant distress or impairment in social, occupational, or other important areas of functioning" [1994 *DSM-IV*: 528].

Chapter 1

1. Robert S. McNamara with Brian VanDeMark, *In Retrospect: The Tragedy and Lessons of Vietnam* (New York: Times Books 1995), xvi–xvii.
2. Modern translations omit this statement, but ancient authorities include it.
3. Greg Hernandez and Tony Perry, "Broken Romance Writes Tragic End to Bright Future," *Los Angeles Times*, 2 December 1993, 1.
4. What follows is adapted from "An Evening Run to Victory through Surrender," *The Priest*, February 1989, 29–32.

Chapter 2

1. Greg Louganis with Eric Marcus, *Breaking the Surface* (New York: Random House, 1995).

Chapter 3

1. Walter Trobisch, *All a Man Can Be* (Downers Grove, Ill.: InterVarsity Press, 1983), 61.

Chapter 4

1. This analogy was suggested by the Reverend Jim Kermath, formerly of the Santa Monica Vineyard Church.
2. Joe Maxwell, "Looking for a Few Good Men," *Christianity Today*, 26 April 1993, 40.

3. Robert C. Girard, *Brethren, Hang Loose* (Grand Rapids, Mich.: Zondervan, 1972), 110–113.

Chapter 6
1. Leith Anderson, "The Trouble with Legalism," *Moody*, October 1994, 13.
2. Stu Weber, *Tender Warrior* (Sisters, Oreg.: Multnomah Books), 203–4.

Chapter 7
1. I owe this exegesis to John Sandford.
2. John Dawson, *Healing America's Wounds* (Ventura, Calif.: Regal Books, 1994), 28–9.

Chapter 8
1. Woody Allen, "Standup Comic" (audiocassette), Casablanca Record and FilmWorks, Inc., 1979.
2. Leanne Payne, *Crisis in Masculinity* (Wheaton, Ill.: Crossway Books, 1986), 46.
3. David H. Hackworth, "The War without End," *Newsweek*, 22 November 1993, 44–8.

Chapter 9
1. *Webster's New World Dictionary* (New York: The World Publishing Company, 1973), 7.
2. Anne Schaef, *When Society Becomes an Addict* (Harper & Row: San Francisco, 1987).
3. Mike Downey, *Los Angeles Times*, 6 April 1994, C1.
4. "Still Carrying a Torch," *Newsweek*, 21 February 1994, 46.
5. Randy Harvey, "He's Faced Highest Hurdle," *Los Angeles Times*, 29 June 1993, C1.

Chapter 10
1. Mike Flynn & Doug Gregg, *Inner Healing* (Downers Grove, Ill: InterVarsity Press: 1994), 137.
2. E. James Wilder, *Life Passages for Men* (Ann Arbor, Mich: Servant Publications: 1993), 66.
3. Ibid., 67.
4. Ibid., 74.

Chapter 11
1. "B-a-a-a-d Dudes," *People*, 18 October 1993, 98.
2. Michael Meyer, "Be Kinder to Your 'Kinder'," *Newsweek*, 16 December 1991, 43.
3. Elizabeth Mehren, "It's Bad News for America's Kids," *Los Angeles Times*, 12 April 1994, E1–2.
4. William Sears, M.D., and Martha Sears, R.N., *The Baby Book* (Boston: Little, Brown, and Company, 1993), 16, 520.

5. Philip Greven, *Spare the Child: The Religious Roots of Punishment and the Psychological Impact of Physical Abuse* (New York: Vintage Books, 1990), 15.
6. Ibid., 16.
7. Ibid., 194.

Chapter 12

1. Portions of this chapter are adapted from my article, "Teach Us to Be Weeping Prophets," *The Pentcostal Minister,* winter 1988, 19–21.
2. Don Martinez, "Legislators Hear Chilling Testimony on Hate Groups," *Santa Barbara News Press,* 16 December 1993, B4.
3. Elie Wiesel, *A Jew Today* (New York: Random House, 1978), 180.
4. Keith Thompson, "The Meaning of Being Male: A Conversation with Robert Bly," *L.A. Weekly,* 5–11 August 1983, 17.
5. Kevin Springer, "Applying the Gift to Everyday Life," *Charisma,* September 1985, 32.
6. Ben Kinchlow, *Plain Bread* (Dallas: Word Books, 1985), 20, 154.
7. *SCRC Vision Magazine,* January 1986, 11.

Chapter 13

1. The chief surgeon is the boy's mother.
2. Donna Britt, "Pseudo-Equality," *Santa Barbara News Press,* 16 April 1994, A13.

Chapter 14

1. Dr. John Gray, in an address to Santa Barbara City College, 9 May 1994.
2. Keith Thompson, "The Meaning of Being Male/ A Conversation with Robert Bly," *L.A. Weekly,* 5–11 August 1983, 17.
3. Ibid.
4. Leigh Hagan, editor, *Women Respond to the Men's Movement* (San Francisco: HarperCollins, 1992).
5. Thus, in her book *Motherhood Deferred* (New York: G. Putnam's Sons, 1994), *New York Times* columnist Anne Taylor Fleming critiques secular feminism from within.
6. E. James Wilder, *Life Passages for Men* (Ann Arbor, Mich.: Servant Pblications, 1993), 100.

Chapter 15

1. I derived the gist of this argument from Don Basham's chapter, "Tongues and the Chronic Seeker," in his booklet *Ministering the Baptism of the Holy Spirit* (Monroeville, Pa.: Whitaker Books, 1971).

ABOUT THE AUTHOR

GORDON DALBEY, author of the widely acclaimed *Healing the Masculine Soul,* is a popular speaker at retreats and conferences around the country. A graduate of Duke University, Gordon holds an M.A. in journalism from Stanford University and an M.Div. from Harvard Divinity School. He was a news reporter, a Peace Corps volunteer, and a high school teacher before pastoring churches in southern California.

Gordon has appeared on many radio and television programs, including *Focus on the Family, The 700 Club,* and *The Minirth-Meier Clinic.* His articles have been published in a wide variety of journals, magazines, and newspapers, including *Reader's Digest, Los Angeles Times, Catholic Digest, Leadership,* and *Christian Herald.*

Gordon lives in Santa Barbara, California, with his wife, Dr. Mary Andrews-Dalbey, and their son, John-Miguel.

For more information on speaking engagements or further resources, contact:

Gordon Dalbey
Box 61042
Santa Barbara, CA 93160